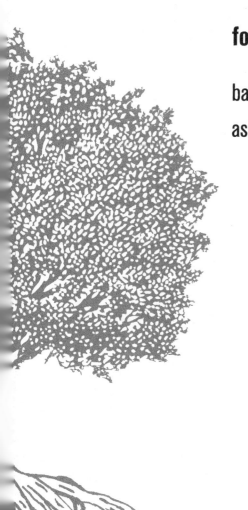

Handbook

for the ministry of Biblical discipleship/counseling

based on the Old and New Testaments

as the only authoritative source of faith and conduct

HANDBOOK
FOR THE MINISTRY OF BIBLICAL DISCIPLESHIP/ COUNSELING

This reference/teaching handbook in biblical discipleship/counseling is published by the Biblical Counseling Foundation, Inc., a non-profit, non-stock corporation founded in 1974 and incorporated in 1977 in the Commonwealth of Virginia, USA.

Scripture taken from the New American Standard Bible, © 1960, 1962, 1963, 1968, 1971, 1972, 1973, 1975, 1977 by The Lockman Foundation. Used by permission.

ISBN 978-1-60536-035-5

First printing, August 2001
Second printing, January 2002
Third printing, March 2005
Fourth printing, April 2006
Fifth printing, August 2007
Sixth printing, January 2010
Seventh printing, July 2010
Eighth printing, January 2012
Ninth printing, June 2017
Tenth printing, June 2024

Biblical Counseling Foundation
42550 Aegean Street
Indio, CA 92203-9617, USA

760.347.4608 telephone
760.775.5751 fax
orders@bcfministries.org e-mail for orders
admin@bcfministries.org e-mail for other
877.933.9333 (in USA) telephone for orders only
http://www.bcfministries.org webpage for orders and information

TABLE OF CONTENTS

SECTION I:
BIBLICAL PRINCIPLES FOR DISCIPLESHIP/ COUNSELING

SECTION II:
MASTER PLAN FOR THE MINISTRY OF BIBLICAL DISCIPLESHIP/COUNSELING

SECTION III:
ESSENTIAL PRECEPTS FOR BIBLICAL DISCIPLESHIP/COUNSELING

Part 3: The Biblical Discipleship/Counseling Process

SECTION IV:
RESOURCE HELPS AND FORMS
FOR BIBLICAL DISCIPLESHIP/
COUNSELING

PREFACE

This pioneer undertaking to re-establish the Word of God as the sole authority for life and as the only basis for discipling/counseling others has been a labor of love by many of God's people. The core team of writers used by the Lord to develop this handbook consists of John Broger, Bob Schneider, and Shashi Smith. The BCF teachers and trainers used by the Lord to edit and revise this volume consist of Cathy Barshinger, Carrie Brown, Woody Church, Joe Dyer, Irene Evers, Joe Gearo, Gary and Linda Hays, Jim Johnson, Ron and Sally Lee, Lindy Ko, Gerald Nygren, Steve Smith, and Lee Weeder. All of these individuals have given sacrificially of their time, talents, and energies without financial remuneration of any kind.

In addition, BCF staff members, including Cindy Johnson, Kate O'Donnell, Spencer Smith, and Stuart Smith have devoted extensive time to editing, graphics design, and printing of these materials.

The team of writers and editors has devoted years of intensive study and writing in the preparation of this work. The Lord has used the gifts and talents of each team member to contribute in a unique way to insure biblical accuracy and internal integrity.

In addition, the members of the BCF Board of Directors have been chosen because of their full commitment to the complete sufficiency of the Scriptures. They are all skilled in the teaching of BCF materials and are committed to discipleship/counseling ministry development and training.

Our wholehearted desire is to help prepare the body of believers in the church of Jesus Christ to enjoy the fullness and abundance of the Christian life but also to be able to face, deal with, and where necessary, to endure the tests and tribulations of this earthly life in a victorious manner.

God bless you as you pursue this training in righteousness (*II Timothy 3:16-17*).

INTRODUCTION

The *Handbook for the Ministry of Biblical Discipleship/Counseling* has been developed to help the biblical discipler/counselor maintain his biblical focus in ministering to those with problems. It is a reference/teaching handbook for biblical disciplers/counselors and for all BCF training courses starting with Biblical Discipleship/Counseling Course II. Information is divided into four sections as follows:

I. **SECTION I: BIBLICAL PRINCIPLES FOR DISCIPLESHIP/COUNSELING**

This section consists of biblical principles for the focus and conduct of both the disciple/counselee and the discipler/counselor. The first portion contains biblical principles for disciples/counselees. They are taken from the *Self-Confrontation* manual and are listed in the same order in which they appear in the manual. The second portion contains biblical principles for disciplers/counselors. They start with number 106 and apply to discipleship/counseling situations.

II. **SECTION II: MASTER PLAN FOR THE MINISTRY OF BIBLICAL DISCIPLESHIP/ COUNSELING**

This section contains essential helps for planning and evaluating the entire discipleship/counseling process with all individuals to whom you minister. The **MASTER PLAN FOR THE MINISTRY OF BIBLICAL DISCIPLESHIP/ COUNSELING** is an outline of the procedure you can follow as you progress in your ministry with individuals. The **EXPLANATION OF THE MASTER PLAN** provides the detailed guidance you need to implement the biblical guidelines listed in the **MASTER PLAN**.

III. **SECTION III: ESSENTIAL PRECEPTS FOR BIBLICAL DISCIPLESHIP/ COUNSELING**

This section contains essential scriptural teaching for all aspects of your ministry as a biblical discipler/counselor. It consists of three parts: **THE DISCIPLE/ COUNSELEE, THE BIBLICAL DISCIPLER/COUNSELOR,** and **THE BIBLICAL DISCIPLESHIP/COUNSELING PROCESS.** Throughout the years you spend ministering to others, this section will provide a valuable reference for your own discipleship/counseling and for training others.

IV. **SECTION IV: RESOURCE HELPS AND FORMS FOR BIBLICAL DISCIPLESHIP/ COUNSELING**

This section includes forms for discipleship/counseling, guidelines for completion of the forms, guidelines for completing homework assignments, guidance for how to carry out discipler/counselor training responsibilities and standards of conduct for biblical disciplers/counselors. In many informal discipleship/ counseling situations, it will not be appropriate to use some of these forms; however, even then, the information on the forms provides valuable guidance for gathering information during your discipleship/counseling meeting.

An important item in Section IV is the **BCF SELF-STUDY BIBLE COURSE IN BIBLICAL DISCIPLESHIP/COUNSELING**. It is designed to acquaint the prospective discipler/counselor with principles and precepts from the Old and New Testaments that apply to dealing with problems and achieving maturity in Christ. The course consists of five major sections: 1) a study of twelve key scriptural doctrines that have direct application to biblical discipleship/counseling, 2) a study of 24 Old Testament characters from a biblical discipler/counselor's perspective, 3) a biblical discipleship/counseling perspective of poetic and prophetic books in the Old Testament, 4) a variety of discipleship/counseling topics, and 5) studies on the way that Jesus discipled.

A SPECIAL NOTE ON THE SCRIPTURE REFERENCES FOUND IN THIS HANDBOOK

As you study and use this *Handbook*, you will find that the biblical principles and precepts presented are substantiated with Scripture references that you are encouraged to look up as you study. The Scripture references are listed in the order they are found in the Bible, not necessarily in the order of importance or clarity.

As in the *Self-Confrontation* manual, whenever you see italicized parentheses with Scripture references listed, the passages substantiate the principle or teaching directly. Whenever the Scripture reference is prefaced with the words *"based on,"* the principle or teaching is a clear inference or specific application of the passage, or the references must be studied together as a whole.

BIBLICAL COUNSELING IS IN-DEPTH DISCIPLESHIP

> The disciples of Jesus Christ are to be His witnesses to the uttermost part of the earth and they also are to teach disciples of all nations to practice all that Jesus taught. These two missions are principal characteristics of biblical discipleship *(based on Matthew 28:19-20; Acts 1:8)*. Because biblical counseling deals with every aspect of a person's life, it can be described as in-depth discipleship. It includes evangelizing, baptizing, teaching, admonishing, instructing, comforting, encouraging, restoring, strengthening, reproving, rebuking, and exhorting others to follow a biblical pattern of life *(based on Matthew 28:19-20; Romans 15:14; II Corinthians 1:4; Galatians 6:1; I Thessalonians 3:2; II Timothy 4:2; Hebrews 3:13; 10:24).*

BIBLICAL DISCIPLESHIP IS GOD'S PLAN

We know from the Bible that God desires for all to come to Him — He does not desire for any to perish *(II Peter 3:9)*. Furthermore, He has a plan and a method for reaching the world. His plan is to send His children to the uttermost part of the earth to be His witnesses *(Acts 1:8)*. The Lord not only tells us what His plan is, but He also reveals to us His method for carrying out that plan.

In *Matthew 28:19-20* God describes His method for reaching the world is for His witnesses to make disciples. Note, in this passage, that there are two parts to making disciples: baptizing and training. Of course, only believers are to be baptized, so evangelism is included as part of making disciples. The second part of this "Great Commission" is to train believers to live victoriously. This is not only important for the believers' maturity, but it also enables them to fulfill their part in making other disciples.

The discipleship process must be so thorough that each disciple learns to teach others in the same way he was taught. God's plan is that every one of His children be involved in making disciples. God's plan is for each person being discipled then responds to his training by discipling others. This multiplication process is to be continued until the whole world is won.

To illustrate the wisdom of God's plan for reaching the world, let us compare the difference between "increasing numbers by multiplying" and "increasing numbers by adding." Suppose that you were able to use radio, television, and the internet to present the Gospel to very large groups of people on an ongoing basis. And suppose that as you preached the Gospel, you were able to lead 100,000 people to Christ every day. By the end of one year over 36 million people (365 days in a year x 100,000 per day) would be added to the kingdom of Christ. (See the first two columns of the following chart.)

COMPARISON OF ADDING VERSUS MULTIPLYING

Year	Adding 100,000 each day	Multiplying by 2 each year
1	36.5 million	2
2	73 million	4
3	109.5 million	8
.	.	.
.	.	.
.	.	.
32	1.168 billion	4.3 billion
33	1.204 billion	8.6 billion*
.	.	.
.	.	.
.	.	.
181	6.6 billion	3×10^{45}

* The world's population is approximately 6.6 billion

In contrast, suppose that you concentrated on discipleship in the same way that Jesus discipled. The Lord, while He was on this earth, concentrated His ministry on only a few disciples with the goal of training them in depth. He trained them so thoroughly that they were then able to repeat His example in reaching others. Now, suppose that you were privileged to lead someone to the Lord, and then, you concentrated primarily on discipling just that one person. And suppose that you spent an entire year discipling this new believer, so that by the end of the year, he was able, not only to lead another to the Lord, but was able to disciple the new convert in the same way he was discipled.

For the first few years, the "increase by multiplying" plan seems to achieve extremely low results in comparison to the "increase by adding" plan. But by doubling the number of disciples each year it would take less than 33 years to reach the world of approximately 6.6 billion people. (See the third column of the chart.) In contrast, the method of adding to the church would reach only a little over a billion people in 33 years. Following this method would take a total of 181 years to reach the same number of people.

Of course, this comparison does not take into account the fact that some people choose not to be involved in discipleship, but it does illustrate dramatically the effectiveness of God's plan. The in-depth discipleship that Jesus taught, established, and practiced is the key to spreading the Gospel because it keeps the spiritual reproduction going from generation to generation.

God's method for spreading the Gospel is very powerful. You can see from this illustration why Jesus put such heavy emphasis on discipleship. Most of his time with the disciples was spent preparing them to overcome the hindrances to victorious living knowing that the key to reaching the world is by winning the lost through multiplication.

BIBLICAL COUNSELING IS IN-DEPTH DISCIPLESHIP

As we have already seen in *Matthew 28:19-20*, biblical discipleship is God's method. But biblical discipleship as described and demonstrated in the Scriptures is much broader and deeper than the "discipleship" that is often practiced today. Let's go back to *Matthew 28:20*. Jesus made it clear in this passage that making disciples includes teaching disciples to observe *all* that He taught. Notice the topics Jesus dealt with in the Sermon on the Mount *(Matthew 5 - 7)*. In teaching the disciples, He talked much about the difficulties of life, such as anger, persecution, reconciliation, lustful temptations, retaliation, divorce, hatred, worry and hypocrisy. He was preparing His disciples to deal with and endure the problems of life. So, the word "all" in *verse 20* indicates that biblical discipleship is thorough. Biblical discipleship includes all of what is often categorized as counseling since it deals with every aspect of a person's life. It is in-depth discipleship.

Biblical discipleship, which includes restoration of those ensnared in problems, is the responsibility of all believers *(Romans 15:14; Galatians 6:1-2)*. This ministry is not just for those who have "the gift of counseling." When believers begin to deal with their own problems God's way, He gives them the privilege and responsibility to restore others to His way *(based on Matthew 7:5; Galatians 6:1)*.

In summary, biblical discipleship includes evangelism as the first step, basic follow-up of new believers as the second step, and finally restoration of those who are in the midst of difficulties. Jesus, our supreme example for how to disciple, concentrated most of His effort on training His twelve disciples to deal the difficulties of life. Yes, He taught the masses; however, His primary objective in teaching was to train His disciples so thoroughly that they would not only be victorious over all hindrances, but they, in turn, would prepare those they were training to continue the process of making disciples after He returned to heaven. Surely, we should learn from Him.

THE FRAMEWORK OF
BIBLICAL DISCIPLESHIP/COUNSELING

> Biblical discipleship/counseling is founded, not on the opinions of man, but on the unchanging Word of God and is rooted in God's dealings with man *(based on Job 12:13; Psalm 33:11; 73:24; Isaiah 9:6; 11:2; 28:29; 55:8-11; John 14:16, 26; 16:7-13)*. It is critically important for the biblical counselor to understand clearly what he is called to do and how he is to counsel others.

THE FOUNDATION OF BIBLICAL DISCIPLESHIP/COUNSELING

Biblical discipleship/counseling is dramatically different from all of man's philosophies about life *(based on Isaiah 55:8-11)* because it relies solely on the Scriptures as the authoritative hope, structure, and guide for living, and God's grace and power. Biblical discipleship/counseling reflects the absolute nature of God's authoritative Word. Therefore, it is characterized by an absolute (non-negotiable and unchanging) set of standards governing behavior and relationships. Right and wrong are clearly defined according to God's decrees, not according to man's fluctuating situational ethics. Consequently, biblical discipleship/counseling focuses on pleasing God and loving others — not on pleasing or exalting self.

Biblical discipleship/counseling is not a new concept; it is as old as man's problems, which began with Adam. All three persons of the Trinity are involved. In *Psalm 73:24*, God, the Father, is the counselor; in *Isaiah 9:6*, Jesus Christ is named the Wonderful Counselor; and in *John 14:16, 26; 16:7-13*, the Holy Spirit is identified as the Comforter and Guide.

Throughout the Old Testament, God counseled those in need by giving constant instruction, guidance, and supervision as man's creator and supreme judge. God Himself directly counseled Adam, both before and after the fall *(based on Genesis 2:15-25; 3:8-24)*, Cain *(based on Genesis 4:3-15)*, and many others. He also counseled people through His prophets and the judges. During the four thousand years covered by the Old Testament, He instituted the discipleship/counseling relationship in every area of life, individually and collectively.

In the book of Proverbs, God clearly identifies the importance of counseling and the responsibility of the counselor:

A wise man will hear and increase in learning,
And a man of understanding will acquire wise counsel
　　　　　　(Proverbs 1:5).

Where there is no guidance, the people fall,
But in abundance of counselors there is victory
　　　　　　(Proverbs 11:14).

The way of a fool is right in his own eyes,
But a wise man is he who listens to counsel
　　　　　　(Proverbs 12:15).

Without consultation, plans are frustrated,
But with many counselors they succeed
　　　　　　(Proverbs 15:22).

Listen to counsel and accept discipline,
That you may be wise the rest of your days
                    (Proverbs 19:20).

Oil and perfume make the heart glad,
So a man's counsel is sweet to his friend
                    (Proverbs 27:9).

God also clearly predicts the results of the refusal or acceptance of His counsel:

Because I called, and you refused;
I stretched out my hand, and no one paid attention;
And you neglected all my counsel,
And did not want my reproof;
I will even laugh at your calamity;
I will mock when your dread comes,
When your dread comes like a storm,
And your calamity comes on like a whirlwind,
When distress and anguish come on you.
Then they will call on me, but I will not answer;
They will seek me diligently, but they shall not find me,
Because they hated knowledge,
And did not choose the fear of the Lord.
They would not accept my counsel,
They spurned all my reproof.
So they shall eat of the fruit of their own way,
And be satiated with their own devices.
For the waywardness of the naive shall kill them,
And the complacency of fools shall destroy them.
But he who listens to me shall live securely,
And shall be at ease from the dread of evil
                    (Proverbs 1:24-33).

The New Testament, from Matthew through Revelation, is filled with discipleship/counseling standards, precepts, and illustrations, as well as direct guidance and admonitions. Every position of leadership in the church of the Lord Jesus Christ carries with it the responsibility of spiritual oversight of believers, which includes training all believers to do the work of service for the building up of the body of Christ *(based on Ephesians 4:11-13)*. This responsibility of training includes the ministry of discipleship/counseling as identified and practiced in the Scripture *(based on Matthew 28:19-20; Galatians 6:1-5; Romans 15:14; II Timothy 2:2)*. It is essential for ministry leaders to train up believers to disciple/counsel biblically.

The church must re-assume the God-given responsibility for restoring individuals and helping them to minister as maturing and working parts of the body of Christ *(based on Galatians 6:1-2; Ephesians 4:12-16)*. If believers apply any less than the authoritative scriptural principles to the problems of individuals, they cannot be assured that their counsel will lead to lasting biblical change *(based on Isaiah 55:8-11; II Timothy 3:16-17; Hebrews 4:12)*. Man's attempts at formulating counseling theories and psychotherapies do not even begin to compare with the authority, the wisdom, and the power of God's counsel, and further, are doomed to disorder and confusion *(based on Romans 1:21-25; I Corinthians 1:20-21; II Timothy 3:1-9, 13; 4:1-5)*.

The danger of seeking and offering the world's counsel is graphically illustrated in *Isaiah 30:1-15*. God declares:

In *verse 1*, woe to those who execute plans that are not His;

In *verses 9-10*, that those seeking instruction from sources other than the Lord are rebellious, seeking pleasant words;

In *verses 2-5*, that the result will be shame when the people turn for help to Egypt which was considered then the center of the world's wisdom;

In *verse 7*, that help from Egypt is vain and of no profit; and

In *verses 12-14*, that the consequences of rejecting God's counsel are calamitous.

THE FRAMEWORK OF BIBLICAL DISCIPLESHIP/COUNSELING

What is a biblical description of both the disciple/counselee and the discipler/ counselor? What is the discipler/counselor's mission and purpose as identified from Scripture?

A scriptural study of first-century biblical discipleship/counseling reveals problems as more than a manifestation of secular or humanistic struggles. Conflict in the Christian life is not against flesh and blood, but against the rulers, against the powers, against the world forces of darkness, against the spiritual forces of wickedness in heavenly places *(based on Ephesians 6:12)*. Therefore, those who are entrapped, oppressed, and defeated must learn how to put on the full armor of God *(based on Romans 13:12; Ephesians 6:10-13; I Thessalonians 5:8)*, that each one may be able to stand firm against the schemes and temptations of our adversary, the enemy of our salvation *(based on Ephesians 6:12-13)*.

The global setting of this conflict may be illustrated, at least partially, by the drama that takes place in a courtroom. In this manner we may better understand the position of the disciple/counselee and of the biblical discipler/counselor. The following describes the relationship of conflicts to the Lord, the biblical discipler/counselor, the disciple/ counselee, and biblical discipleship/counseling.

The Supreme Judge, Chief Advocate, and Chief Witness — The Lord acts in all three of these capacities. He is the righteous Judge of all things *(Psalm 7:9-11; 96:13; II Timothy 4:8; Hebrews 12:23)*. No one is hidden from His sight and all things are open and laid bare to His eyes *(Hebrews 4:13)*. He has established His throne to execute judgment in righteousness *(Psalm 9:7-8)*. He will bring every act to judgment, everything which is hidden, whether it is good or evil *(Ecclesiastes 12:14)*. God has fixed a day of judgment through Jesus, whom He appointed, having furnished proof to all men by raising Him from the dead *(Acts 17:31)*. Each person living or dead shall be judged and held accountable at the day of judgment for every careless word spoken and every deed performed *(based on Matthew 12:36-37; II Corinthians 5:10; I Peter 4:5; Revelation 20:12)*.

The Lord Jesus Christ is the Chief Advocate *(I John 2:1-2)*, who died for the accused (mankind) and paid the price for his sin, his guilt, and his redemption *(Romans 3:23-25)*. He is the one who intercedes continually for the accused *(Romans 8:34; Hebrews 7:25; I John 2:1-2)* and who sits at the right hand of the throne of God *(Luke 22:69; Acts 7:55-56; Romans 8:34; Ephesians 1:20; Colossians 3:1; I Peter 3:22)*. All authorities and powers have been subjected to Jesus *(based on I Corinthians 15:27; Ephesians 1:22; I Peter 3:22)*. He is the one, the only hope of the accused that he may live *(based on I Timothy 2:5; Hebrews 2:14-15)*.

The Holy Spirit of God is the unimpeachable witness and guide to all that is true and right *(based on John 16:13; I John 5:6-7)*. He convicts all men of sin and righteousness and judgment *(based on John 16:7-8)*. He also teaches believers all things *(based on John 14:26; 15:26; I John 2:27)*.

The Basis of Judgment — The law, the testimony, the precepts, and the judgments of the Lord are intended for teaching, for reproof, for correction and for training and are collectively called the Word of God *(based on Psalm 19:7-9; II Timothy 3:16-17)*. It is sharper than any two-edged sword and is able to judge the thoughts and intentions of the heart *(Hebrews 4:12-13)*. God's law and the examples given in His Word are consistent throughout the Bible and have been written for our instruction *(based on Romans 15:4; I Corinthians 10:5-11; Hebrews 11:4-40)* that we may know the peace and freedom that comes through obedience *(based on John 8:30-32; 16:33)*.

The Accuser and the Adversary — The adversary, the accuser, the enemy is Satan *(based on Job 1:6-12; 2:1-7; Zechariah 3:1; Revelation 12:10)*. He is hostile to God and everything good. His objective is to deceive all mankind *(based on Revelation 12:9)*. He is the adversary of the disciple/counselee and the discipler/counselor and as a roaring lion is seeking to devour and destroy them *(based on I Peter 5:8)*. He is a murderer and a liar, and the truth is not in him *(John 8:44)*. Disguised as an angel of light, he seeks to deceive all individuals by his craftiness and lead their minds astray from the simplicity and purity of devotion to Christ *(based on II Corinthians 11:3, 14)*.

Further, let us investigate Scripture's view of the disciple/counselee:

The Accused — The disciple/counselee is heavily burdened normally by his problems; otherwise, he would not have come for help.

If the one seeking help is an unbeliever, he is enmeshed in his own fleshly desires *(Romans 8:5-8)* and entrapped by the snares and temptations of the accuser and adversary *(based on II Timothy 2:26)*. He needs to have his eyes opened *(I Corinthians 2:14; II Corinthians 3:14-16; 4:3-4)* so that he may turn from darkness to light and from the dominion of Satan to God *(based on Acts 26:18)*.

If the one seeking help is a believer, he needs to know the hope of His calling and the riches of His inheritance *(based on Ephesians 1:18)*. The accused needs to be cleansed from his unrighteousness *(based on Psalm 51:2; I John 1:9)*, and to be restored to the joy of God's salvation *(based on Psalm 51:8-12)*.

As a believer does those things that are pleasing to the Lord, he becomes an effectual doer of the Word, and he will be blessed in what he does *(James 1:22-25)*. By being sober and alert, firm in the faith, and resisting the accuser, the disciple/counselee will see God perfect, confirm, strengthen and establish him *(I Peter 5:8-10)*.

In light of all the above, what is the responsibility of the biblical discipler/counselor?

The Biblical Discipler/Counselor — As the Lord's bondservant, the discipler/counselor is to teach patiently and correct gently those who are in opposition in the hope that God will grant them repentance leading to a knowledge of the truth, and that they may come to their senses and escape from the snare of the devil *(II Timothy 2:24-26)*. If the accused is a Christian, the biblical discipler/counselor is to be God's instrument to restore the accused *(based on Galatians 6:1-2, 5)* so that he will focus on pleasing God in every aspect of his life *(based on Colossians 1:10; 3:17, 23-24)*.

This is the framework of biblical discipleship/counseling. Only the Holy Spirit can provide the wisdom and power to live victoriously in the way He has designed us to live. This training is not a blend of theology and psychology; rather, it is a return to a straightforward recognition that the Bible, God's Word, is the only fully adequate and complete authority for discipleship/counseling. Rejecting it brings serious consequences *(based on Proverbs 1:22-33)*. Accepting and following its guidance and admonitions brings the rewards of peace and joy in spite of all trials and tests.

SECTION I

BIBLICAL PRINCIPLES FOR DISCIPLESHIP/COUNSELING

SECTION I

BIBLICAL PRINCIPLES FOR DISCIPLESHIP/COUNSELING

INTRODUCTION

As a biblical discipler/counselor you are to study and apply God's Word as the only standard, hope, and authority for helping others face, deal with, and endure all of life's problems. It is therefore necessary for you to investigate all the biblical principles and precepts that apply to disciples/counselees' circumstances, so that you may help them become established in a Christlike pattern of life.

This section consists of biblical principles for the focus and conduct of both the disciple/counselee and discipler/counselor. The first portion contains biblical principles for disciples/counselees. They are taken from the *Self-Confrontation* manual and are listed in the same order in which they appear in the manual. The second portion contains biblical principles for disciplers/counselors. They start with number 106 and apply to discipleship/counseling situations.

BIBLICAL PRINCIPLES
FOR DISCIPLES/COUNSELEES
(FROM THE *SELF-CONFRONTATION* MANUAL)

YOU CAN CHANGE BIBLICALLY
(PART ONE)
(Lesson 1)

God's plan for you to change in a biblical way centers on His Son, Jesus Christ.

(Principle 1)   Because God's standard is one of perfection *(Leviticus 19:2; Matthew 5:48)*, you cannot meet it by your own efforts *(Psalm 143:2; Ecclesiastes 7:20; Romans 3:23)*. You cannot save yourself *(Proverbs 20:9)* nor depend on any other human being to redeem you *(Psalm 49:7)*. You need to recognize your helplessness to meet God's standard *(Isaiah 64:6; Romans 3:9-12)* and need to repent of your sin *(Luke 15:7; Acts 2:38, 3:19, 17:30-31, 26:19-20; Romans 2:4; II Peter 3:9)*. By God's grace and mercy, you recognize your lost condition and believe wholeheartedly and sincerely on the Lord Jesus Christ to receive the gift of eternal life *(John 3:16, 36; 5:24; 11:25-26; Romans 6:23; Ephesians 2:8-9; Titus 3:5-7; I John 5:11-13)* and forgiveness for your sins *(Mark 16:16; John 3:16-18, 8:24; Acts 2:38, 4:12; Romans 10:9-13; Ephesians 1:7)*.

YOU CAN CHANGE BIBLICALLY
(PART TWO)
(Lesson 2)

You are to establish a biblical pattern of life.

(Principle 2)   You are to be rooted, built up, and established in the Lord Jesus Christ and are not to be conformed to the world *(Romans 12:1-2; Colossians 2:6-10)*. You must practice God's Word to grow into maturity *(Matthew 7:24-27; II Timothy 3:16-17; Hebrews 5:12-14; James 1:22-25; I Peter 2:2; II Peter 1:4-11; I John 2:5)*.

You are to prepare yourself to help others.

(Principle 3)   Practicing God's Word begins with judging yourself and removing sinful obstructions from your own life *(Matthew 7:1-5; I Corinthians 11:28-31; Hebrews 12:1)*. Then, you have the privilege and responsibility of restoring others to victorious living *(Matthew 7:5; Romans 15:14; II Corinthians 1:3-4; Galatians 6:1-5)*.

MAN'S WAY AND GOD'S WAY
(PART ONE)

(Lesson 3)

The Bible is adequate.

(Principle 4)   Since God's Word is the only authority for faith and conduct and is the sole, legitimate standard by which all aspects of living are evaluated, you are to rely on no other source. God's Word provides hope and gives direction for change in deeds (thoughts, speech, and actions) and is adequate to equip you for every good work *(Psalm 19:7-11; Proverbs 30:5-6; Colossians 2:8; II Timothy 3:16-17; Hebrews 4:12; II Peter 1:2-4)* and to develop a Christlike attitude of servanthood within you *(II Corinthians 3:5-6; Philippians 2:5-8).*

The Holy Spirit is necessary.

(Principle 5)   Only through the power of the Holy Spirit are you able to live an abundant life *(John 14:26, 16:7-14; Romans 8:5-11; I Corinthians 2:9-14; Ephesians 1:13-14, 5:18).*

Prayer is vital.

(Principle 6)   Prayer is essential to a Spirit-controlled life *(Psalm 145:18-19; Matthew 7:7-8; Ephesians 5:18-20; 6:18; I Thessalonians 5:17; I John 3:22).* You are to be devoted to prayer, according to God's will, and to bring everything and everyone unceasingly before the Lord in prayer *(Luke 18:1; Ephesians 6:18; Philippians 4:6; Colossians 4:2; I Thessalonians 5:17; I Timothy 2:1; I John 5:14-15).*

MAN'S WAY AND GOD'S WAY
(PART TWO)

(Lesson 4)

Man's way

The natural man is inadequate.

(Principle 7)   You cannot live according to God's design in your own way or by your own wisdom *(Proverbs 14:12; Isaiah 55:8-9; I Corinthians 2:14).*

The natural man is rebellious.

(Principle 8)   The natural man is self-centered and rebels against God's way *(Genesis 3:1-6; Romans 1:20-32; 3:9-18, 23; 10:1-3).* Furthermore, partial obedience to God is just as unacceptable to Him as even your deliberate rebellion *(based on I Samuel 15:1-23, esp. verses 22-23; Isaiah 1:10-20; Hosea 6:6; Micah 6:6-8; Mark 12:28-33, esp. verse 33).*

God's way

Man needs to be changed.

(Principle 9)   It is necessary to be born again (to be born from above; to have a spiritual birth) in order to recognize, admit, and solve your problems in a biblical manner. Only God's solutions, grace, empowering, and wisdom are completely adequate for abundant living *(Ecclesiastes 12:13-14; John 3:3-8; 10:10; 14:16-17, 26; Romans 8:5-14; I Corinthians 2:10-14; Ephesians 2:8-10).*

BIBLICAL DYNAMICS OF CHANGE

(Lesson 5)

The downward spiral

(Principle 10)   God's thoughts and ways are far higher (superior) than yours *(Isaiah 55:8-9)*, and His Word is truth *(Psalm 119:160; John 17:17).* If you neglect or refuse God's ways or His truth, you will experience ever-increasing problems; and the problems you have will grow worse *(Proverbs 1:25-32, 13:15, 28:13-14; Romans 1:20-32; Galatians 5:16-21; Hebrews 3:7 19; James 1:14-15).*

Beginnings of biblical change

(Principle 11)   A transforming new birth is necessary for you to live victoriously and to be empowered to overcome the world and problems of life *(John 3:3-7; Romans 12:1-2; II Corinthians 5:17-21; Titus 3:3-7; I John 5:4-5).*

(Principle 12)   The whole duty of man is to fear (reverence) God and keep His commandments *(Ecclesiastes 12:13-14; I Peter 1:17).* You are to love God and others in response to God's love for you *(Matthew 22:37-39; John 15:9-14; I John 4:11, 19).* You are to walk in a manner worthy of God and to please Him in every area of your life *(II Corinthians 5:9; Colossians 1:10)* by being a doer of the Word *(John 14:15; James 1:22; I John 2:3-4).* As you obediently respond to God's love, you become mature in the Lord and are blessed with peace and joy *(John 15:10-11, 16:33).* Numerous other blessings from the Lord follow *(Matthew 6:33; James 1:25; I John 3:22).* If you do not obey God's Word, He will judge and discipline you *(I Corinthians 11:31-32; Hebrews 12:5-10).*

(Principle 13)   To appropriate God's gracious wisdom in facing and dealing with your problems, you must ask in faith *(Hebrews 4:16; James 1:5-8)*, live according to God's Word *(James 1:22-25)*, and depend on His power *(II Corinthians 3:4-5; Philippians 4:13).*

The upward path

(Principle 14)   You must obey God's Word consistently *(I John 2:3-6)* to grow increasingly into godliness *(I Timothy 4:7-8; II Peter 1:3-11)* and to realize true peace *(Psalm 119:165; John 16:33)* and joy *(John 15:10-11).*

BIBLICAL BASIS FOR CHANGE

(Lesson 6)

Understanding your problems at the:

Feeling level (often reflects your focus in life and may also reveal upon whom or what you are depending for your peace and joy)

(Principle 15)   Feelings of being mistreated indicate a focus on self and not on Jesus Christ *(Philippians 2:14-15; II Timothy 2:24-25; Hebrews 12:3).*

(Principle 16)   The way you feel and the way you view yourself, your relationships, and your circumstances are often indications of whether you are living to please yourself or living to please God *(Genesis 4:6-7; Psalm 119:165; John 14:27, 15:10-11; Romans 14:17-18; II Corinthians 7:10; Philippians 4:6-7; I John 4:18-21).*

Doing level (reveals the extent of your faithfulness to the Lord)

(Principle 17)   If you hear God's Word and do it, you will be blessed *(Joshua 1:8; Psalm 19:11; Proverbs 29:18; Matthew 7:20-27; James 1:25; I John 3:22),* and your ability to discern good and evil will be increased *(Hebrews 5:14).*

(Principle 18)   If you do not become a doer of the Word, you deceive yourself *(James 1:22-24),* show your lack of love for the Lord *(John 14:23-24),* place yourself under the corrective discipline of the Lord *(I Corinthians 11:32; Hebrews 12:5-11),* and deny the reality of His life within you *(Romans 6:11-13, 17-18; I John 2:3-4; 3:7, 10).*

Heart level (partially revealed by your thoughts, words, and actions)

(Principle 19)   Since even you cannot fully understand your heart *(Jeremiah 17:9),* God's own Word is the measure and the instrument by which the heart level of your problems is discerned *(Hebrews 4:12).* Your responses to problems need not be dependent on people, circumstances, or things. Your deeds (thoughts, speech, and actions) in any situation are used by God to reveal the condition of your heart *(Matthew 15:18-20; Mark 7:20-23; Luke 6:45).*

Your hope in the midst of trials

(Principle 20)   Those in Christ are freed from the power and penalty of sin *(Romans 6:6-7, 14, 18, 23).*

(Principle 21)   God will not allow believers to be tested or tempted beyond what they can bear. He gives you His grace and strength to endure every test and resist every temptation so that you never have to sin *(Romans 8:35-39; I Corinthians 10:13; II Corinthians 4:7-10, 12:9-10; Philippians 4:13; Hebrews 4:15-16; II Peter 2:4-9).*

(Principle 22)   Our Lord Jesus Christ will grant mercy and provide grace to help in every need. He constantly intercedes as an advocate for you to God the Father and fully understands your weaknesses *(Hebrews 2:18, 4:15-16, 7:25; I John 2:1).*

(Principle 23)   Trials and tests will develop and mature you in Christ if you respond to them in God's way *(Romans 5:3-5; James 1:2-4).* He never devises evil or harm for you; rather His plans for you are for good *(Genesis 50:20; Deuteronomy 8:2, 5, 16; Psalm 145:17; Ecclesiastes 7:13-14; Jeremiah 29:11-13; Romans 8:28-29; James 1:13-17).*

(Principle 24)   God's peace and joy are available to believers regardless of others, possessions, or circumstances *(Psalm 119:165; Matthew 5:3-12; John 14:27; 15:11; 16:33; 17:13; Romans 14:17; Philippians 4:4-7; I Peter 1:6-9).*

(Principle 25)   Only God can change people *(Ezekiel 36:26-27; Philippians 1:6, 2:13),* so you are not and cannot be responsible for changing them. You are accountable to God solely for your own deeds *(Jeremiah 17:10; Ezekiel 18:1-20, especially verse 20; Matthew 16:27; Romans 2:5-10; Colossians 3:23-25; I Peter 1:17)* and are to do your part in living at peace with others *(Matthew 5:23-24; Mark 11:25; Romans 12:9-21, 14:19; I Peter 3:8-9, 4:8).*

(Principle 26)   When you confess your sins, God forgives and cleanses you *(I John 1:9).*

BIBLICAL STRUCTURE FOR CHANGE

(Lesson 7)

Your steps for biblical change

The process

(Principle 27)   Effective and lasting biblical change is a continuing process. You are to obey the commands and guidelines in God's Word for every area of your life (your thoughts, speech, and actions) *(Romans 15:4; II Timothy 3:16-17; James 1:21-25; II Peter 1:2-4).* As you stop (put off) the old continuing pattern of sin and begin (put on) the new practice of righteousness and holiness, you are renewed in the spirit of your mind *(Romans 6:11-14, 16-23; 12:1-2; Ephesians 4:22-24; Philippians 2:12-13; Colossians 3:5-17; II Timothy 2:19).*

The "put-offs"

(Principle 28)   In order to put off the old sinful habits, you must first identify them by examining (judging) your life in light of God's Word *(Matthew 7:1-5; I Corinthians 11:28-31; II Timothy 3:16-17; Hebrews 4:12).* Once you have specifically identified sins in your life, you must repent of them *(Proverbs 28:13; II Corinthians 7:9-10; Revelation 2:5),* confess them *(I John 1:9),* and immediately put them aside *(Romans 6:12-13a; II Corinthians 10:5; Ephesians 4:25, 29, 31; 5:4; Colossians 3:2, 5-9; II Timothy 2:22a).*

The "put-ons"

(Principle 29)   As you put on righteous deeds (II Timothy 2:22b; Titus 2:11-12) in the power of the Holy Spirit (Galatians 5:16; Ephesians 3:16-21, 5:18), you will glorify God (I Corinthians 10:31; I Peter 4:11), demonstrate your love for Him (Deuteronomy 10:12; Matthew 22:37; I John 5:3; II John 1:6), and please Him in all things (II Corinthians 5:9; Colossians 1:10).

BIBLICAL PRACTICE ACHIEVES LASTING CHANGE
(Lesson 8)

Your practice of biblical change

Starting

(Principle 30)   Change results when you remember from where you have fallen, repent, and do the deeds you did when you first received the Lord Jesus into your life (Revelation 2:4-5). Acknowledge the Lordship of Jesus Christ and make a commitment to be a doer of the Word (Luke 6:46-49). If you are merely a hearer and not a doer of the Word, then you remain foolish (Matthew 7:24-27), spiritually deluded (James 1:22), and spiritually immature (I Corinthians 3:1-3; Hebrews 5:11-13; James 1:22-24).

Continuing

(Principle 31)   To continue the process of biblical change, you must faithfully practice your daily responsibilities (Ephesians 5:15-16; Colossians 3:23-24; James 4:17) and discipline yourself toward godliness (I Timothy 4:7-11; II Peter 1:5-11; I John 3:7). As you continue to be a doer of the Word, your senses will be trained to discern good and evil (Hebrews 5:14). Your spiritual growth is a sovereign work of God (Galatians 5:22-23; Philippians 1:6, 2:13; Hebrews 12:2a, 13:20-21) that is divinely linked to your living in a biblical manner (Ephesians 2:10, 4:14-16; I Timothy 4:7-8; Hebrews 13:20-21; I Peter 2:2; II Peter 1:5-11).

Maturing

(Principle 32)   In order to mature (grow up) in Christ, you must persevere in doing what is good in the Lord's sight by being obedient to Scripture (Luke 17:10; John 14:15; Romans 2:7; I Corinthians 15:58; Galatians 6:9; James 1:22-25). Instead of living according to your self-centered feelings and desires (II Corinthians 5:15; Galatians 5:16-17; I Peter 2:19-20, 4:1-6), continue to press forward to your high calling in Christ Jesus (Ephesians 4:1; Philippians 3:12-14; Hebrews 6:1-3). Discipline your thought life (II Corinthians 10:5; Colossians 3:1-2; Philippians 4:8), speak in a manner that is helpful to others (Ephesians 4:29; Colossians 4:6), and faithfully love others in a biblical manner (Matthew 22:39; I Corinthians 13:4-8a; I John 4:7-8, 10-11, 20). Do not focus on physical or immediate results; instead, focus on eternal values in order to mature in Christ (II Corinthians 4:17-18; Colossians 3:1-2; I Timothy 4:7-8;

II Peter 1:4-10), to glorify God (I Corinthians 10:31), and to please the Lord in all things (II Corinthians 5:9; Colossians 1:10).

DEALING WITH SELF (PART ONE)

(Lesson 9)

God's view

(Principle 33)   No one hates himself; rather, he loves, cherishes, and nourishes himself *(Matthew 22:39; Ephesians 5:29).* Man's problem is that he pays too much attention to self, not too little *(Luke 9:24; Philippians 2:19-21; II Timothy 3:1-5).*

(Principle 34)   A proper view of self comes from an understanding of who you are in Christ *(Romans 8:14-17; Ephesians 1:3-14; Colossians 2:9-12; I Peter 2:9-10).* As a child of God, you have the assurance that your Heavenly Father, out of His grace and mercy, is involved actively in your life *(Philippians 1:6, 2:13; I Peter 2:9-10; II Peter 1:3-4)* in spite of your natural inadequacies *(Psalm 62:9; Isaiah 64:6; John 15:4-5; II Corinthians 3:5).* While you are totally inadequate to live God's way in your own strength, God has chosen you to be a testimony of His power to the world *(I Corinthians 1:26-31).* He gives you a purpose for living by conforming you to the image of Christ *(Matthew 5:16; Romans 8:28-29; I Corinthians 1:26-31; II Corinthians 5:17-20; Ephesians 2:10).*

(Principle 35)   Your contentment in all circumstances is dependent on your obedient response to God in your deeds (thoughts, speech, actions) *(Genesis 4:7; Psalm 119:165; Isaiah 26:3; Luke 11:28; John 15:10-11; II Corinthians 4:7-10, 16-18; Philippians 4:6-11).* By obeying the Lord in your daily walk, you show your love for the Lord Jesus Christ *(John 14:15, 21, 23-24; I John 2:4-5)* and demonstrate His Lordship in your life *(Matthew 7:21).* God has delight and pleasure in your obedience of faith *(I Samuel 15:22; Hebrews 11:6),* not merely in your protestations of loyalty *(Proverbs 20:6; Matthew 7:21; I John 2:4),* your expressions of remorse *(for example, I Samuel 15:24-26),* or your good but meaningless activities *(Psalm 40:6, 51:16-17; Jeremiah 6:20; Hebrews 10:1-4).*

Your hope

(Principle 36)   You should be thankful to God because you are fearfully and wonderfully made *(Psalm 119:73, 139:13-14).* Even though you might have physical deformities or a chronic affliction, God's plan is to use them for your good and His glory *(Romans 5:3-5, 8:28; I Corinthians 10:13; II Corinthians 12:9-10).* God loves you with perfect love regardless of any weaknesses and "limitations" you may have, even though you do not merit, do not deserve, and cannot earn His love *(Isaiah 53:6; Luke 15:4-7; John 3:16; Romans 5:8; I John 4:10).*

(Principle 37)   You can quickly overcome self-belittlement, self-exaltation, or self-pity. This is possible when you realize that a preoccupation with self is sin *(Matthew 23:12; Luke 9:23; Romans 14:7-8; II Corinthians 5:15; Galatians*

2:20; Philippians 2:3-4; James 4:16-17). You are to confess this unbiblical focus and begin immediately to live in accordance with His Word (Psalm 51:10; Philippians 3:12-14; I John 1:9).

(Principle 38)   You have been freed from the power of all sins (Romans 6:6, 12-13; 12:21; Colossians 3:2-17), including those of envy, jealousy, covetousness, and greed, which have a pronounced self-focus. You can be content in any circumstance (Philippians 4:11-13) and can have the attitude of Christ developed within you (Philippians 2:5).

DEALING WITH SELF (PART TWO)

(Lesson 10)

Your change

(Principle 39)   You must take the focus off yourself in daily situations and relationships (Luke 9:23-24; John 3:30, 12:24-26; Romans 12:3, 14:7-8; II Corinthians 5:15) by following God's commandments (Matthew 22:37-39). Instead of sinning through self-belittlement, self-exaltation, or self-pity, you are to regard others as more important than yourself and be a servant to God and others (Matthew 20:26-28; Luke 4:8; John 13:3-17, esp. verses 14-15; Romans 15:1-3; I Corinthians 9:19; 10:24, 32-33; Philippians 2:3-8; Colossians 3:23-24; I Peter 4:10).

(Principle 40)   You are to put off the sins of envy, jealousy, covetousness, and greed, which characterized your life apart from Jesus Christ. Rather, you are to delight yourself in the Lord, commit your ways to Him, and wait patiently for Him (Psalm 37:1-9). Instead of being jealous and having selfish ambition, you are to be pure, peaceable, gentle, reasonable, full of mercy and good fruits, and unwavering without hypocrisy (James 3:16-17).

(Principle 41)   Since you have been bought with the precious sacrifice of Jesus Christ and are not your own (I Corinthians 6:19-20; I Peter 1:17-19), you are God's possession and a steward (managing servant) of all that the Lord has provided for you. As the Lord's servant, you have the privilege and responsibility to be faithful with all that He has placed in your care (Matthew 25:14-30; Luke 16:10-13; I Corinthians 4:1-2; I Peter 4:10). As a servant of the Lord, you should not seek to be served (Mark 10:42-45) or to receive credit from men (Colossians 3:23; I Thessalonians 2:4-6) but instead should seek only to please the Lord (I Corinthians 10:31; II Corinthians 5:9; Hebrews 13:20-21).

Your practice

(Principle 42)   Examine (judge) yourself continually in a biblical manner (Matthew 7:5; I Corinthians 11:26-32) and do not compare yourself with others (II Corinthians 10:12; Galatians 6:3-4) to determine whose approval you ultimately seek (II Corinthians 5:9; Galatians 1:10; Colossians 3:23-24; I Thessalonians 2:4).

(Principle 43)   Thank God for "apparent deficiencies" that you cannot correct *(II Corinthians 12:7-10; Ephesians 5:20; I Thessalonians 5:18)* and correct all actual deficiencies in your life that hinder you from serving God and edifying others *(Matthew 22:37-39; Romans 6:19, 14:12-13; I Corinthians 10:31-33; Philippians 2:12-16; Colossians 3:2-15; Hebrews 12:1-2; James 4:8)*.

(Principle 44)   You are to practice love without hypocrisy (play-acting) *(Romans 12:9)*, demonstrating the fruit of Christ's life in your thoughts, speech, and actions *(Matthew 5:16; Galatians 5:22-23; Ephesians 5:1-2)*.

ANGER AND BITTERNESS

(Lesson 11)

God's view

(Principle 45)   Anger (great displeasure, animosity) that is quickly aroused or quickly expressed is characteristic of your old self apart from Jesus Christ and is contrary to Scripture *(Galatians 5:19-20; Colossians 3:8; James 1:19-20)*. Bitterness is related to anger and demonstrates a great dissatisfaction with God's sovereignty in your life. Bitterness arises out of living to please self instead of living to please the Lord *(Acts 8:18-23; Romans 3:10-18, esp. vs. 14)* and causes much trouble *(Hebrews 12:15)*.

Your hope

(Principle 46)   Since God's Word commands you to put away anger and bitterness *(Psalm 37:8; Ephesians 4:31; Colossians 3:8)*, it is possible to do so *(I Corinthians 10:13; Hebrews 2:17-18, 4:15-16)*.

(Principle 47)   You do not need to defend or preserve what you perceive to be your "rights" *(based on Psalm 37:23, 84:11-12; I Peter 2:19-25)*, because God causes all things to work together for good to those who belong to Him and love Him *(Romans 8:28-29)*.

Your change

(Principle 48)   You are to control your spirit *(Proverbs 25:28)*, be slow to anger *(James 1:19)*, and deal with anger quickly *(Ephesians 4:26-27)*. You are to put off anger, wrath, bitterness, quick-temperedness, dissension, abusive speech, and strife; and you are not to take into account a wrong suffered *(Matthew 5:21-22; I Corinthians 13:5; Ephesians 4:31; Colossians 3:8; I Timothy 2:8; Titus 1:7)*. Instead, you are to put on patience, kindness, humility, bearing with one another, tenderheartedness, forgiveness, love, and self-control *(Ephesians 4:31-32; Colossians 3:12-14)*.

Your practice

(Principle 49) List the circumstances or relationships in which you are (or have been) tempted to become angry or bitter *(based on Proverbs 9:6, 14:16; Matthew 7:1-5; Galatians 5:16-21)*. Develop a **"Daily Practices" Plan** for overcoming anger or bitterness and formulate an **"Overcoming Temptations" Plan** for dealing with anger or bitterness that may arise quickly or unexpectedly *(based on Proverbs 28:13; Ephesians 4:26-27; I Thessalonians 5:22; II Timothy 2:15, 22; James 1:19; I Peter 1:13-16)*. As you rely on God's power and provisions *(John 15:5; Galatians 5:24-25; II Timothy 3:16-17)*, diligently do what you have planned to avoid further sin with regard to anger or bitterness *(James 1:22-25, 4:17)*.

(Principle 50) Practice biblical love *(Proverbs 10:12; I Corinthians 13:4-8a; I Peter 1:22, 4:8; I John 4:11)* by forgiving others just as God has forgiven you *(Mark 11:25; Ephesians 4:32; Colossians 3:13)* and by doing kind and tenderhearted deeds to the very individuals with whom you become irritated *(Ephesians 4:32; I Peter 3:8-9)*.

INTERPERSONAL PROBLEMS (PART ONE) (LEARNING HOW TO LOVE YOUR NEIGHBOR)

(Lesson 12)

God's view

(Principle 51) If you do not love others, you do not love God *(I John 4:20-21)*. If you do not biblically forgive others, you will not be forgiven by God *(Matthew 6:14-15, 18:21-35; Mark 11:25-26)*. Your forgiveness of others demonstrates your obedience to God's Word *(Ephesians 4:32; Colossians 3:13)* and, thus, your love for the Lord *(John 14:15; I John 5:3; II John 1:6)*. When you forgive others, you indicate your gratefulness to God for His gracious forgiveness of you through the Lord Jesus Christ *(based on Matthew 18:21-35, esp. verses 32-33)*.

(Principle 52) Do not judge others by your own standards, perspectives, or experiences *(John 7:24; Romans 14:1-13; James 4:11-12)*. You will be judged in the very same way you judge others *(Matthew 7:1-2; Luke 6:36-38)*.

(Principle 53) Even when you are worshipping the Lord and remember that someone (spouse, brother, neighbor, co-worker, etc.) has something against you, you are to cease your worship, go and seek reconciliation, and then return to your worship *(Matthew 5:23-24)*. You are commanded in the Name of the Lord Jesus Christ to eliminate divisions among believers, since the unity of the body of Christ is from and in the Holy Spirit. Unity of mind and purpose should characterize believers *(John 17:20-23; I Corinthians 1:10, 12:22-27; Philippians 2:1-2)*.

Your hope

(*Principle 54*)   God has enabled you to forgive others *(based on Ephesians 4:32)*. You can love even your enemies *(Matthew 5:43-48; Luke 6:27-35)*. Both forgiveness and biblical love are not dependent upon your feelings *(based on I Corinthians 13:4-8a; Colossians 3:13)* but upon an act of your will *(John 14:15; II Corinthians 5:14-15; I John 3:18-24; 4:10-11, 21)* as you respond to God's love to you *(I John 4:19)*.

INTERPERSONAL PROBLEMS (PART TWO) (LEARNING HOW TO LOVE YOUR NEIGHBOR)

(Lesson 13)

Your change

(*Principle 55*)   Do unto others as you would want them to do for you *(Matthew 7:12)*. In your relationships, you must be careful to remove anything from your life that could become a stumbling block to others *(Matthew 18.7, Romans 14:13; I Corinthians 8:9, 13)*.

(*Principle 56*)   Put off arguing, quarreling, and returning evil for evil; put on kind speech and gentle behavior by giving a blessing instead *(Philippians 2:14-16; Colossians 4:6; I Thessalonians 5:15; II Timothy 2:23-25; I Peter 3:8-9)*.

Your practice

(*Principle 57*)   Confess your sins to the Lord *(I John 1:9)* and, in a completely biblical manner, confess sins to others against whom you have sinned *(James 5:16)*. Express sorrow and repentance *(Matthew 3:8; Acts 26:20; II Corinthians 7:9; James 4:8-10)*, formulate a specific biblical plan to change, and begin to implement the plan *(II Corinthians 7:9-11; Ephesians 4:31-32; Colossians 3:12-17; James 1:25; I Peter 4:8-11)*.

(*Principle 58*)   When communicating with someone, first establish the habit of listening carefully *(Proverbs 18:2, 13; James 1:19-20)*. Then, speaking the truth in love, bless those with whom you speak *(Ephesians 4:15, 25, 29; Colossians 4:6)*. Follow God's directives for biblical communication: be honest, be kind and tender-hearted, keep current, speak no unwholesome words, and use only words that build up and make for peace *(Proverbs 12:18, 15:1; Romans 14:19; Ephesians 4:25, 29, 32; Colossians 4:6)*.

(*Principle 59*)   Actively seek reconciliation with others *(Matthew 5:9, 23-24; 18:15-18; Romans 12:18; Colossians 3:14-15)*.

THE MARRIAGE RELATIONSHIP
(PART ONE)
(Lesson 14)

God's view

(Principle 60)   Marriage is not a social convenience nor simply an invention for living together. It is ordained by God to be a covenant of companionship and mutual complement *(based on Genesis 2:18, 22-25; Malachi 2:14; Matthew 19:3-6; I Corinthians 7:10-11)*, and it is meant to keep you set apart in your physical relationship for one another *(I Corinthians 7:2-5)*.

(Principle 61)   The marriage relationship is designed to be one of unity and one-flesh permanency *(Genesis 2:24; Mark 10:6-9; Ephesians 5:31)* that reflects the loving relationship between Christ and His Church *(Ephesians 5:21-33)*.

Your hope

(Principle 62)   If you are married, God's Word instructs you to love your spouse *(Ephesians 5:25; Titus 2:4)*; and, if you are a believer in Jesus Christ, you have already been enabled to do so *(Romans 5:5)*. Even if your spouse never practices biblical love, you can still be at peace *(Psalm 119:165; John 14:27, 16:33; Romans 12:18; Galatians 5:22-23)* and can do your part to foster harmony in your home *(I Peter 3:8-9)*. Remember that you are not responsible to change others *(based on Ezekiel 18:20; Philippians 1:6, 2:13)*, but you are responsible to examine yourself continually in a biblical manner *(Matthew 7:1-5; I Corinthians 11:31)*.

(Principle 63)   As you continue to be a biblical servant and be a blessing to your spouse *(based on Romans 12:9-21; Ephesians 5:21-33; Philippians 2:3-4)*, you can be assured that God will work all things for good in your relationship with your spouse. No one, not even an unbelieving or unloving or rebellious spouse, can prevent it *(based on Romans 8:28-29)*.

THE MARRIAGE RELATIONSHIP
(PART TWO)
(Lesson 15)

Your change

(Principle 64)   Husbands, put off being harsh or embittered towards your wives. Put on love and understanding just as Christ also loved the church and gave Himself up for her *(Ephesians 5:25; Colossians 3:19; I Peter 3:7)*. Being a true leader requires being a true servant in attitude and action *(Matthew 20:25-28; John 15:11-13; Ephesians 5:21, 25-33; Philippians 2:3-8)*.

(Principle 65)   Wives, put off being quarrelsome and contentious with your husbands. Put on love, submission, and respect for them *(Proverbs 21:9; John 15:11-13; Ephesians 5:21-24, 33; Colossians 3:18; Titus 2:3-5; I Peter 3:1-6).*

(Principle 66)   To love one's spouse as God commands *(I John 3:23)* requires that you die daily to your own selfish desires *(Luke 9:23-24)* and live to please God and serve your spouse *(Matthew 22:37-39; Ephesians 5:21; Philippians 2:3-8).*

Your practice

(Principle 67)   In order to fulfill your marriage responsibilities faithfully, you must rely on the Lord's strength and the wisdom of His Word. Do not depend on your natural strength or wisdom *(based on Proverbs 3:5-6; Isaiah 55:8-11; John 15:1-5; II Timothy 3:16-17; I John 2:4-6, 3:23-24).* As you lovingly and faithfully carry out these responsibilities, you demonstrate your love for God *(Matthew 22:37-38; I John 5:3)* and your spouse *(I Corinthians 13:4-8a; I John 3:18, 4:7-8).*

(Principle 68)   When you fail to love your spouse as you should, you can be restored to fellowship with both the Lord and your spouse *(based on Psalm 145:14; Proverbs 24:16; Matthew 5:23-24).* To be restored to the Lord, you must confess your sin to Him *(Psalm 51:1-4; I John 1:9)* and return to your initial commitment to live for Him by: (a) remembering from where you have fallen, (b) repenting, and (c) doing again the deeds you did at first which show your love for the Lord *(John 14:15; I John 5:3; Revelation 2:4-5).*

PARENT-CHILD RELATIONSHIPS
(PART ONE)

(Lesson 16)

God's view

(Principle 69)   Children are a gift (heritage) of the Lord *(Psalm 127:3).* They are to be brought up according to the directives of God's Word *(based on Psalm 19:7-11; II Timothy 3:14-17)* and not according to the arbitrary decisions of parents or the philosophies of man *(Proverbs 3:5; 16:2; Isaiah 55:8-11; I Corinthians 3:18-20).* Parents are to train up their children in the discipline and instruction of the Lord *(Deuteronomy 4:9; 6:6-7, 20-25; Proverbs 22:6; Ephesians 6:4).*

(Principle 70)   Children are to honor and obey their parents in the Lord, because this is right and is pleasing to the Lord *(Deuteronomy 5:16; Mark 7:8-10; Ephesians 6:1-2; Colossians 3:20).*

Your hope

(*Principle 71*)   As you study and follow God's Word for your life and the training of your children (*based on Ecclesiastes 12:13-14; Isaiah 55:8-11; II Timothy 2:15; 3:16-17*) and decisively put off any reliance on yourself, your background, or your upbringing (*Proverbs 3:5, 14:12, 28:26a; I Corinthians 3:20*), you will gain the wisdom and direction that you need to be a godly parent (*based on Proverbs 3:5-6, 15:33; James 1:25*).

(*Principle 72*)   Children, when you put off disobedience, stubbornness, and rebellion (*based on Deuteronomy 21:18-21; Romans 1:28-32, esp. verse 30; 2:5-11; II Timothy 3:1-5, esp. verse 2; Titus 1:6*) and put on honor and obedience to the Lord and your parents (*Ephesians 6:1-2; Colossians 3:20*), God will bless you (*Ephesians 6:2-3*). Heed (take seriously) your parents' instruction and discipline, that you may be wise (*based on Proverbs 13:1, 19:20, 23:19*).

PARENT-CHILD RELATIONSHIPS
(PART TWO)
(*Lesson 17*)

Your change

(*Principle 73*)   Parents, stop provoking your children (*Ephesians 6:4; Colossians 3:21*) but instead provide them with discipline and instruction in the Lord (*Deuteronomy 6:6-7; Ephesians 6:4*). While continuing to judge yourself in all areas of life (*Matthew 7:1-5*), you are to train your children (*Proverbs 22:6; Ephesians 6:4*) to delight in the Lord and to walk faithfully in His ways (*based on Psalm 1:1-6; Ephesians 4:1-3; II Timothy 3:14-17*).

(*Principle 74*)   As parents, you are to serve your children lovingly (*based on Philippians 2:3-4*) through your faithful biblical teaching and discipline (*based on Deuteronomy 4:9, 6:4-9; I Corinthians 4:14-16, 11:1; Philippians 3:15-17; II Thessalonians 3:7*) in order to train up your children in the ways of the Lord (*based on Proverbs 4:1-4, 22:6; Ephesians 6:4*). You are not to insist on your children's obedience merely on the basis of your parental authority, nor are you to rely upon any adequacy as coming from yourself. Rather, you are to minister to your children faithfully as a servant of the Lord Jesus Christ (*based on John 13:12-17; II Corinthians 3:5-6*).

(*Principle 75*)   Children, you are to learn from your parents willingly as they teach you the precepts, the principles, and the ways of the Lord (*Proverbs 1:2-5; 2:1-9; 6:20-23*). You are to heed as from the Lord the teaching, reproof, and discipline from your parents and other spiritually mature individuals. In doing this, you will gain wisdom and will not be ensnared by the deceit or wickedness of others and their false ways (*based on Proverbs 2:10-15; 3:13-26, 4:10-27; 5:1-23, 13:1, 20:11; Colossians 1:9-12*). Put off being wise in your own eyes (*Proverbs 12:15; 21:2*) and put on the fear (reverence) and love of the Lord that results from being obedient to His Word *(Psalm 111:10; Proverbs 3:5-7; John 14:15; 21; I John 5:3)*. In addition, put off abandoning or neglecting the teaching of your parents and put on heeding their teaching and reproof *(based on Proverbs 4:1-6; 15:32-33, 19:26; Ephesians 6:1; Colossians 3:20)*.

Your practice

(Principle 76) Based on God's standards for life as revealed in His Word *(Psalm 19:7-11; 119:105, 160; II Timothy 3:16-17; II Peter 1:3-4)*, you, as a parent, are to determine biblical responsibilities and tasks that will lead you and your children to discipline yourselves toward godliness *(based on I Timothy 4:7-8; II Peter 1:3-10)*, resulting in glory to God *(based on Psalm 29:1-2, 145:10-13; Matthew 5:16; I Peter 1:7)*.

(Principle 77) Even though you may not yet be an adult, you are to live in a manner that is pleasing to the Lord as you seek to be an example of a godly believer *(based on Proverbs 20:11; Colossians 1:10; I Timothy 4:12)*. Stubbornness and rebellion are not to be part of your life as you continuously honor and obey your parents *(based on Ephesians 6:1-2; Philippians 2:14-16; Colossians 3:20)*. Be a good steward, even in your youth, of all the Lord has provided you in order to demonstrate your faithfulness to Him *(based on I Corinthians 4:2; Colossians 3:23-24)*.

DEPRESSION

(Lesson 18)

God's view

(Principle 78) Symptoms defined as "depression" are sometimes precipitated by sin *(based on Genesis 4:3-14; Psalm 32:3-5, 38:1-10)*, which means you are living to please yourself instead of living to please the Lord. If you do not repent, confess your self-centeredness, and return to living in a biblical manner, you will experience even further difficulties *(based on Psalm 32:3-4, 38:1-4; Colossians 3:25; Hebrews 12:5-11)*.

(Principle 79) To love life and see good days, you must turn from doing evil and be obedient to God's Word *(I Peter 3:10-12)*. In spite of "feeling depressed," you can live biblically because of the divine resources that God graciously provides for you *(based on Psalm 19:7-11; 34:18-19; 119:28, 105, 143; 145:14; Matthew 11:28-30; Romans 8:11-14, 26; II Corinthians 12:9-10; Philippians 4:6-7, 13; Hebrews 4:15-16)*.

Your hope

(Principle 80) No matter how difficult any situation appears, the Lord Jesus Christ has overcome it *(John 16:33)*. God will not allow anything into your life that is beyond His control or beyond your ability to endure without sinning *(based on Genesis 50:20; Jeremiah 29:11; Romans 8:28-29; I Corinthians 10:13; II Corinthians 12:9-10; Philippians 4:13)*. Trials are

for your good *(Romans 5:3-5; James 1:2-4; I Peter 1:6-7)*; and, as you respond biblically, give opportunity for the power of God to show forth in your life *(II Corinthians 4:7-18, 12:9-10)*.

(Principle 81)   In difficulties, God's comfort *(Psalm 119:50; II Corinthians 1:3-5, 7:6a)* and sustaining care are available to you *(Psalm 34:8, 42:11, 46:1-3, 55:22, 145:14; Lamentations 3:32; Matthew 11:28-30; Hebrews 4:15-16)*.

Your change

(Principle 82)   Put off disobedience to God's Word; put on living a disciplined, faithfully obedient life *(Genesis 4:7; Romans 6:11-13, 19; I Timothy 4:7-11)* out of a commitment to please God instead of yourself *(II Corinthians 5:14-15; Galatians 5:16-17)*.

Your practice

(Principle 83)   Establish a biblical schedule for fulfilling your God-given responsibilities and keep the schedule regardless of any feelings of depression you may experience *(Ephesians 5:15-17; James 4:17)*. Do all your responsibilities and tasks heartily as to the Lord and for His glory *(Matthew 5:16; I Corinthians 10:31; Colossians 3:17, 23-24)*. If you sin, confess this to the Lord *(I John 1:9)* and, following biblical guidelines, confess your sins to those against whom you have sinned *(James 5:16)*.

FEAR AND WORRY

(Lesson 19)

God's view

(Principle 84)   Overwhelming fear and worry result from living to please yourself instead of living to please the Lord *(based on Matthew 6:25-34; 25:14-30, esp. verses 25-26; Luke 12:4; I Peter 3:13-16; I John 4:15-19)*. Instead of a sinful self-focus, you are to fear (reverence) God *(Deuteronomy 5:29, 13:4; Psalm 25:14, 33:8; 147:11; Proverbs 10:27; Luke 1:50, 12:5; II Corinthians 7:1; I Peter 2:17)* and have a responsive concern (care) for others *(based on I Corinthians 12:25; II Corinthians 11:24-30, esp. verse 28; Philippians 4:10)*.

Your hope

(Principle 85)   God has not given you a spirit of timidity (fear) but of power and love and discipline (sound judgment) *(II Timothy 1:7)*.

(Principle 86)   God has promised to provide all the necessities of life as you seek to please Him *(Proverbs 3:5-10; Luke 12:22-34; Philippians 4:19)*. God is always available to help you *(Psalm 55:22, 94:17-19, 145:14)*, and He is firmly in control of every aspect of your life *(based on Psalm 139:1-18; Jeremiah 17:7-8, 29:11; Lamentations 3:32; Romans 8:28-29, 35-39)*.

Your change

(Principle 87) Put off timid, fearful, and troubled thinking. Put on love and sound judgment in the power of the Holy Spirit *(based on II Timothy 1:7; I John 4:9-19, esp. verse 18).* Recognize that in Christ Jesus you have peace *(John 14:27, 16:33).*

(Principle 88) Put off self-centered concern about the future *(Matthew 6:25, 34; Luke 12:22-34, esp. verses 22-23).* Put on "doing the Word" *(based on Psalm 119:165; Matthew 6:33-34; Philippians 4:9; Hebrews 5:14; James 1:22-25),* with special emphasis given to prayer with thanksgiving *(Philippians 4:6-7; I Thessalonians 5:17-18)* and dwelling on the things of God *(Philippians 4:8; Colossians 3:2).*

Your practice

(Principle 89) In order to deal biblically with fear, you must confess your self-centered fear to the Lord *(I John 1:9)* and fulfill your responsibilities in Christ-like love *(I Corinthians 13:4-8a; Colossians 3:12-14),* regardless of your feelings *(based on II Corinthians 5:14-15; Philippians 4:6-9; I John 4:18).*

(Principle 90) To overcome worry, make a plan to accomplish today's tasks and do each task heartily as unto the Lord *(Proverbs 16:9; Ephesians 5:15-17; Philippians 4:6-9; Colossians 3:17, 23-24).*

LIFE-DOMINATING PRACTICES OF SIN
(PART ONE)
(Lesson 20)

God's view

(Principle 91) God holds you responsible for all your deeds (thoughts, speech, and actions), including those that are life-dominating or those that are thought to be "genetically predisposed" or "addictive" *(based on Ecclesiastes 12:13-14; Ezekiel 18:2-20, esp. verse 20; Matthew 12:35-37; Romans 2:1-11; I Corinthians 3:8; II Corinthians 5:10; Colossians 3:23-25; I Peter 1:17; Revelation 22:12).* You become a slave to whatever controls you *(Romans 6:16-18; II Peter 2:19b).*

Your hope

(Principle 92) No matter how serious or long-standing your sin, it can be overcome completely and in a very short period of time as you follow God's plan for all of life *(based on Romans 6:17-18; I Corinthians 6:9-11, esp. verse 11; 10:13; II Corinthians 5:17; II Timothy 3:16-17; I John 5:3-5).*

LIFE-DOMINATING
PRACTICES OF SIN (PART TWO)
(Lesson 21)

Your change

(Principle 93) You are immediately to stop (put off) yielding to or placing yourself under the control of any sin that has you enslaved. Instead, determine to place yourself under the powerful control of the Holy Spirit and wholeheartedly commit to obey God's Word (put on) in every area of your life *(Romans 6:11-18, 22; 8:2-16, esp. verses 2, 5-6, 14; Galatians 5:16-17; Ephesians 5:18; II Timothy 3:16-17; I Peter 2:11; II Peter 1:2-11).*

Your practice

(Principle 94) Since God's Word teaches that those who continually practice sin shall not inherit the Kingdom of God *(I Corinthians 6:9-10; Galatians 5:19-21; I John 3:6-9)*, make a thorough examination of yourself to determine if you are in the faith (i.e., whether you are truly a believer in Jesus Christ) *(based on John 3:3, 16-21, 36; Romans 10:8-11; II Corinthians 13:5; I John 2:3-6, 3:4-9, 5:11-13).*

(Principle 95) Make a thorough biblical evaluation of when, where, how, and with whom you commit the sin by which you are being dominated *(based on Psalm 139:23-24; Matthew 7:1-5; I Corinthians 11:31)* and develop a biblical plan to be an overcomer in all of these situations by putting on the full armor of God *(based on Romans 6:12-13; I Corinthians 6:9-12; Ephesians 2:10; 4:1-3, 25-32; 6:10-18; Colossians 2:6, 3:1-17).*

(Principle 96) Take immediate steps to eliminate, resist, or flee from temptations that arise unexpectedly, especially in the area of your life-dominating sin *(based on Psalm 1:1; Proverbs 4:14-19, 27:12; I Corinthians 15:33; II Timothy 2:22; James 4:7; I Peter 5:8-9).*

(Principle 97) Continually be a faithful doer of the Word in every area of your life. Be especially diligent to follow your biblical plan to overcome your life-dominating sin(s) so that you can mature in Christlikeness in all your deeds (thoughts, words, and actions) *(based on Psalm 19:7-11; II Timothy 3:16-17; Hebrews 5:14; James 1:22-25; I Peter 1:13-22; II Peter 1:2-11).*

GOD'S STANDARDS FOR LIFE

(Lesson 22)

God's view

(Principle 98)   God's standards are always consistent and are never subject to the whim of the moment. His commands are changeless *(Isaiah 40:8; I Peter 1:25);* they do not fluctuate with the age in which you live *(based on Psalm 19:7-11; 119:89, 160; Proverbs 30:5-6)* because God Himself is changeless *(based on Exodus 3:14-15; Malachi 3:6; John 8:57-58; Hebrews 1:10-12, 13:8).*

(Principle 99)   God's standards are the same for all individuals, in all cultures, and at all age levels, regardless of personality or background *(based on II Chronicles 19:7; Proverbs 20:11; Acts 10:34-35; Romans 1:16, 2:2-11, 3:21-30; Galatians 3:26-29; Ephesians 6:9; Colossians 3:25; II Timothy 3:14-15).* Therefore, no "double standard" exists for adults, children, the rich, the poor, nationalities, different occupations, either gender, or any other distinction.

(Principle 100)   The key to fruitfulness in your life is to fear (have reverence for) God *(Psalm 111:10, 145:19; Proverbs 1:7, 3:7-8, 9:10, 14:27, 19:23; Ecclesiastes 8:12-13, 12:13-14)* and consistently keep His commandments in every aspect of your life (be a doer of the Word) *(based on Exodus 20:1-17; Deuteronomy 11:26-28; Matthew 7:24-27; John 14:21, 23; 15:10-11; James 1:25; I John 3:22).*

Your hope

(Principle 101)   God's plans for you are for your benefit *(based on Psalm 145:17; Jeremiah 29:11-13; Romans 8:28)* and have as their goal your maturity in Christ *(based on Romans 8:29; II Corinthians 3:18).* If you keep God's commandments, He will bless you; if you do not keep them, He will judge you with a view to discipline *(Deuteronomy 11:8-9, 13-17, 26-28; Psalm 32:3-5; I Corinthians 11:31-32; Hebrews 12:5-11; James 1:22-25).*

(Principle 102)   God's standards are not burdensome *(Matthew 11:28-30)* for He will strengthen, uphold, and keep you from stumbling as you walk in His way, cooperating with the change He is accomplishing in your life *(based on Joshua 1:8-9; Psalm 103:1-5, 121:1-8; Proverbs 3:5-6; Isaiah 40:29-31; Matthew 28:18-20; John 6:37; Ephesians 1:13-14; Philippians 2:12-13; Colossians 2:6-7; II Peter 1:10; Jude 1:24-25).*

Your change

(Principle 103)   Put off the deeds of darkness; put on the Lord Jesus Christ and make no provision for fleshly lusts *(Romans 13:12-14).* Put on the full armor of God to withstand the schemes of the devil *(Ephesians 6:10-18).*

(Principle 104) Do not be surprised at trials, even if they seem fiery; instead, rejoice in them because God uses them to develop Christ-like maturity in your life *(based on Romans 5:3-5; II Corinthians 4:7-18; James 1:2-4; I Peter 4:12-13).* Be prepared to be reviled and to suffer persecution because of your commitment to Jesus Christ and your faithfulness in being obedient to God's Word *(based on Matthew 5:10-12, 10:16-28; II Timothy 3:12; I Peter 4:12-19).* If you should endure suffering for the sake of righteousness, you are blessed of the Lord *(based on Matthew 5:10-12; Luke 6:22-23; James 5:10-11; I Peter 3:13-17, esp. verse 14; I Peter 5:6-10).*

Your practice

(Principle 105) Establish and maintain biblical standards that will encourage you and your children (if any) toward godliness. Identify godly traits that need to be developed within you, along with corresponding biblical responsibilities and activities which will demonstrate Christlikeness *(based on Galatians 5:22-23; Ephesians 1:4, 4:1, 4:17 - 6:9; Philippians 2:12-13; Colossians 3:12-24; I Timothy 4:7-8; II Peter 1:2-10).*

BIBLICAL PRINCIPLES FOR DISCIPLERS/COUNSELORS

BIBLICAL COUNSELING IS IN-DEPTH DISCIPLESHIP

Biblical discipleship involves evangelism and teaching.

(Principle 106) The disciples of Jesus Christ are to be His witnesses to the uttermost part of the earth and they also are to teach disciples of all nations to practice all that Jesus taught. These two missions are principal characteristics of biblical discipleship *(based on Matthew 28:19-20; Acts 1:8).*

Biblical counseling is in-depth discipleship.

(Principle 107) Because biblical counseling deals with every aspect of a person's life, it can be described as in-depth discipleship. It includes evangelizing, baptizing, teaching, admonishing, instructing, comforting, encouraging, restoring, strengthening, reproving, rebuking, and exhorting others to follow a biblical pattern of life *(based on Matthew 28:19-20; Romans 15:14; II Corinthians 1.4, Galatians 6:1; I Thessalonians 3:2; II Timothy 4:2; Hebrews 3:13; 10:24).*

A BIBLICAL UNDERSTANDING OF THE DISCIPLE/COUNSELEE

Unbelievers have no capability to change biblically.

(Principle 108) Unbelievers are not able to understand the things of God *(I Corinthians 2:6-14, esp. verse 14),* and they do not have the power that comes from God to live victoriously *(based on John 15:4-5; Romans 5:5-8; 8:8-9).* Therefore, they do not have the steadfast hope that comes from obedient faith in Jesus Christ *(Ephesians 2:12).*

Believers can change quickly and dramatically.

(Principle 109) Believers have available all that they need to change quickly and dramatically because they have the authority of the Scriptures *(John 17:17; Acts 20:32; I Thessalonians 2:13; II Timothy 3:16-17; Hebrews 4:12),* the empowering of the Holy Spirit available to them *(Romans 8:9-14; Ephesians 1:13-14; 5:18),* and the privilege of prayer to approach the throne of God in time of need *(Hebrews 4:15-16).* Since God commands His children to walk by the Spirit, which implies His empowerment, believers are able to exhibit the fruit of the Spirit at all times *(based on Galatians 5:16, 22-25).*

YOUR RESPONSIBILITY AS A BIBLICAL DISCIPLER/COUNSELOR

Every maturing believer is to disciple/counsel biblically.

(Principle 110) God gives you the privileged responsibility to disciple/counsel others *(based on Romans 15:14; Galatians 5:25; 6:1-2)*. He has already taught you much about His work and His provisions as He, by the Holy Spirit, has worked in your own life. He already has given you His empowering grace and wisdom through Jesus Christ to live abundantly and victoriously *(based on John 1:16; 10:10; Romans 5:1-2; 8:31-37; I Corinthians 1:18-30; II Corinthians 1:3-4, 12:9; I John 5:4-5)*.

Maintain an obedient walk with the Lord.

(Principle 111) Maintain a faithful and obedient walk with the Lord *(based on Matthew 7:1-5; John 14:15; Ephesians 4:1-3; Colossians 1:9-12; 2:6-7)*. Your deeds should set an example for others to follow *(based on Matthew 5:13-16; I Corinthians 11:1; I Thessalonians 1:6; I Timothy 4:12, 15-16; Hebrews 6:12; 13:7)* and demonstrate your commitment to the Lord Jesus Christ *(based on Mark 8:34-38; John 14:15)*. Your manner in every circumstance and with every person should exemplify the gentle and humble character of Jesus *(based on Matthew 11:29-30; Ephesians 5:1-2; Colossians 2:6; I Peter 2:21; I John 2:3-6, esp. verse 6)*.

Be a servant to those you disciple/counsel.

(Principle 112) Serve those you disciple/counsel with fond affection *(based on Mark 10:42-45; John 13:3-17; I Corinthians 9:19; I Thessalonians 2:8)*. Your ministry to others is to be a labor of love and not that of merely expounding facts or imparting your own wisdom *(based on I Corinthians 3:18-20; II Corinthians 3:5-6; I Thessalonians 1:2-5; 2:1-12)*. As a servant of Jesus Christ, you are not to try to win praise or worldly gain from men *(based on I Corinthians 9:17-18; II Corinthians 2:17; Galatians 1:10; I Thessalonians 2:3-9)*.

The Lord disciplines those who are unfaithful.

(Principle 113) If you are disobedient to the Lord in your own life while you are attempting to disciple/counsel others, you face the discipline of the Lord *(based on Proverbs 1:20-33; 15:10a; Matthew 18:15-17; I Corinthians 10:12; 11:31-32; Hebrews 12:5-11)* and will one day have to account to the Lord for your lack of faithfulness *(Jeremiah 17:10; Matthew 16:27; II Corinthians 5:10; Colossians 3:23-25)*.

Pray for your co-laborers and those you are counseling.

(Principle 114) You are to pray at all times for everyone including those involved in the biblical discipleship/counseling process *(based on Ephesians 6:18; Philippians 4:6-7; I Thessalonians 5:17)*.

Your speech is always to be edifying.

(*Principle 115*) Your speech is to be gracious and edifying in all aspects of the discipleship/counseling process (*based on Proverbs 16:21; Ephesians 4:29; Colossians 4:6*). You are not to participate in arguments or foolish speculations (*Proverbs 15:1-2; II Timothy 2:22-26*). When it is biblically appropriate to correct others, do so patiently and in a spirit of gentleness (*based on Proverbs 15:1; Galatians 5:22-23; 6:1; II Timothy 2:23-24*) with the goal of establishing them in biblical love (*I Timothy 1:5*).

TEAM DISCIPLESHIP/COUNSELING

In team discipleship/counseling, there is wisdom and victory.

(*Principle 116*) There is wisdom and victory in a multitude of counselors (*Proverbs 11:14; 15:22; 24:6b*). Team members working in unity with one another are stronger and have a better return for their labor than one individual working alone (*based on Ecclesiastes 4:9-10, 12*). Team members can sharpen one another's discipleship/counseling skills (*based on Proverbs 27:17*).

Team discipleship/counseling provides protection from false accusation.

(*Principle 117*) With multiple team members ministering as co-laborers in the discipleship/counseling process, any false accusations that may be made by others can be dealt with in a forthright and biblical manner (*based on Deuteronomy 19:15*).

Team members are to consider others as more important than themselves.

(*Principle 118*) Disciplers/counselors are to give preference in honor to one another and to disciples/counselees, stimulating them to love and good deeds (*based on Romans 12:10-11; Philippians 2:1-8; Hebrews 10:24*).

BIBLICAL HOPE AND AUTHORITY FOR DISCIPLERS/COUNSELORS

Do not measure your "success" by worldly standards.

(*Principle 119*) You are not to focus on the "results" you might wish to see in lives of others (*based on Romans 14:10-12*). Furthermore, you are not to depend on this world's wisdom to measure your supposed "success" (*based on I Corinthians 1:18-31; 3:19-20; II Corinthians 10:12, 18*). Your success consists of remaining faithful to God's Word (*Joshua 1:8-9*).

OVERVIEW OF THE BIBLICAL DISCIPLESHIP/COUNSELING PROCESS

Teach disciples/counselees the biblical pattern for living, not just how to fix the current problem.

(Principle 120) It is not your task to help disciples/counselees deal with all the problems in their lives *(based on Galatians 6:5; Philippians 2:12-13)*. Rather, your objective is to help disciples/counselees biblically face, deal with, and endure their current problems with a view to helping them become established in a pattern of righteousness that encompasses loving God and others in every area of their lives *(based on Matthew 22:37-39; II Corinthians 7:1; Galatians 5:22-25; Ephesians 4:1-3; Titus 2:11-14; II Peter 1:2-11)*.

Follow-up and encourage each disciple in his walk with the Lord Jesus Christ.

(Principle 121) Remain diligent so that you may present each disciple/counselee complete in Christ *(based on Colossians 1:28-29)*. Demonstrate your concern for each person entrusted to you by the Lord, by following-up and encouraging each one in his walk in the Lord Jesus Christ *(based on examples of the Apostles' continuing work with individuals and groups, such as seen in Philippians 1:3-11; 2:19-28; Colossians 1:3-12; I Thessalonians 2:5-12; 4:1; 5:11; I Timothy 1:5; II Timothy 1:1-14; II Peter 1:13-15)*.

APPLYING SCRIPTURES IN DISCIPLESHIP/ COUNSELING

Rely on God's Word alone as your authority.

(Principle 122) As a biblical discipler/counselor you are to rely on the Scriptures alone as your basis of authority; not on your opinions or experiences no matter how relevant they may seem *(based on Isaiah 55:8-9; II Timothy 3:16-17; Titus 2:1)*. You are to be a diligent worker who accurately handles the Word of truth *(II Timothy 2:15)*. This means first, that you need to know and obey the Scriptures *(Joshua 1:8)*, and second, that you need to know how to point disciples/counselees continually to the Word as their only authority for living *(based on Titus 1:9)*.

Teach disciples/counselees to accept nothing less than God's truth for their lives.

(Principle 123) Teach disciples/counselees that God's standards and perspective on life are in direct contrast to man's standards and perspective *(based on Isaiah 55:8-9)*. Remind them also that God regards man's wisdom as foolishness *(I Corinthians 1:20; 3:18-20)*. He expects His children to reject man's deceitful philosophies *(based on Proverbs 14:12; Galatians 3:3-5; Colossians 2:8)* and to trust only in Him and His Word *(based on Proverbs 3:5-6; II Timothy 3:16-17; I Peter 1:24-25)*.

UNDERSTANDING PROBLEMS BIBLICALLY

Accurately assess the disciple/counselee's present condition.

(Principle 124) You are to help disciples/counselees compare their lives with God's Word so that they may gain a biblical understanding of their problems *(based on Psalm 19:7-11; 119:105; II Timothy 3:16-17; Hebrews 4:12; James 1:25)*. Ask questions to help them identify the areas of their lives in which there is a focus on pleasing self instead of pleasing the Lord *(based on Proverbs 18:13, 17; 20:5)*.

Our standard for living is Jesus Christ.

(Principle 125) The example of Christ's perfect life must be the standard in evaluating the disciple/counselee's life *(Philippians 2:5; I Peter 2:21)*. This standard provides a clear picture of God's goal for each disciple/counselee *(Romans 8:29; Philippians 2:5-8; I Peter 2:21-25)*.

Avoid sinful discussions.

(Principle 126) Avoid listening to descriptions of the faults of other people *(based on Proverbs 11:9, 12; 20:19)*. Do not dwell on the specific details about sinful activities that might encourage sinful thinking *(based on Galatians 6:1; II Timothy 2:22)*.

Listen and judge carefully.

(Principle 127) Listen attentively to the information given by the disciple/counselee *(based on Proverbs 10:19; 15:28; 18:2)*. Be careful that you focus on what the disciple/counselee is saying rather than seeking to come up with your next response *(based on Proverbs 18:2, 13)*. Do not come to hasty conclusions (e.g., making a judgment after hearing only one side of a story involving other individuals whose side you have not heard) *(based on Proverbs 18:13, 17; 29:20; James 1:19)*.

Gather information primarily on the disciple/counselee's known failures to live in a godly way.

(Principle 128) When gathering information about the disciple/counselee's problem, move quickly from the feeling level to the doing level. The disciple/counselee may have much to say about his feelings and perceptions about the problem, but until he deals biblically with his known sinful deeds, he deludes himself and is unable to discern good and evil *(based on Hebrews 5:12-14; James 1:22-25; I John 2:9-11)*. Therefore, concentrate on known failures to live in a godly way.

HELPING A DISCIPLE JUDGE SELF

Help the disciple/counselee recognize his sin.

(Principle 129) At the biblically appropriate time, humbly and lovingly present your observations of scriptural violations and perceived sinful patterns to those who need to know *(based on Psalm 37:30-31; Proverbs 9:9; 12:17-18; 25:11-12; 27:5-6; Galatians 6:1-2).* Offer biblical counsel in a manner that will bring honor to the Lord and will help those who hear to repent of these deeds *(based on Proverbs 15:2; 22:17-21; Romans 14:19; 15:1-7; I Timothy 1:5; II Timothy 2:25-26).*

As necessary, describe the consequences of persistent disobedience.

(Principle 130) Teach disciples/counselees that a lack of obedience to God may result in a loss of peace and joy and even great distress *(based on Genesis 4:6-7; Psalm 32:3-5; 38:3-8).* In fact, if the individual professes to be a believer, counsel him that he will remain under the corrective discipline of the Lord when he persists in being disobedient to God's Word *(based on I Corinthians 11:31-32; Hebrews 12:5-11)* and may face church discipline *(Matthew 18:15-17).* More importantly, persistent disobedience to the Lord may demonstrate the need for salvation *(Matthew 7:21-23; I Corinthians 6:9-10; Galatians 5:19-21; I John 3:4-10).*

BIBLICAL HOPE FOR DISCIPLES/COUNSELEES

Our hope is in the Lord and His Word only.

(Principle 131) Keep the focus on the Lord and on His Word as the sole sources of hope *(based on Psalm 33:18; 119:49; 130:5; Lamentations 3:21-25; Romans 15:4, 13; I John 3:3)* since all other foundations will fail *(based on Job 8:13; 27:8; Psalm 33:16-17; Proverbs 11:7; Ephesians 2:12; I Thessalonians 4:13).*

Discuss often the blessings of obedience.

(Principle 132) Help the disciple understand that no matter how difficult the circumstances, the Lord will bless those who are doers of the Word *(based on Deuteronomy 30:8-10; Psalm 119:165; John 15:10-11; James 1:22-25).*

Avoid false hope.

(Principle 133) Avoid encouraging the disciple to base his hope on opinions or man's philosophies *(based on Proverbs 3:5-8; Isaiah 55:8-9; I Corinthians 3:18-20; I Thessalonians 5:21-22).* Remind him that lasting hope is not based on changes in others around him or in his circumstances, but on the Lord's work in his situation to mature him in Christlikeness *(based on Romans 5:3-5; 8:18-39; Colossians 1:27; I John 3:3).*

STRUCTURING FOR BIBLICAL CHANGE

Recognize that only God causes lasting biblical change in the lives of people.

(Principle 134) You can confidently expect that the Lord will honor His Word and will accomplish His will in the lives of His people within the circumstances they face *(based on Isaiah 55:10-11; II Corinthians 3:18; Philippians 1:6; 2:12-13; I Thessalonians 2:13; II Timothy 3:16-17; James 1:2-4).* You cannot cause change in the lives of disciples/counselees. Only God can accurately judge the entire condition of the heart *(based on I Samuel 16:7; Psalm 139:23-24; Jeremiah 17:9-10; I Corinthians 4:5; I Thessalonians 2:4),* and only He provides the power for lasting biblical change *(based on John 15:5; Romans 8:3-13; Philippians 4:13).*

Biblical change is not possible without salvation.

(Principle 135) Without salvation through faith, biblical change is not possible *(based on John 15:4-5; I Corinthians 2:14-16).* Therefore, it is vital that you establish the biblical basis for the counselee's salvation. This is demonstrated in a person's life by his righteous deeds *(based on James 2:14-19; I John 2:3-6).*

ASSIGNING BIBLICAL HOMEWORK

Biblical homework assignments are characterized by having their foundation in biblical principles.

(Principle 136) Assigning biblical homework is a means of encouraging the disciple/counselee to take purposeful action to establish the practice of obeying the Word of God in his life *(based on Matthew 7:24-27; Romans 6:12-13; Titus 2:11-12; James 1:22-25).*

(Principle 137) Completing biblical homework assignments — doing the Word — is an indication of the disciple/counselee's commitment or lack of commitment to please the Lord. Bearing fruit in every good work brings great blessing *(based on Matthew 7:16-20, 24-27; Colossians 1:10; James 1:22-25).*

SECTION II

MASTER PLAN
FOR THE MINISTRY OF
BIBLICAL DISCIPLESHIP/COUNSELING

SECTION II

MASTER PLAN
FOR THE MINISTRY OF
BIBLICAL DISCIPLESHIP/COUNSELING

INTRODUCTION

This section contains essential helps for planning and evaluating the entire discipleship/counseling process with all individuals to whom you minister. The **MASTER PLAN FOR THE MINISTRY OF BIBLICAL DISCIPLESHIP/ COUNSELING** is an outline of the procedure you can follow as you progress in your ministry with individuals. The **EXPLANATION OF THE MASTER PLAN** provides the detailed guidance you need to implement the biblical guidelines listed in the **MASTER PLAN**.

Before you examine these helps for the first time, be sure that you read **HOW TO USE THE MASTER PLAN AND THE EXPLANATION OF THE MASTER PLAN**.

HOW TO USE THE MASTER PLAN AND THE EXPLANATION OF THE MASTER PLAN

> The **MASTER PLAN** and the **EXPLANATION OF THE MASTER PLAN** are designed to help you plan and conduct biblical discipleship/counseling so that you not only know how to help someone face, deal with, and endure the tests and trials of life but also so that you can help him progressively mature in Jesus Christ.

I. **Purposes of the MASTER PLAN and the EXPLANATION OF THE MASTER PLAN**

   A. The **MASTER PLAN** and the **EXPLANATION OF THE MASTER PLAN** have been prepared to assist the biblical discipler/counselor in evaluating problems according to biblical principles and constructing a personal but completely biblical plan that will lead to peace and joy in spite of all circumstances, conditions, or responses of others. The **MASTER PLAN** and its explanation cover major hindrances to spiritual growth, and when used in conjunction with the *Self-Confrontation* manual, supply the key biblical procedures contained in God's Word to help individuals face, deal with, and endure problems, be overcomers, and enjoy abundant life in Christ Jesus.

   B. Specifically, the **MASTER PLAN** and the **EXPLANATION OF THE MASTER PLAN** are designed to:

   1. Increase your effectiveness in applying the Scriptures when discipling/ counseling others.

   2. Provide you with guidance in investigating, identifying, facing, dealing with, and enduring situations and problems in light of God's Word. Whether the problem is simple or complicated, you can utilize these tools to evaluate how the disciple thinks, speaks, and acts. The perceived problems (e.g., fear, depression, worry, anxiety, marital problems, anger, substance abuse) are usually only symptoms of deeper spiritual problems. You, as a biblical discipler/counselor, must examine all information with a view to discerning the problem biblically.

   3. Direct you to specific biblical principles that encourage continuing spiritual growth as you begin to become a doer of the Word. In using the **MASTER PLAN** and its explanation, you will learn systematically how to help disciples/counselees to deal with problems and become more effective doers of the Word.

   4. Assist you in identifying specific failures, either on your part or on the part of the disciple, in dealing with aspects of life related to the problem, and in formulating specific plans for change.

   C. The **MASTER PLAN** and the **EXPLANATION OF THE MASTER PLAN** have been developed to serve as guides for discipleship/counseling. They are meant to be used systematically, not rigidly or legalistically. You should not assume that every item on the chart must be dealt with in the sequence given.

Under the Holy Spirit's sovereign direction, you must deal with problems according to the demands of each situation.

II. **Overview of the MASTER PLAN**

A.   The **MASTER PLAN** consists of three pages that describe specific areas of progressive spiritual growth in the life of a disciple of Christ, especially in relationship to facing, dealing with, and enduring problems. Each successive page reflects increasing depth in faith and practice. The three pages are entitled and described as follows:

1.   **The Foundation for Biblical Discipleship/Counseling**

The first page of the **MASTER PLAN**, containing Boxes 1-8, focuses on establishing a basic foundation for facing, dealing with, and enduring all problems while growing as a disciple of the Lord Jesus Christ. Primary emphasis is on:

a.   Gathering information that will provide a biblical understanding of the problems,

b.   Developing initial hope and recognition of personal sins, and

c.   Dealing with the disciple/counselee's relationship with the Lord.

2.   **Biblical Reconciliation with God and Man**

The second page of the **MASTER PLAN**, containing Boxes 9-14, describes how to establish a biblical structure for change. The primary tool, the **VICTORY OVER FAILURES PLAN**, is a biblically based tool that can help the disciple/counselee apply God's Word in the power of the Holy Spirit, so that he may overcome any difficulty of life with the full expectation of complete and lasting victory. It explains the specific steps necessary to develop biblical plans for living God's way beginning with helping the disciple/counselee to identify a problem area in his life to work on. Part of the process involves putting off the old manner of life and putting on new, righteous practices in their place (*Ephesians 4:22-24*). The **VICTORY OVER FAILURES PLAN** describes how to do that in very practical ways and gives the disciple/counselee a format he can follow. Very important steps of change on this page are to forgive others, reconcile relationships, and respond biblically in the current situation.

3.   **The Maturing Disciple of Jesus Christ**

The third page of the **MASTER PLAN**, containing Boxes 15-18, provides guidelines for practicing the plans established previously and persevering daily as a faithful servant of God. It describes the believer who is reordering his entire life to conform to what God commands and is beginning to minister to others, thus fulfilling the Great Commission to make disciples. From this point on, most of the counsel will be to prepare the disciple/counselee for continuing his growth in discipleship after the structured discipleship/counseling phase ends.

B.   The italicized references within the boxes cite biblical principles found in Section I of this *Handbook*. All references outside the boxes cite lessons, supplements, or sections in either the *Self-Confrontation* manual or this *Handbook*. These references are not meant to be exhaustive. They are key references that you should review to help you minister to others.

III. **Overview of the EXPLANATION OF THE MASTER PLAN**

A. For each box in the **MASTER PLAN**, the **EXPLANATION OF THE MASTER PLAN** provides a commentary, essential discipleship/counseling Scriptures, cross references, suggested topics for discipleship/counseling meetings, and suggested homework assignments.

1. *Biblical focus and guidelines:* This portion expands on the narrative in the box. It includes explanations, warnings, suggestions, and insights.

2. *Essential Scriptures:* Only a few key verses are noted here; you may refer to a concordance, the *Self-Confrontation* manual, and other parts of this volume for more Scriptures.

3. *Cross references:* These are references to the other boxes in the **MASTER PLAN** that are related to the subject.

4. *Suggested topics for discipleship/counseling meetings:* Included here are examples of topics that you may desire to use when you meet with the counselee. Choose only the topics or portions of topics that will be useful. The first topic listed is typically related to the relevant biblical principles. This is a reminder of the importance of the Scriptures as your basis for discipleship/counseling. Note that some of the suggested topics are directly related to the homework assignments listed in the next section.

5. *Key homework assignments:* The homework assignments listed are not meant to be exhaustive, but are key to helping disciples develop biblical change in their lives. If you choose to use other sources for homework assignments, make sure that they are thoroughly biblical. Explain fully how to complete the assignment and cover necessary details as one of your topics. The first homework assignment is usually a Scripture memory passage.

MASTER PLAN

FOR THE MINISTRY OF
BIBLICAL DISCIPLESHIP/COUNSELING

"If we live by the Spirit, let us also walk by the Spirit."
(Galatians 5:25)

The Foundation for Biblical Discipleship/Counseling

MASTER PLAN FOR THE MINISTRY OF BIBLICAL DISCIPLESHIP/COUNSELING — FIRST PAGE

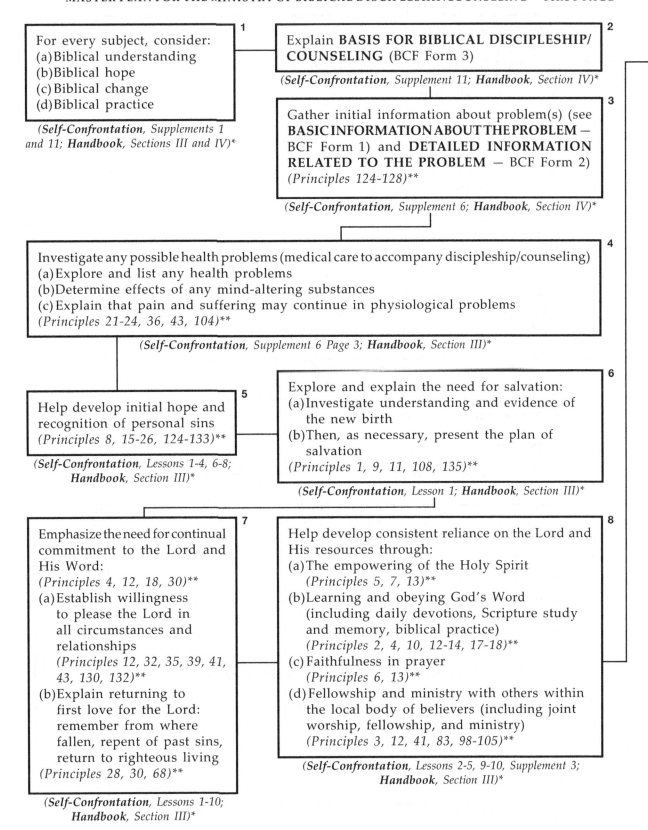

1

For every subject, consider:
(a) Biblical understanding
(b) Biblical hope
(c) Biblical change
(d) Biblical practice

(Self-Confrontation, Supplements 1 and 11; Handbook, Sections III and IV)*

2

Explain **BASIS FOR BIBLICAL DISCIPLESHIP/ COUNSELING** (BCF Form 3)

(Self-Confrontation, Supplement 11; Handbook, Section IV)*

3

Gather initial information about problem(s) (see **BASIC INFORMATION ABOUT THE PROBLEM** — BCF Form 1) and **DETAILED INFORMATION RELATED TO THE PROBLEM** — BCF Form 2)
(Principles 124-128)**

(Self-Confrontation, Supplement 6; Handbook, Section IV)*

4

Investigate any possible health problems (medical care to accompany discipleship/counseling)
(a) Explore and list any health problems
(b) Determine effects of any mind-altering substances
(c) Explain that pain and suffering may continue in physiological problems
(Principles 21-24, 36, 43, 104)**

(Self-Confrontation, Supplement 6 Page 3; Handbook, Section III)*

5

Help develop initial hope and recognition of personal sins
(Principles 8, 15-26, 124-133)**

(Self-Confrontation, Lessons 1-4, 6-8; Handbook, Section III)*

6

Explore and explain the need for salvation:
(a) Investigate understanding and evidence of the new birth
(b) Then, as necessary, present the plan of salvation
(Principles 1, 9, 11, 108, 135)**

(Self-Confrontation, Lesson 1; Handbook, Section III)*

7

Emphasize the need for continual commitment to the Lord and His Word:
(Principles 4, 12, 18, 30)**
(a) Establish willingness to please the Lord in all circumstances and relationships
(Principles 12, 32, 35, 39, 41, 43, 130, 132)**
(b) Explain returning to first love for the Lord: remember from where fallen, repent of past sins, return to righteous living
(Principles 28, 30, 68)**

(Self-Confrontation, Lessons 1-10; Handbook, Section III)*

8

Help develop consistent reliance on the Lord and His resources through:
(a) The empowering of the Holy Spirit
(Principles 5, 7, 13)**
(b) Learning and obeying God's Word (including daily devotions, Scripture study and memory, biblical practice)
(Principles 2, 4, 10, 12-14, 17-18)**
(c) Faithfulness in prayer
(Principles 6, 13)**
(d) Fellowship and ministry with others within the local body of believers (including joint worship, fellowship, and ministry)
(Principles 3, 12, 41, 83, 98-105)**

(Self-Confrontation, Lessons 2-5, 9-10, Supplement 3; Handbook, Section III)*

*   All references outside the boxes cite Sections or Supplements in either the *Self-Confrontation* manual or the *Handbook*.

**   References within boxes cite biblical principles found in Section I of the *Handbook*.

Section II, Handbook

Biblical Reconciliation with God and Man

9

Teach how to judge self through the development of personal failures lists (e.g., keeping account of wrongs suffered, inflicting wrongs, or neglecting to demonstrate biblical love toward God and others) using *Worksheet 2: Lists of Specific Failures to Live Biblically,* **VICTORY OVER FAILURES PLAN** (BCF Form 102)
(Principles 3, 4, 19, 28, 30, 42, 52, 94-95)**

*(**Handbook**, Section III and IV)**

10

Explain the necessity to repent and confess these sins to the Lord, demonstrated by asking for His forgiveness and showing the fruit of repentance
(Principles 26, 28, 30, 57)**

*(**Self-Confrontation**, Lesson 5 and 8; **Handbook**, Section III)**

11

Provide guidance on how to complete *Worksheet 3: "Put-offs" and "Put-ons."*
(Principles 27-29, 56, 93, 103)**

*(**Self-Confrontation**, Lessons 5-8; **Handbook**, Section III)**

12

Provide guidance on how to complete *Worksheet 4: "Daily Practices" Plan* and *Worksheet 5: "Overcoming Temptations" Plan.*
(Principles 30-32, 49, 50, 57, 83, 95-97, 105)**

*(**Self-Confrontation**, Lesson 8; **Handbook**, Sections III and IV)**

13

Teach how to restore unreconciled relationships and develop biblical relationships by:
(a) Forgiving others biblically using *Worksheet 6a: My Plan for Demonstrating Forgiveness*
   (Principles 48, 50-51)**
(b) Being reconciled to others in accordance with biblical principles of communication using *Worksheet 6b: My Plan for Asking Forgiveness*
   (Principles 53, 57-59, 68)**

*(**Self-Confrontation**, Lessons 12-13; **Handbook**, Section III)**

14

Explain how to treat others biblically by teaching principles for:
(a) Not retaliating when wronged
(b) Seeking ways to bless them
(c) Eliminating stumbling blocks
(Principles 50, 55-56, 63, 104)**

*(**Self-Confrontation**, Lessons 9-13, Supplements 15-17; **Handbook**, Section III)**

---

*   All references outside the boxes cite Sections or Supplements in either the *Self-Confrontation* manual or the *Handbook*.

** References within boxes cite biblical principles found in Section I of the *Handbook*.

15

Encourage to stand firm in the midst of sufferings, tests, and trials and to put on the full armor of God
(Principles 12, 21, 23, 24, 32, 80, 95, 103-104)**

(Self-Confrontation, Lessons 5-8, 21; Handbook, Section III)*

16

Explain how to continue to mature in God's standards for life through:
(a) Elimination of unprofitable activities — using **MY PRESENT SCHEDULE** (BCF Form 107)
(b) Addition of activities necessary to carry out God-given responsibilities — using **MY PROPOSED BIBLICAL SCHEDULE** (BCF Form 108)
(c) Periodic evaluation of the plans made
(Principles 12, 31-32, 83, 88, 98-103, 105)**

(Self-Confrontation, Lesson 22, Supplements 15, 16; Handbook, Section III)*

17

Encourage ministry as a working part of the local body of believers through:
(Principle 41)**
(a) Practice of spiritual gifts and cooperation with God's Spirit in bearing spiritual fruit as a faithful steward
(Principles 12, 39, 41, 43-44, 83, 98-105)**
(b) Submission to the spiritual leaders
(Principles 116-118)**
(c) Meeting the needs of the afflicted
(Principle 3)**

(Self-Confrontation, Lessons 10, 22)*

18

Teach how to disciple others toward spiritual maturity and, as applicable, train how to restore those caught up in sin by:
(a) Standing ready to give them a reason for the hope within
(b) Exercising a spirit of gentleness
(c) Assisting in bearing their burdens
(d) Encouraging and stimulating them to love and good deeds
(e) As necessary, admonishing, reproving, and disciplining
(Principle 3, 105, 129-130)**

(Self-Confrontation, Lessons 13, 17, 21; Handbook, Section III)*

*   All references outside the boxes cite Sections or Supplements in either the *Self-Confrontation* manual or the *Handbook*.
**   References within boxes cite biblical principles found in Section I of the *Handbook*.

EXPLANATION OF THE MASTER PLAN

EXPLANATION OF THE MASTER PLAN

THE FOUNDATION FOR BIBLICAL DISCIPLESHIP/COUNSELING
MASTER PLAN — FIRST PAGE

OVERVIEW

The first page of the **MASTER PLAN**, containing Boxes 1-8, focuses on establishing a basic foundation for facing, dealing with, and enduring all problems while growing as a disciple of the Lord Jesus Christ. Primary emphasis is on:

1. Gathering information that will provide a biblical understanding of the problems,
2. Developing initial hope and recognition of personal sins, and
3. Dealing with the disciple/counselee's relationship with the Lord.

NOTES FOR BOX 1

> 1
> For every subject, consider:
> (a) Biblical understanding
> (b) Biblical hope
> (c) Biblical change
> (d) Biblical practice

I. Biblical focus and guidelines:

The purpose of Box 1 is to remind you that in every topic you cover with disciples/counselees you must consider the four basic elements for how to face, deal with, and endure every problem of life. They are essential to discipleship/counseling.

A. Always seek to attain and then to lead the disciple/counselee to a biblical understanding of his problems *(based on Isaiah 55:8-11)*.

B. Consistently emphasize hope from God's Word for each trial in the disciple/counselee's life *(based on Romans 15:4)*.

C. Assist the disciple/counselee in identifying and beginning to practice the specific biblical changes that need to be made to overcome sin in his life. This will involve putting off the old practices of sin and putting on new practices of righteousness *(based on Ephesians 4:22-24; Colossians 3:9-10)*.

D. Encourage the disciple/counselee to establish biblical changes in his life through faithful, persevering obedience. Emphasize that obeying the Word faithfully is essential to maturing as a disciple of Jesus Christ *(based on James 1:22-25)*.

E. For guidance, study *Handbook*, Section III, Part 3, Pages H123-H154.

II.   **Essential Scriptures:**

    A.   For understanding the problems biblically — *Isaiah 55:8-9,*

    B.   For biblical hope — *Romans 15:4,*

    C.   For biblical change — *Ephesians 4:22-24,* and

    D.   For biblical practice — *James 1:22-25.*

III. **Cross references:**

    All other boxes

IV.   **Suggested topics for discipleship/counseling meetings:**

    A.   Ensure that you include all four elements when covering each topic during discipleship/counseling meetings.

    B.   In the first counseling meeting, highlight the four essential elements in Paragraph 8 of **BASIS FOR BIBLICAL DISCIPLESHIP/COUNSELING** *(Handbook,* Page H164, BCF Form 3).

V.   **Key homework assignments:**

    Assign only biblical homework.

NOTES FOR BOX 2

> Explain **BASIS FOR BIBLICAL DISCIPLESHIP/ COUNSELING** (BCF Form 3)

2

I.   Biblical focus and guidelines:

The purpose of Box 2 is to establish a foundation upon which to begin discipling. The **BASIS FOR BIBLICAL DISCIPLESHIP/COUNSELING** (*Handbook*, Pages H163-H166, BCF Form 3) communicates to the disciple/counselee how you will proceed throughout the discipleship/counseling process.

II.   Essential Scriptures:

A.   Regarding **TRAINING OF THE BIBLICAL DISCIPLER/COUNSELOR** — *II Timothy 3:16-17*

B.   Regarding **TEAM DISCIPLESHIP/COUNSELING** — *Proverbs 11:14; 15:22*

C.   Regarding **THE MINISTRY OF THE HOLY SPIRIT** — *John 14:26; 16:13*

III.   Cross references:

Boxes 1, 18

IV.   Suggested topics for discipleship/counseling meetings:

Explain the **BASIS FOR BIBLICAL DISCIPLESHIP/COUNSELING** (*Handbook*, Pages H163-H166, BCF Form 3) and introduce the Victory Over Failures Plan booklet as follows:

In Paragraph 2:   Emphasize that the Bible is the only authority to be used throughout the discipleship/counseling process; then read **II Timothy 3:16-17**. Tell the disciple/counselee that if he does not understand the biblical basis for anything you say, he should ask you for the biblical basis.

In Paragraph 3:   Note that there is no charge for biblical discipleship/counseling. It is a labor of love.

In Paragraph 4:   Explain that you are working as a team in accordance with *Proverbs 11:14* and other Scriptures. Emphasize that the most important member of the team is the Holy Spirit.

NOTE: Use this last point to emphasize the need for prayer and lead the group in prayer.

In Paragraph 5:   Explain that the purpose of the ministry is to accomplish much more than overcoming the current problem. Biblical discipleship/ counseling is a ministry that teaches how to deal with all of life's problems no matter how serious.

In Paragraph 6:   State that biblical confidentiality is quite different from the world's definition and practice. While believers are commanded

NOTES FOR BOX 2 (Continued)

by God not to gossip, you may need to talk to others from time to time to get additional information or counsel.

In Paragraph 8: Briefly explain each of the four elements of biblical discipleship/counseling.

Read the last paragraph, beginning with "In order to help you ..." and give the counselee a copy of the *Victory Over Failures Plan* booklet.

In Paragraph 10: Read only the first sentence.

In Paragraph 13: Emphasize the importance of bringing the Bible to each meeting since it is the only standard and authority to be used for discipleship/counseling.

Also, it is important to bring a notebook and pencil. Explain that taking notes helps the disciple/counselee remember key Scripture passages, important counsel given, and homework assignments. Notes are important to you and the assistants because notes help in recalling important points after the meeting and also help in preparation for future meetings.

V. **Key homework assignments:**

A. Read the **BASIS FOR BIBLICAL DISCIPLESHIP/COUNSELING** (*Handbook*, Pages H163-H166, BCF Form 3). Write down any questions that I have.

B. Read *Victory Over Failures Plan* booklet, Pages 1-10. Write down any questions I have.

NOTES FOR BOX 3

> **3**
>
> Gather initial information about problem(s) (see **BASIC INFORMATION ABOUT THE PROBLEM —** BCF Form 1) and **DETAILED INFORMATION RELATED TO THE PROBLEM —** BCF Form 2) *(Principles 124-128)***

I.   **Biblical focus and guidelines:**

   A.   The **BASIC INFORMATION ABOUT THE PROBLEM** *(Handbook,* Page H157, BCF Form 1) and the **DETAILED INFORMATION RELATED TO THE PROBLEM** *(Handbook,* Pages H159-H162, BCF Form 2) provide you with initial information that will help you know how to proceed with the disciple/counselee.   These forms will help you to:

   1.   Gather detailed information about the disciple/counselee's problems (in keeping with *Proverbs 18:2, 13, 15, 17*).

   2.   Gain a biblical understanding of the problems at the feeling, doing, and heart levels (refer to *Self-Confrontation,* Pages 99-100).

   3.   Examine the basis for his profession of faith and commitment to please the Lord (refer to **A BIBLICAL UNDERSTANDING OF THE DISCIPLE/ COUNSELEE,** *Handbook,* Pages H109-H110).

   4.   Check thoroughly his involvement with the local body of believers beginning with his closest relationships.

   B.   Gathering information at all three levels of the problem:

   1.   *Feeling level* — Carefully explore the feeling level of a problem because feelings are often indicators of deeper problems *(based on Psalm 38:3-10).* A person preoccupied with self tends to allow his feelings to dictate his behavior rather than live according to biblical principles *(see examples in Genesis 4:5-8, I Samuel 18:8-11; Mark 10:21-22).*

   2.   *Doing level* — When gathering information about the disciple/counselee's problem, move quickly from the feeling level to the doing level.   The disciple/counselee may have much to say about his feelings and perceptions about the problem, but until he deals biblically with his known sinful deeds, he deludes himself and is unable to discern good and evil *(based on Hebrews 5:12-14; James 1:22-25; I John 2:9-11).*

   3.   *Heart level* — God is primarily concerned about the heart *(I Samuel 16:7);* however, no human being (including a biblical discipler/counselor) can fully understand the heart *(based on I Kings 8:39; Jeremiah 17:9-10).* But since deeds come out of the heart *(based on Matthew 12:34; 15:18-19),* you may gain insights about whether or not the disciple/counselee's heart is focused on pleasing God or pleasing self when you observe patterns of repetitive righteous or sinful deeds *(based on I John 3:4-10).*

NOTES FOR BOX 3 (Continued)

C. For further guidance, study *Principles 124-128* (*Handbook*, Page H47), **A BIBLICAL UNDERSTANDING OF THE DISCIPLE/COUNSELEE,** and **UNDERSTANDING PROBLEMS BIBLICALLY** (*Handbook*, Pages H109-H110 and H133-H138).

II. **Essential Scriptures:**

Proverbs 18:2, 13, 17; Matthew 15:18

III. **Cross references:**

Boxes 1, 4-6, 18

IV. **Suggested topics for discipleship/counseling meetings:**

A. Gather information.

1. Review the counselee's completed **BASIC INFORMATION ABOUT THE PROBLEM** form (*Handbook*, Page H157, BCF Form 1).

2. Ask questions using the **DETAILED INFORMATION RELATED TO THE PROBLEM** form (*Handbook*, Pages H159-H162, BCF Form 2).

B. Thoroughly check the individual's profession of faith.

C. Gather information at all three levels of the current problem, but concentrate on the doing level.

V. **Key homework assignments:**

If you do not have sufficient time in the first meeting to ask all the pertinent questions, either assign homework designed to gather answers to additional questions or plan to ask them in subsequent meetings (*this assignment refers to IV. A. above*). Some homework assignments useful for gathering further information about the disciple/counselee's situation and problems are as follows:

1. (*To gather further information about relationships*) list all current relationships in which there may be problems, strains, or concerns. Briefly identify the nature of the problems in the relationships.

2. (*To gather information about current responsibilities, in the case of an individual who says he is overwhelmed by his work*) list all current responsibilities. Write a "D" next to the ones that must be done on a daily basis. Then, place a star or asterisk next to the ones not being accomplished on a regular basis.

3. (*To gather information about involvement in church activities or ministries*) list all church or ministry-related activities currently involving time, and identify next to each the amount of time spent on a daily or weekly basis.

NOTES FOR BOX 4

> 4
>
> Investigate any possible health problems (medical care to accompany discipleship/counseling)
> (a) Explore and list any health problems
> (b) Determine effects of any mind-altering substances
> (c) Explain that pain and suffering may continue in physiological problems
> *(Principles 21-24, 36, 43, 104)***

I.   **Biblical focus and guidelines:**

A.   When there is a physical health problem, you can help the disciple face, deal with, and endure his spiritual problems *(based on Romans 8:28-29; II Corinthians 4:7-18)* at the same time that a primary-care physician or health specialist deals with his physical difficulties.

B.   Seek to help the disciple refrain from taking substances that lead to dependence or that substantially affect or alter the mind or behavior *(based on I Corinthians 6:12, 19-20)*.

C.   If the disciple experiences mood swings on a recurrent basis and a health problem has not been investigated yet, check for deeds that may demonstrate failure to be responsible in the care of the body (such as intake of alcohol, drugs, or other mind-altering substances, working continuously without sleep). Also, investigate unknown bodily problems (such as hormonal changes, severe headaches). *NOTE: Jesus indicated a need for physicians to take care of bodily problems (Matthew 9:12). Luke was a physician (Colossians 4:14).*

D.   Help the disciple become confident that God's plan is for good in their lives whether the physical problem changes or not *(based on Psalm 145:17; Jeremiah 29:11; Romans 8:28-29)*. You may need to assure the disciple that the Sovereign God of the universe will accomplish His purposes in the disciple's life *(based on Isaiah 46:9-11; Romans 8:29; Philippians 1:6; 2:13)*.

E.   Recognize that God may or may not choose to heal the believer in this life.

1.   In this life we may undergo testing for which we can find no clear earthly explanation *(based on the book of Job)*, and

2.   The Lord is sovereign and in complete control of life and every segment of it *(based on Deuteronomy 32:39; Psalm 115:3; Romans 8:28-39)*.

F.   The disciple's peace and joy must not be dependent on anything (including mind-altering substances) other than the Lord (refer to *Principle 24*, **Handbook**, Page H27, *Self-Confrontation*, Pages 103-105).

G.   The Lord may, in His sovereign will, allow the physical problem to remain, for the disciple's increasing maturity and effectiveness in ministry *(based on II Corinthians 12:7-10; James 1:2-4)*.

H.   Explain to the disciple that enduring trials (which may include pain and suffering) with patience produces maturity *(based on Romans 5:3-5; James 1:2-4; I Peter 1:6-7)*.

NOTES FOR BOX 4 (Continued)

I.   Even while the health specialist is helping the disciple deal with physical problems physiologically, assist him in identifying and beginning to institute the biblical changes necessary to overcome sin in his life. This will involve putting off the old practices of sin and putting on new practices of righteousness *(based on Ephesians 4:22-24; Colossians 3:9-10).*

J.   Encourage the disciple to establish biblical changes in his life through faithful, persevering obedience *(based on I Corinthians 15:58).* Emphasize that obeying the Word faithfully is essential to being blessed as a disciple of Jesus Christ *(based on James 1:22-25;* also, refer to *Principle 17, Handbook,* Page H26). He must change his life practice so that he may please God which includes remaining free from mind-altering substances.

K.   For further guidance, study *Principles 21-24 (Handbook,* Pages H26-H27) and **UNDERSTANDING PROBLEMS BIBLICALLY** *(Handbook,* Pages H133-H138).

II.   **Essential Scriptures:**

I Corinthians 6:12, 19-20; II Corinthians 12:7-10

III. **Cross references:**

Boxes 1, 3, 6-7, 15, 18

IV.   **Suggested topics for discipleship/counseling meetings:**

A.   Explain relevant portions of *Principles 21-24 (Handbook,* Pages H26-H27).

B.   Explore any health problems identified by the disciple.

C.   Explore all prescriptive, non-prescriptive, and illegal substances that affect the ability to perform daily responsibilities.

D.   Investigate the degree of dependence on mind-altering substances.

E.   Deal with any continual physical suffering.

1.   Explain Job's response to his physical suffering in *Job 42:1-6.*

2.   Explain Paul's response to his physical suffering in *II Corinthians 6:3-10; 12:7-10.*

V.   **Key homework assignments:**

A.   If necessary, go to a primary-care health specialist for a medical checkup *(this assignment refers to IV. B. above).*

B.   List by name all prescribed, non-prescribed, and illegal substances I have taken, giving the dosage, the frequency, the reason for taking them, and the period of time taken *(this assignment refers to IV. C. above).*

NOTE: The disciple/counselee may neglect to mention some frequently overlooked substances such as allergy medication, mild pain relievers, birth control pills, cold medications, sleep aids, vitamin and herbal supplements, or potions. You may need to ask about these specifically if the disciple's mood/behavior seems to be affected.

NOTES FOR BOX 4 (Continued)

C.   *(If the disciple/counselee is not falling asleep after going to bed)* keep a written record of the things about which I think while awake.

NOTES FOR BOX 5

> **5**
>
> Help develop initial hope and recognition of personal sins
> *(Principles 8, 15-26, 124-133)***

I. **Biblical focus and guidelines:**

   A.   You are to help the disciple learn how to compare his life with the standards of God's Word in order to gain a biblical understanding of his problems *(based on Psalm 19:7-11; 119:104-105; II Timothy 3:16-17; Hebrews 4:12; James 1:22-25).* Especially emphasize to the disciple that thoughts, speech, and actions reveal the condition of the heart *(based on Matthew 12:34; 15:18-20; Mark 7:20-23; Luke 6:45).*

   B.   The disciple may not even be aware that many of his failures are described in God's Word as sins *(based on Proverbs 12:15; 14:12; 16:2, 25; 21:2).* Help him understand that his problems (e.g., marriage difficulties, depression, worry, fear, anger, substance abuse) are being used by the Lord to show the necessity for change in his life *(based on Psalm 119:67, 71, 75; Hebrews 12:5-11).*

   C.   Be careful not to deal merely with circumstances. If you concentrate on changing the circumstances, the disciple may become temporarily relieved and not see the necessity of dealing with the deeper problem that led to the difficulties.

   D.   God's plan for believers is to use all things in their lives for their good, the good being to conform them to the image of His Son *(Romans 8:28-29).*

   E.   Believers are not under bondage to sin *(Romans 6:11-13).* The Lord will not give a believer more than he can bear; therefore, it is possible for a disciple to deal with his problems without sinning in the process *(I Corinthians 10:13).*

   F.   If the disciple is not experiencing victory in the face of difficulties, it may be that he is:

      1.   Not a believer and lacks the power to change biblically *(based on Romans 8:5-11; I Corinthians 2:9-14),*

      2.   A believer who is ignorant of how to apply God's Word to his life *(I Corinthians 3:1-3; Hebrews 5:11-14),* or

      3.   A believer who is not demonstrating love and, therefore, is being disciplined by God *(based on Hebrews 12:5-8).*

   G.   The disciple may be hardened and not willing to change. Help him see the seriousness of his condition by describing the consequences of continued, deliberate sin *(Proverbs 1:22-33; 13:15; 15:6; Hebrews 10:26-31).*

   H.   For further guidance, study *Principles 8, 15-26, 124-133* (**Handbook**, Pages H24, H26-H27, H47-H48) and appropriate portions of **Handbook**, Section III, Pages H105-H154.

II.   **Essential Scriptures:**

Proverbs 14:12; Romans 8:28-29; I Corinthians 10:13

III.   **Cross references:**

Boxes 1, 3, 6-9, 18

IV.   **Suggested topics for discipleship/counseling meetings:**

A.   Explain relevant portions of *Principles 8, 15-26* (**Handbook**, Pages H24, H26-H27).

B.   Help develop initial hope and recognition of personal sins.   Explain that:

1.   God uses trials for the believer's good.   He causes all things to work together for good to those who love God and are called according to His purpose *(based on Romans 8:28-29)*.

2.   If the counselee is:

a.   Not a believer — present the plan of salvation (see *Victory Over Failures Plan* booklet, Page 7, Paragraph A. 2.).

b   A believer who is not demonstrating love — show that:

1)   His major problem is failure to love *(Romans 8:28; Matthew 22:37-39)*, and

2)   His need is to evaluate whether or not he is a loving person *(I Corinthians 13:4-8a)*.

c.   Hardened and is not willing to change — describe the consequences of continued, unrepentant sin *(Proverbs 1:22-33; 13:15; 15:6; Matthew 7:24-27; Hebrews 10:26-31; James 1:22)*.

V.   **Key homework assignments:**

Evaluate whether or not I have been a loving person using *I Corinthians 13:4-8a* as a guide *(to help the disciple recognize sin in his life)*.

NOTES FOR BOX 6

> 6
>
> Explore and explain the need for salvation:
> (a) Investigate understanding and evidence of the new birth
> (b) Then, as necessary, present the plan of salvation
> *(Principles 1, 9, 11, 108, 135)***

I.   **Biblical focus and guidelines:**

   A.   Your first priority, after gathering initial information about the problem(s), is to investigate understanding and evidence of the new birth. As necessary, present the message of salvation [refer to *Principle 1 (**Handbook**, Page H23)*] and emphasize the need for a counselee to receive Jesus Christ as Lord and Savior *(based on Romans 1:16-17; II Corinthians 5:14-21; I Timothy 2:3-4)*. Remember that unbelievers are not able to understand the things of God *(I Corinthians 2:6-14, esp. verse 14)*, and they do not have the power that comes from God to live victoriously *(based on John 15:4-5; Romans 5:5-8; 8:8-9)*. Therefore, they do not have the steadfast hope that comes from obedient faith in Jesus Christ *(Ephesians 2:12)*.

   B.   If a counselee has experienced a genuine conversion, there should be evidence that his life has changed *(based on II Corinthians 5:17; Ephesians 2:8-10; James 2:14, 17-19; I John 4:6-21)*.

   C.   If the counselee's salvation is questionable *(based on Matthew 7:21-23; I John 2:3-6; 3:8-10)*, explain that it is impossible to deal biblically with life's problems without the help, assurance, and strength of God and His Word [refer to *Principle 1 (**Handbook**, Page H23)*]. During each meeting, describe the failure of man's way and the power of God's way.

   D.   Those who commit themselves to Christ become new creations *(II Corinthians 5:17)* and receive assurance that the Lord will never leave them *(Matthew 28:20; Hebrews 13:5)*.

   E.   For further guidance, study *Principles 1, 9, 11, 108, 135 (**Handbook**, Pages H23, H25, H43, H49)* and **A BIBLICAL UNDERSTANDING OF THE DISCIPLE/ COUNSELEE** *(Handbook, Pages H109-H110)*.

II.   **Essential Scriptures:**

   II Corinthians 5:17, 21; Ephesians 2:8-10; James 2:14, 17-19; I John 2:3-4

III. **Cross references:**

   Boxes 1, 3-5, 7, 10, 18

IV.   **Suggested topics for discipleship/counseling meetings:**

   A.   Explain relevant portions of *Principles 1, 9, 11, 108, 135 (**Handbook**, Pages H23, H25, H43, H49)*.

B.   Investigate understanding and evidence of the new birth.

    1.   For an unsaved counselee:

        a.   Present the plan of salvation using the *Victory Over Failures Plan* booklet, Page 7, Paragraph A. 2.

            NOTE: For a more detailed explanation of the plan of salvation, refer to **YOU CAN CHANGE BIBLICALLY (PART ONE)** *(Self-Confrontation, Pages 20-24).*

        b.   Where the counselee expresses genuine conviction of his need, lead him in a prayer of commitment to the Lord Jesus Christ for salvation.

    2.   For a disciple who is doubtful about his salvation:

        a.   Investigate what events (particularly sinful patterns) have led to the lack of assurance of salvation *(based on I John 2:3-6; 3:9-10).*

        b.   Examine the type of changes, if any, that took place in the disciple's life as a result of his profession of faith in Christ. As appropriate, address the matter of having left his first love for the Lord *(based on Revelation 2:4-5).*

        c.   Emphasize the need for continual commitment to the Lord and His Word (see **NOTES FOR BOX 7**).

C.   Show a new believer the need to testify of salvation to family members and close friends *(based on II Corinthians 5:17-20).*

V.   **Key homework assignments:**

A.   Describe how I can have eternal life through Jesus Christ [refer to *Principle 1* (**Handbook**, Page H23), or refer to **IV. God empowers you to choose His solution to your spiritual problem** *(Self-Confrontation,* Page 21)]. Write at least one Scripture reference for each point *(this assignment refers to **IV. B. 1.** above).*

B.   Tell my family about my decision to receive Jesus Christ as Lord and Savior *(this assignment refers to **IV. C.** above).*

C.   *(For the disciple/counselee about whose salvation you are doubtful)* — Read the book of *I John*, one chapter each day. List all the verses that use the words "You know," "We know," "That you might know," etc., and next to each verse reference, tell how I personally know or can know that I am a child of God *(this assignment refers to **IV. B. 2.** above).*

NOTES FOR BOX 7

> **7**
>
> Emphasize the need for continual commitment to the Lord and His Word:
> *(Principles 4, 12, 18, 30)***
> (a) Establish willingness to please the Lord in all circumstances and relationships
> *(Principles 12, 32, 35, 39, 41, 43, 130, 132)***
> (b) Explain returning to first love for the Lord: remember from where fallen, repent of past sins, return to righteous living
> *(Principles 28, 30, 68)***

I. Biblical focus and guidelines:

A. You are to help a disciple understand that making a commitment to the Lord Jesus Christ for salvation is the first step in following Jesus wholeheartedly *(based on Luke 9:23-26; Colossians 2:6-7)*. Genuine salvation is demonstrated by obeying God's Word in every area of his life *(based on John 14:15, 23-24; I John 2:3-6)*. A disciple must learn to depend solely on God *(Proverbs 3:5-12; Isaiah 26:3-4)*, Jesus Christ *(John 14:1; 15:1-11)*, God's Word *(all of Psalm 119; II Timothy 3:16-17; Hebrews 4:12)*, and His Holy Spirit *(John 16:7-13; I Corinthians 2:10-13)* as the only source, hope, authority, and standard for righteous living.

B. If the individual professes to be a believer, remind him that he will remain under the corrective discipline of the Lord when he persists in being disobedient to God's Word *(based on I Corinthians 11:31-32; Hebrews 12:5-11; Revelation 3:19)*. Teach him that his only hope is to repent wholeheartedly and faithfully obey Scripture in every area of his life *(based on II Corinthians 7:10; James 4:6-10; Revelation 3:19)*.

C. Help the disciple understand that no matter how difficult the circumstances, the Lord will bless those who are doers of the Word *(based on Deuteronomy 30:8-10; Psalm 119:165; John 15:10-11; James 1:22-25)*.

D. Explain to the disciple that change results when he remembers from where he has fallen, repents, and does the deeds he did when he first received the Lord Jesus into his life *(based on Revelation 2:4-5)*. Help him to see that he must acknowledge the Lordship of Jesus Christ and make a commitment to be a doer of the Word *(Luke 6:46-49)*. If he is merely a hearer and not a doer of the Word, then he deludes himself *(James 1:22)*, is spiritually immature *(I Corinthians 3:1-3; Hebrews 5:11-14)*, and will remain foolish *(Matthew 7:24-27)*.

E. Focus on the problems of those who want to be counseled and are committed to please the Lord. Avoid gathering information about the problems of people who are not present, since that information will often be distorted *(Proverbs 18:17)* and may constitute gossip.

F.   Evaluate the commitment of the disciple/counselee on the basis of his deeds, not his intellectual knowledge or verbal professions *(based on Matthew 7:21-23; 21:28-32; James 1:22; 2:14-20; I John 2:4; 3:18)*. (The one who is most committed to find a biblical solution may not necessarily be the one who knows the most Scripture).

G.   Continually emphasize the believer's hope in Christ *(Colossians 1:27)* and that God provides hope based on His character and His Word for every trial, test, or temptation *(based on Psalm 119:49-50; Jeremiah 29:11-13; Lamentations 3:21-25, 31-40; I Corinthians 10:13; Romans 8:28-29; 15:4; I John 3:3)*.

H.   Avoid encouraging the disciple to base his hope on opinions or man's philosophies *(based on Proverbs 3:5-8; Isaiah 55:8-9; I Thessalonians 5:21-22; I Corinthians 3:18-20)*.

I.   Commitment to God involves living to please Him *(based on II Corinthians 5:9; Ephesians 5:8-10; Colossians 1:10; I Thessalonians 4:1)* in every area of life. It is demonstrated by denying one's self daily *(based on Luke 9:23-25; 14:27)*, loving God with all one's heart, and loving one's neighbor as one's self *(Matthew 22:37-39; John 14:15; I John 5:2-3)*.

J.   For further guidance, study *Principles 4, 12, 18, 28, 30, 32, 35, 39, 41, 43, 68, 130, 132* (**Handbook**, Pages H24-H31, H35, H48) and **Handbook**, Section III, Pages H105-H154.

II.   **Essential Scriptures:**

Luke 6:46-49; 9:23-25; Colossians 1:10; James 1:22-25; Revelation 2:4-5

III.   **Cross references:**

Boxes 1, 4-6, 8-9, 12, 18

IV.   **Suggested topics for discipleship/counseling meetings:**

A.   Explain relevant portions of *Principles 4, 12, 18, 28, 30, 32, 35, 39, 41, 43, 68, 130, 132* (**Handbook**, Pages H24-H31, H35, H48).

B.   Explore details of the disciple/counselee's profession of faith — where, when, what changes took place in his life, what activities he began at church, what new friends he made, how his relationship to old associates and places changed. The objective is to remember what his first love was like and how far he has strayed from the Lord.

C.   Explain the need to repent *(Revelation 3:19)*.

D.   Explain the need for commitment to please God in every area of life *(Colossians 1:10)*.

E.   Explain to the uncommitted person the consequences of unforsaken sin.

NOTES FOR BOX 7 (Continued)

1. The way of the treacherous (transgressor) is hard *(Proverbs 13:15)*.

2. God disciplines those who continue to sin *(Hebrews 10:26-31; 12:1-29)*.

3. Explain appropriate portions of **IV. God empowers you to choose His solution to your spiritual problem** *(Self-Confrontation, Pages 21-22)*.

V. **Key homework assignments:**

A. List all that the Lord has provided to live in a meaningful way, using as a guide **YOU CAN CHANGE BIBLICALLY (PART TWO)** *(Self-Confrontation, Pages 32-34) (this assignment refers to IV. E. above)*.

B. List those practices that I followed during my "first love" relationship with the Lord just after my salvation. Then, write a plan to reestablish these practices in my life.

NOTES FOR BOX 8

> **8**
>
> Help develop consistent reliance on the Lord and His resources through:
> (a) The empowering of the Holy Spirit
>   (*Principles 5, 7, 13*)**
> (b) Learning and obeying God's Word
>   (including daily devotions, Scripture study
>   and memory, biblical practice)
>   (*Principles 2, 4, 10, 12-14, 17-18*)**
> (c) Faithfulness in prayer
>   (*Principles 6, 13*)**
> (d) Fellowship and ministry with others within
>   the local body of believers (including joint
>   worship, fellowship, and ministry)
>   (*Principles 3, 12, 41, 83, 98-105*)**

I. **Biblical focus and guidelines:**

A. The Holy Spirit is fully divine and is identified as being equal with God the Father and Jesus Christ the Son (*based on Matthew 28:19; John 14:16-18; Acts 5:3-4; 16:6-7; II Corinthians 13:14*). He is the Helper, Guide, and Instructor who reveals the wisdom of God to the disciple (*based on John 14:16-17, 26; 16:7-13; I Corinthians 2:6-13*). Only through the power of the Holy Spirit is the disciple able to live a victorious life (*based on Romans 8:5-11; I Corinthians 2:9-14; Galatians 5:16-17; Ephesians 5:18*).

B. God's Word is changeless, powerful, and applicable to whatever circumstances the disciple faces (*based on Joshua 1:8; Psalm 19:7-11; 119:160; Isaiah 55:11; Matthew 24:35; Romans 15:14; II Timothy 3:16-17; Hebrews 4:12; I Peter 1:24-25*). Encourage the disciple to study and apply the Scriptures (*based on Joshua 1:8; Psalm 1:1-2; all of Psalm 119; II Timothy 2:15; James 1:22-25*) to his present situation.

C. Prayer is essential to a Spirit-controlled life (*based on Psalm 145:18-19; Matthew 7:7-8; Ephesians 5:18-20; 6:18; I Thessalonians 5:17; I John 3:22*). Encourage the disciple to be devoted to prayer (*Colossians 4:2*) and to bring everything and everyone unceasingly before the Lord in prayer (*based on Luke 18:1; Ephesians 6:18; Philippians 4:6; I Thessalonians 5:17; I Timothy 2:1*) asking according to His will (*I John 5:14-15*). Especially encourage the disciple to pray for God's grace and wisdom in the current tests and trials (*based on Hebrews 4:16; James 1:5*).

D. Biblical fellowship and ministry are the privileged responsibility of every Christian (*based on Romans 12:3-8; I Corinthians 12:11-27; I Peter 4:8-11*) and are a means of growth for the body of Christ (*based on Ephesians 4:13-16*). Encourage the disciple to participate in fellowship and ministry to other believers (*based on Hebrews 3:12-13; 10:24-25*).

E. Teach the disciple that God's teaching about man's problems are in direct contrast to man's understanding (*based on Isaiah 55:8-9*). Remind him also that God regards man's wisdom as foolishness (*I Corinthians 1:20; 3:18-20*) and expects him to reject man's deceitful philosophies (*based on Proverbs 14:12; Colossians 2:8*).

NOTES FOR BOX 8 (Continued)

F.   It is imperative that you help the disciple establish consistency in daily devotions and Scripture memory at the very beginning of your discipleship/ counseling. The daily pattern of looking to the Holy Spirit for guidance and empowering through God's Word and prayer is vital to facing and dealing with the problems of life [based on **BIBLICAL BASIS FOR DAILY DEVOTIONS AND SCRIPTURE MEMORY** (*Self-Confrontation*, Pages 38-40)].

G.   For further guidance, study *Principles 2-7, 10, 12-14, 17-18, 41, 83, 98-105* (*Handbook*, Pages H23-H26, H30, H38, H41-H42).

II.   **Essential Scriptures:**

A.   For the empowering of the Holy Spirit — *John 16:7-13; I Corinthians 2:11-13;*

B.   For learning and obeying God's Word — *II Timothy 2:15; Hebrews 4:12; James 1:22-25;*

C.   For faithfulness in prayer — *I Thessalonians 5:17; Hebrews 4:15-16; James 1:5;* and

D.   For fellowship and ministry with other believers — *Ephesians 4:13-16; Hebrews 3.12-13, 10.24-25.*

III.   **Cross references:**

Boxes 1, 5, 7, 12, 15-18

IV.   **Suggested topics for discipleship/counseling meetings:**

A.   Explain relevant portions of *Principles 2-7, 10, 12-14, 17-18, 41, 83, 98-105* (*Handbook*, Pages H23-H26, H30, H38, H41-H42).

B.   Explain the biblical basis for devotions using *Psalm 1:1-3* as your text.

C.   Show the need for Scripture memory using *Psalm 119:9-11* as your text.

D.   Show the need for fellowship in the local body of believers and involvement in ministry using *Hebrews 3:13; 10:24-25* as your text.

V.   **Key homework assignments:**

A.   Memorize the Scripture passage that will best help me in my present situation.

B.   Develop a prayer list, including topics for praise and thanksgiving in regard to my current situation, requests for help in dealing with specific trials, and specific people for whom I should pray. Then, faithfully pray for the items on my list all week during my devotions as well as during idle moments throughout the day.

C.   Take notes of the message at the next worship service and write out how I will apply what the Lord convicts me to change in my life.

D.   Meet with my discipler/counselor for a midweek check on my homework.

BIBLICAL RECONCILIATION WITH GOD AND MAN
MASTER PLAN — SECOND PAGE

OVERVIEW

The second page of the **MASTER PLAN**, containing Boxes 9-14, describes how to establish a biblical structure for change. The primary tool, the **VICTORY OVER FAILURES PLAN**, is a biblically based tool that can help the disciple/counselee apply God's Word in the power of the Holy Spirit, so that he may overcome any difficulty of life with the full expectation of complete and lasting victory. It explains the specific steps necessary to develop biblical plans for living God's way beginning with helping the disciple/counselee to identify a problem area in his life to work on. Part of the process involves putting off the old manner of life and putting on new, righteous practices in their place *(Ephesians 4:22-24)*. The **VICTORY OVER FAILURES PLAN** describes how to do that in very practical ways and gives the disciple/counselee a format he can follow. Very important steps of change on this page are to forgive others, reconcile relationships, and respond biblically in the current situation.

9

Teach how to judge self through the development of personal failures lists (e.g., keeping account of wrongs suffered, inflicting wrongs, or neglecting to demonstrate biblical love toward God and others) using *Worksheet 2: Lists of Specific Failures to Live Biblically*, **VICTORY OVER FAILURES PLAN** (BCF Form 102) *(Principles 3, 4, 19, 28, 30, 42, 52, 94-95)***

NOTES FOR BOX 9

I.   **Biblical focus and guidelines:**

The purpose of Box 9 is to help a person take the first step in reordering his life before the Lord: judging himself without simultaneously judging others. This is often the most difficult challenge in discipleship/counseling. Only after the disciple has dealt biblically with himself, is he ready to help others *(based on Matthew 7:1-5)*. Refer to *Principle 124 (**Handbook**, Page H47)*.

     A.   Learning how to complete *Worksheet 2: Lists of Specific Failures to Live Biblically* of the **VICTORY OVER FAILURES PLAN** (***Handbook***, Pages H227-H231, BCF Form 102) will:

         1.   Help the disciple/counselee learn how to examine (test, judge) himself in order to establish a pattern of judging himself biblically *(Psalm 139:23-24; Matthew 7:1-5; I Corinthians 11:31; Galatians 6:4)*; and

         2.   Provide a basis for identifying "put-offs" and "put-ons."

     B.   It is vital that *Worksheet 2: Lists of Specific Failures to Live Biblically* be biblical and complete since it is the basis for identifying "put-offs" and "put-ons." Help the disciple/counselee:

---

1. **Be specific.** The disciple/counselee should describe exactly how he demonstrated his failures in each situation.

    a. Change takes place in specific ways, i.e., specific changes in thoughts, speech, and actions. Change does not take place in generalities. For example, the disciple/counselee should not just say "I was angry." Rather, he should list the specific ways in which he has demonstrated his anger. He should list specific unbiblical thoughts (such as grumbling inside self, devising sarcastic responses, etc.), speech (including the tone and volume of his voice), and actions (including looks, gestures, etc.).

    b. When developing a specific list, the disciple/counselee should:

        1) Not include specific details about sinful thoughts that may present a stumbling block to himself or others to whom he may need to show the list. It is enough to list the kinds of thoughts (e.g., grumbling, arguing, reviling). Keeping a written record of exact words can serve as a reminder to keep him thinking those sinful thoughts.

        2) Not list emotions (i.e., feelings) because God does not hold the disciple/counselee responsible for how he feels, and the disciple/counselee cannot change his feelings by a direct act of his will.

2. **Be thorough.** For each situation it is important to consider thoughts, speech, and actions. Remember that it is possible to sin in many ways in a very short period of time. The lists must be comprehensive and specific enough to identify the patterns of sin ("put-offs") which will be dealt with as part of his biblical plans for change. If this step is not accomplished thoroughly before moving on to the other worksheets of the **VICTORY OVER FAILURES PLAN**, you are in danger of encouraging false hope and artificial change in the disciple/counselee.

3. **Not shift blame.** Each person must take full responsibility for his sins committed against God and against others, with a commitment to forsake those sins *(based on Psalm 51:1-4; Proverbs 28:13; I John 1:9)*. It is important that *Worksheet 2* be free from blameshifting *(based on Ezekiel 18:20; Matthew 7:5)*. Refer to **VICTORY OVER FAILURES PLAN: GUIDELINES AND WORKSHEETS** *(Handbook,* Pages H227-H231, BCF Form 102).

4. **Not minimize sin.** In listing his failures, the disciple/counselee should take care not to minimize away his sin *(based on Proverbs 28:13; Ezekiel 18:20; I John 1:5-9)*.

C. When discipling/counseling more than one person:

    1. First, deal with each person's individual sins *(based on Matthew 7:1-5)*.

    2. In the case of parents who have problems with their children, first deal with the sins of each spouse *(based on Matthew 7:1, 5)*; then help the parents train (which includes counsel) their children *(Deuteronomy 6:6-7; Proverbs 22:6; Ephesians 6:4)*.

D. For further guidance, study *Principles 3, 4, 19, 28, 30, 42, 52* **(Handbook,** Pages H23-H24, H26-H28, H30, H32) and **Handbook,** Section III, Part 3, Pages H123-H154.

II.   **Essential Scriptures:**

Ezekiel 18:20; Matthew 7:1-5

III. **Cross references:**

Boxes 1, 5, 7, 11, 18

IV.   **Suggested topics for discipleship/counseling meetings:**

A.   Explain relevant portions of *Principles 3, 4, 19, 28, 30, 42, 52* (**Handbook**, Pages H23-H24, H26-H28, H31, H32).

B.   Explain the need to judge self *(Matthew 7:1-5)*.

C.   Show the disciple how to complete *Worksheet 2* using Pages 15-17, 19 of the *Victory Over Failures Plan* booklet.

V.   **Key homework assignments:**

A.   Memorize the Scripture passage that will best help me in my present situation.

B.   Complete *Worksheet 2* using Pages 15-17, 19 of the *Victory Over Failures Plan* booklet.

NOTES FOR BOX 10

> **10**
> Explain the necessity to repent and confess these sins to the Lord, demonstrated by asking for His forgiveness and showing the fruit of repentance
> *(Principles 26, 28, 30, 57)***

I. **Biblical focus and guidelines:**

The purpose of Box 10 is to emphasize that once you have specifically identified sins in your life, you must repent of them *(Proverbs 28:13; II Corinthians 7:9-10; Revelation 2:5)*, confess them *(I John 1:9)*, and immediately put them aside *(based on Romans 6:12-13a; Ephesians 4:22, 25, 29, 31; 5:4; Colossians 3:2, 5-9; II Timothy 2:22a)*.

   A.   Encourage the disciple to confess his sins to the Lord as soon as he recognizes them *(I John 1:9)*. If the disciple/counselee is not willing to deal with known sin, you should not attempt to deal with other areas of his life *(based on Matthew 7:21-27; James 1:22)*.

   B.   While the disciple should confess sins to the Lord quickly, caution him not to ask forgiveness of others until he is properly prepared. This is essential because he needs to learn how to ask forgiveness of others without shifting blame, minimizing sin, or expecting change in others. Refer to Box 13 and *Self-Confrontation*, Pages 199-201.

   C.   For further guidance, study *Principles 26, 28, 30* (**Handbook**, Pages H27-H28).

II. **Essential Scripture:**

I John 1:9

III. **Cross references:**

Boxes 1, 6, 12-13, 18

IV. **Suggested topics for discipleship/counseling meetings:**

   A.   Explain relevant portions of *Principles 26, 28, 30* (**Handbook**, Pages H27-H28).

   B.   Explain the need to confess sins to the Lord as soon as they are recognized *(I John 1:9)*.

V. **Key homework assignments:**

   A.   Memorize the Scripture passage that will best help me in my present situation.

   B.   Ask God's forgiveness for my sins as soon as they are recognized.

NOTES FOR BOX 11

> ¹¹
> Provide guidance on how to complete *Worksheet 3: "Put-offs" and "Put-ons."*
> *(Principles 27-29, 56, 93, 103)***

I.   **Biblical focus and guidelines:**

The purpose of Box 11 is to teach the disciple how to find the biblical "put-offs" and "put-ons" associated with his problem by completing the second two columns of *Worksheet 3: "Put-offs" and "Put-ons"* of the **VICTORY OVER FAILURES PLAN** (*Handbook*, Pages H232-H235, BCF Form 102).

A.   As the disciple puts on righteous deeds (*based on Ephesians 4:24; II Timothy 2:22b; Titus 2:11-12*) in the power of the Holy Spirit (*based on Ephesians 3:16-21; 5:18*), he will glorify God (*I Corinthians 10:31; I Peter 4:11*), demonstrate his love for the Lord (*I John 5:3; II John 1:6*), please Him in all things (*based on Ezekiel 18:23; II Corinthians 5:9; Colossians 1:10*), and will not carry out the desires of his flesh (*Galatians 5:16*).

B.   It is important that:

   1.   The "put-offs" and "put-ons" apply directly to the sins listed in the first column and that they come from the Scriptures (*the Scripture reference should be identified for each one*).

   2.   The "put-offs" listed be accompanied by scripturally based "put-ons" (i.e., normally, "put-ons" from the same verse or passage). There may, however, be "put-ons" without associated "put-offs" [for example, *"... pray without ceasing ..."* (I Thessalonians 5:17)], and "put-offs" without associated "put-ons" [for example, *"Do not lay hands upon anyone to hastily ..."* (I Timothy 5:22)].

   3.   Emphasis is placed on the "put-on" (*based on Galatians 5:16*). When you focus your attention on the "put-on," your mind is not easily distracted to do wrong. When you focus your attention only on the "put-off," the temptation to do wrong is always before you.

C.   Often, sins of omission (i.e., not putting on) are overlooked. Yet sins of omission are just as serious as sins of commission (*James 4:17*).

D.   Lasting change takes self-control, discipline, and time because it involves putting off the practices (habit patterns) of the old self, which is being corrupted, and putting on the practices (habit patterns) of the new self, which has been created in righteousness and holiness of the truth (*Ephesians 4:22-24*). Failure to accomplish lasting, biblical change may be the result of several errors in application of "put-ons" and "put-offs."

   1.   *Superficial change* — A person may attempt to change superficially by selecting a convenient or easy solution.

   2.   *Putting off without putting on* — For example, a person may concentrate merely on eliminating the practice of drunkeness without taking the corresponding step of placing himself under the control of the Holy Spirit (*see Ephesians 5:18*).

NOTES FOR BOX 11 (Continued)

3. *Putting on without putting off* — A person may attempt to put on a righteous practice while maintaining the basic pattern of his old life.

4. *Not dealing with unresolved past sin* — One must deal with any unresolved sin through humble confession *(based on Psalm 51; Proverbs 28:13; I John 1:9)* and thorough repentance *(based on II Corinthians 7:9-11; Ephesians 4:17-32).*

E. For further guidance, study *Principles 27-29* (**Handbook**, Pages H27-H28) and **STRUCTURING FOR BIBLICAL CHANGE** (**Handbook**, Pages H143-H146). *Also refer to* **BIBLICAL CHANGE IS A PROCESS** (**Self-Confrontation**, Pages 112-113).

II. **Essential Scriptures:**

Ephesians 4:22-32; Colossians 3:1-4:6

III. **Cross references:**

Boxes 1, 9, 12, 18

IV. **Suggested topics for discipleship/counseling meetings:**

A. Explain relevant portions of *Principles 27-29* (**Handbook**, Pages H27-H28).

B. Explain God's process for change using *Ephesians 4:22, 24.* Illustrate "put-offs" and "put-ons" using *Ephesians 4:25, 28-29, 31-32.*

C. Explain how to complete *Worksheet 3* using Pages 20-22 of the booklet.

V. **Key homework assignments:**

A. Memorize the Scripture passage that will best help me in my present situation.

B. Complete *Worksheet 3* following the steps listed in the *Victory Over Failures Plan* booklet on Page 20.

NOTE: This homework assignment may take several weeks.

NOTES FOR BOX 12

> Provide guidance on how to complete *Worksheet 4: "Daily Practices" Plan* and *Worksheet 5: "Overcoming Temptations" Plan.* (*Principles 30-32, 49, 50, 57, 83, 95-97, 105*)** **12**

I. **Biblical focus and guidelines:**

The purpose of Box 12 is to provide guidance for developing biblical plans for facing and dealing with the sins listed in *Worksheet 2* of the **VICTORY OVER FAILURES PLAN**. This is a critical step for the disciple because he needs to become a doer of the Word *(Luke 6:46-49)*. If he is merely a hearer and not a doer of the Word, then he deludes himself *(James 1:22)*, is spiritually immature *(I Corinthians 3:1-3; Hebrews 5:11-14)*, and will remain foolish *(Matthew 7:24-27)*.

A. Upon completion of *Worksheet 3: "Put-offs" and "Put-ons,"* the disciple may need to develop up to three kinds of plans in parallel with one another. These plans are: **"Daily Practices" Plan**, **"Overcoming Temptations" Plan**, and **"Forgiveness/Reconciliation" Plan** [see the *Victory Over Failures Plan* booklet (**Handbook**, Pages H237-H250, BCF Form 102) for details].

   1. The purpose of the *"Daily Practices" Plan* is to help the disciple put off a particular ongoing pattern of unrighteous behavior and to put on the appropriate biblical pattern of righteous deeds instead. It includes changes that must be made throughout the day.

   2. The purpose of the *"Overcoming Temptations" Plan* is to help the disciple respond in a godly manner to situations where he has been tempted and has fallen repeatedly. It is for him to use only at the time the temptation occurs, but it is prepared in advance of the temptation so that he will be better prepared to deal with the temptation when it occurs.

   3. The purpose of the *"Forgiveness/Reconciliation" Plan* is to help the disciple deal with relationships that are not reconciled.

B. For further guidance, study *Principles 30-32, 49, 50, 57, 83, 95-97, 105* (**Handbook**, Pages H28, H32-H33, H38, H40, H42), and **Handbook**, Section III, Part 3, Pages H123-H154.

II. **Essential Scriptures:**

Matthew 7:24-27; Hebrews 5:14; James 1:22-25; 4:17

III. **Cross references:**

Boxes 1, 7-8, 10-11, 13-14, 16, 18

IV. **Suggested topics for discipleship/counseling meetings:**

A. Explain relevant portions of *Principles 17-18, 27-32, 39, 48-49, 56-57, 64-66, 72-74, 78-79, 82, 84-85, 87-90, 93, 95-97* (**Handbook**, Pages H26-H41).

B. Explain how to complete *Worksheets 4* and *5* using the *Victory Over Failures Plan* booklet, Pages 24-31 (**Handbook**, Pages H236-H243, BCF Form 102).

V.   **Key homework assignments:**

A.   Memorize the Scripture passage that will best help me in my present situation.

B.   Begin completing *Worksheets 4* and *5* following the steps listed in the *Victory Over Failures Plan* booklet on Pages 24-25 and 28-29 (*Handbook*, Pages H236-H243, BCF Form 102).

NOTES FOR BOX 13

> **13**
>
> Teach how to restore unreconciled relationships and develop biblical relationships by:
> (a) Forgiving others biblically using *Worksheet 6a: My Plan for Demonstrating Forgiveness* (Principles 48, 50-51)**
> (b) Being reconciled to others in accordance with biblical principles of communication using *Worksheet 6b: My Plan for Asking Forgiveness* (Principles 53, 57-59, 68)**

I.   **Biblical focus and guidelines:**

The purpose of Box 13 is to highlight the importance of reconciling relationships. Forgiving others is absolutely vital to a close relationship with God. In fact, the Bible makes it plain that fellowship with God is not possible without it *(based on Matthew 6:14-15; Mark 11:25-26)*. As the disciple forgives others, he demonstrates his obedience to God *(based on Ephesians 4:32; Colossians 3:13)*, and, thus, his love for the Lord *(based on John 14:15; I John 5:3; II John 1:6)*.

A.   The disciple must forgive before he initiates reconciliation *(based on Matthew 6:14-15; Mark 11:25)*.

1.   The disciple's forgiveness of another is much bigger than just his relationship with the other person. His forgiveness of others is essential to unbroken fellowship with his heavenly Father *(Matthew 6:12-15)*.

2.   It is hypocritical to ask others to grant forgiveness when there is an unwillingness to forgive them *(based on Matthew 7:5)*.

B.   To demonstrate forgiveness, the disciple must be taught:

1.   Not to dwell on the offense suffered *(based on Isaiah 38:17)*. The disciple must be taught not to keep account of any wrongs suffered *(I Corinthians 13:5)*. He should not dwell on the evil done to him, but consider how to give a blessing instead *(based on I Peter 3:9)*.

2.   Not to remind the forgiven person of his sin in an accusing manner *(based on Hebrews 10:17)*. There may be times when the disciple will need to remind the person of his sin even after the disciple has forgiven him. For example, if that individual develops a pattern of repeating the sin, the disciple is to exhort that person to repent. The disciple is to make his appeal in a spirit of gentleness, not in an accusing manner *(based on Galatians 6:1)*.

3.   Not to gossip to others about the offense suffered *(II Corinthians 12:20)*. The disciple may need to bring up someone's sins to others but only with the focus on helping the person who is sinning, not to tear him down.

4.   To remove all reminders of the offense that are stumbling blocks, as much as it is physically possible *(based on Matthew 18:7-9)*.

5.   To restore fellowship with the forgiven person, as far as is biblically possible *(based on Romans 12:18; II Corinthians 2:6-8)*. Even if the person

NOTES FOR BOX 13 (Continued)

has not come to ask forgiveness, the disciple must still forgive and stand ready to grant forgiveness if asked.

C. Reconciliation is so important that special care must be taken to ensure that it is accomplished God's way. Even when the one sinning may not demonstrate a desire to rectify his transgressions, the one first recognizing a problem in the relationship needs to initiate reconciliation with the other by:

1. Asking forgiveness for sins committed *(based on Matthew 5:23-24; James 5:16)*;

2. Clearing up misunderstandings that may have occurred *(based on Luke 17:3; I Corinthians 1:10; Ephesians 4:3; Philippians 2:1-4)*; or

3. Restoring him when he has sinned *(based on Matthew 18:15; Galatians 6:1)*.

D. When reconciling, teach the disciple to:

1. Make restitution whenever appropriate *(based on Leviticus 5:15-18; 6:2-5; Numbers 5:5-8; Proverbs 6:30-31; Luke 19:8)*.

2. Demonstrate repentance *(Psalm 51:12-13; Matthew 3:8; Acts 26:20)* by writing and implementing a plan for change.

3. Ask forgiveness. In completing *Worksheet 6b*, under "**C. Words I will use when asking forgiveness**," instruct the disciple to write words to use when asking forgiveness. This should include:

    a. Admission and confession of sin against God and the offended person *(James 5:16; I John 1:9)*.

    b. An expression of repentance which includes:

        1) An expression of sorrow for the sin *(Psalm 51:16-17; II Corinthians 7:9-10; James 4:8-10)*,

        2) An intention not to repeat the sin,

        3) The specific steps the disciple will take to change.

E. The disciple most likely needs to learn more about biblical communication. The type of language that he uses when speaking to others is one of the most important demonstrations of his walk with the Lord *(Matthew 12:34-37; James 3:1-12)*. All speech is to please the Lord *(based on Psalm 19:14; Matthew 12:36; Ephesians 4:29)*.

F. For further guidance, study *Principles 48, 50-51, 53, 57-59, 68* (**Handbook**, Pages H31-H33, H35) and **Handbook**, Section III, Part 3, Pages H123-H154.

II. Essential Scriptures:

Matthew 5:23-24; 6:14-15

III. Cross references:

Boxes 1, 10, 12, 14, 18

IV.   **Suggested topics for discipleship/counseling meetings:**

    A.   Explain relevant portions of *Principles 48, 50-51, 53, 57-59, 68* (***Handbook***, Pages H31-H33, H35).

    B.   *(For a disciple who needs to forgive and/or be reconciled to another)* — Explain how to complete *Worksheets 6a* and *6b* using the steps listed in *Victory Over Failures Plan* booklet on Pages 32-38 (***Handbook***, Pages H244-H250, BCF Form 102).

        For further guidance, study:

        1.   *FORGIVENESS (FORGIVING OTHERS AS GOD HAS FORGIVEN YOU)* (***Self-Confrontation***, *Pages 196-198*).

        2.   *RECONCILIATION (REMOVING ALL HINDRANCES TO UNITY AND PEACE)* (***Self-Confrontation***, *Pages 199-201*).

    C.   *(For a disciple who recognizes a strain in a relationship but does not know the precipitating circumstances)* — Explain to the disciple his responsibility to be reconciled regardless of who cut off communication.

    D.   *(For a disciple who recognizes that his statements precipitated a misunderstanding)* — Help him to go and clear up the matter.

    E.   *(For a disciple who has responded biblically but the other is sinning)* — Teach the disciple how to go to the other person lovingly with a view to restore him.

    F.   *(For a disciple who needs to help another person deal with sin and has already spent considerable time taking the log out of his own eye)* — Explain **RESTORATION/ DISCIPLINE (YOUR BIBLICAL RESPONSE TO THE SIN OF ANOTHER BELIEVER)** (*Self-Confrontation*, Pages 220-221) and **GUIDELINES: THE RESTORATION/DISCIPLINE PROCESS** (*Self-Confrontation*, Pages 222-224).

    G.   Teach principles on biblical communication (*Proverbs 18:2, 13, 15, 17 and Ephesians 4:15, 25-27, 29*).

        *For further guidance, study Sections **II.** through **IV.** of BIBLICAL COMMUNICATION* (***Self-Confrontation***, *Pages 225-226*).

    H.   Explain how to initiate a family meeting using **INITIATING BIBLICAL RECONCILIATION (BY CONDUCTING A FAMILY MEETING)** (*Handbook*, Pages H261-H264, BCF Form 106).   Role-play portions to ensure that the disciple knows how to do it. *If the disciple has a **Self-Confrontation** manual, use **OVERCOMING PROBLEMS THROUGH BIBLICAL COMMUNICATION (USING A CONFERENCE TABLE FOR RECONCILIATION)** (**Self-Confrontation**, Pages 261-264) to explain the conference table.*

    I.   Help the disciples implement their *Worksheets 6a* and *6b* of the *Victory Over Failures Plan* booklet (***Handbook***, Pages H244-H250, BCF Form 102) by asking forgiveness of each other.

V.   **Key homework assignments:**

    A.   Memorize the Scripture passage that will best help me in my present situation.

B.   *(For a disciple who needs to forgive and/or be reconciled)* — Complete *Worksheets 6a* and/or *6b* following the steps listed in the *Victory Over Failures Plan* booklet on Pages 32-38 (***Handbook***, Pages H244-H250, BCF Form 102, Pages 32-38).

C.   *(For a disciple who needs to help another person deal with sin and has already spent considerable time taking the log out of his own eye)* — Using **RESTORATION/ DISCIPLINE (YOUR BIBLICAL RESPONSE TO THE SIN OF ANOTHER BELIEVER)** *(Self-Confrontation*, Pages 220-221) and **GUIDELINES: THE RESTORATION/DISCIPLINE PROCESS** *(Self-Confrontation*, Pages 222-224), develop a specific plan for going to the one who has sinned with a view to restoring him *(this assignment refers to **IV.** F. above)*.

D.   Conduct at least two family meetings this week with my family (or others with whom I have a close relationship) using the format explained in **OVERCOMING PROBLEMS THROUGH BIBLICAL COMMUNICATIONS (USING A CONFERENCE TABLE FOR RECONCILIATION)** *(Self-Confrontation*, Pages 261-264) *(this assignment refers to **IV.** H. above)*.

NOTES FOR BOX 14

> Explain how to treat others biblically by teaching principles for:
> (a) Not retaliating when wronged
> (b) Seeking ways to bless them
> (c) Eliminating stumbling blocks
> *(Principles 50, 55-56, 63, 104)***
>
> **14**

I.   Biblical focus and guidelines:

The purpose of Box 14 is to provide guidance on how to respond to others who are treating the disciple unreasonably. The box is placed right after Box 13 because as the disciple reconciles himself with others, he will often run into resistance. At this point, he may be tempted to retaliate or to grumble about the "unfairness" of his circumstance.

A.   In responding biblically to others, the disciple must not retaliate, but should practice biblical love *(Proverbs 10:12; Romans 12:9-21; I Corinthians 13:4-8a; I Peter 2:21-23; 4:8)* by:

    1.   Forgiving others just as God has forgiven him *(Mark 11:25; Ephesians 4:32; Colossians 3:13);*

    2.   Considering others as more important than self *(Philippians 2:3-4);* and

    3.   Doing kind and tenderhearted deeds to the very individuals with whom he becomes irritated *(Ephesians 4:32; I Peter 3:8-9).*

    Refer also to **THE MEANING OF BIBLICAL LOVE** *(Self-Confrontation, Pages 217-219)* and **BIBLICAL SUBMISSION** *(Self-Confrontation, Page 258).*

B.   Teach the disciple that blessing another is doing whatever is good for him; it may or may not be what the other person wants or expects. The biblical criterion is to do the loving thing — that is — whatever is good for the other according to God's Word *(based on Acts 3:26; I Peter 3:8-12).*

    Refer also to **BIBLICALLY RESPONDING TO SOMEONE WITH A LIFE-DOMINATING SIN** *(Self-Confrontation, Pages 389-392).*

C.   Teach the disciple to remove anything in his life that could be a stumbling block for others *(based on Matthew 18:7; Romans 14:13; I Corinthians 8:9-13).*

D.   For further guidance, study *Principles 50, 55-56, 63, 104* **(Handbook, Pages H32-H34, H42).**

II.   Essential Scriptures:

Matthew 5:3-12; Romans 12:9-21; I Corinthians 13:4-8a; I Peter 2:20-21; 3:8-17

III.   Cross references:

Boxes 1, 12-13, 15, 17-18

IV. **Suggested topics for discipleship/counseling meetings:**

A. Explain relevant portions of *Principles 50, 55-56, 63, 104* (**Handbook**, Pages H32-H34, H42).

B. Show disciples how to treat others biblically by teaching them principles for:

1. Not retaliating when wronged *(I Peter 2:20-23; 3:8-9)*,

2. Seeking ways to bless them *(Romans 12:9-21; I Peter 3:9)*, and

3. Eliminating stumbling blocks *(Romans 14:13; I Corinthians 8:9)*.

C. Depending on the problem in the disciple's life, explain appropriate portions of:

1. **BIBLICAL COMMUNICATION** *(Self-Confrontation*, Pages 225-227),

2. Section **IV.** of **OVERCOMING INTERPERSONAL PROBLEMS** *(Self-Confrontation*, Pages 232-236),

3. **THE MEANING OF BIBLICAL LOVE** *(Self-Controntation*, Pages 217-219), or

4. **BIBLICAL RELATIONSHIPS (LOVING EACH OTHER IN THE BODY OF CHRIST)** *(Self-Confrontation*, Pages 228-231).

D. Items that could be included in the disciple/counselee's plan:

V. **Key homework assignments:**

A. Memorize the Scripture passage that will best help me in my present situation.

B. Based on *Romans 12:9-21* make a list of ways to bless others in my life, beginning with the very person(s) against whom I have previously sinned. Do at least one item on my list on a daily basis, and record what I did to bless others *(this assignment refers to **IV. B.** above)*.

C. After studying **BIBLICAL COMMUNICATION** *(Self-Confrontation*, Pages 225-227), list the changes I need to make in my communication. Incorporate those changes into my **"Daily Practices" Plan** *(this assignment refers to **IV. C. 1.** above)*.

D. After studying **THE MEANING OF BIBLICAL LOVE** *(Self-Confrontation*, Pages 217-219) and **BIBLICAL RELATIONSHIPS (LOVING EACH OTHER IN THE BODY OF CHRIST)** *(Self-Confrontation*, Pages 228-231), list what I should do to bless the person with whom I am having difficulty. Do at least one of the items on my list each day and record what I did that day *(this assignment refers to **IV. C. 3. and 4.** above)*.

THE MATURING DISCIPLE OF JESUS CHRIST
MASTER PLAN — THIRD PAGE

OVERVIEW

The third page of the **MASTER PLAN**, containing Boxes 15-18, provides guidelines for practicing the plans established previously and persevering daily as a faithful servant of God. It describes the believer who is reordering his entire life to conform to what God commands and is beginning to minister to others, thus fulfilling the Great Commission to make disciples. From this point on, most of the counsel will be to prepare the disciple/ counselee for continuing his growth in discipleship after the structured discipleship/ counseling phase ends.

NOTES FOR BOX 15

> **15**
> Encourage to stand firm in the midst of sufferings, tests, and trials and to put on the full armor of God *(Principles 12, 21, 23, 24, 32, 80, 95, 103-104)***

I.   **Biblical focus and guidelines:**

A.   Prepare the disciple for possible reviling and persecution because of his commitment to Jesus Christ and his faithfulness in being obedient to God's Word *(based on Matthew 5:10-12; 10:16-28; John 15:18-20; II Timothy 3:12; I Peter 4:12-19)*. If he should endure suffering for the sake of righteousness, he is blessed of the Lord *(based on Matthew 5:10-12; Luke 6:22-23; James 5:10-11; I Peter 3:13-17, esp. verse 14)*.

B.   The disciple matures in the Lord as tests/trials are dealt with in a godly manner *(based on Romans 5:3-5; James 1:2-4)*. As counseling progresses, however, watch for common temptations.

1.   The disciple may become proud of his initial consistency in obedience to the Lord *(based on I Corinthians 10:12)*. He must learn that any "success" in dealing with circumstances is only because of the Lord's gracious provision and strengthening *(based on II Corinthians 3:5-6; Philippians 2:13; 4:13)*.

2.   He may become discouraged as he recognizes the magnitude of his sin *(based on Psalm 38:1-8; 40:12)*. Remind him that God will never give him more to deal with than he can handle *(I Corinthians 10:13)* and that he does not need to live as a slave to sin because God provides forgiveness and power to live biblically *(Romans 6:6-23)*.

3.   He may be tempted to indulge in self-pity or resentment when others continue to sin *(based on Psalm 37:1-7; 73:1-14)*. Remind him that he is responsible only for his own sin *(Ezekiel 18:20)* and that his joy depends only on his personal relationship with God *(based on John 15:10-11)*. Since only God can accurately judge the entire spiritual condition of the heart *(I Samuel 16:7; Jeremiah 17:10; I Corinthians 4:5; I Thessalonians 2:4)*, the

NOTES FOR BOX 15 (Continued)

disciple should not judge others *(Matthew 7:1-5)*, but continuously commit himself to the Lord who judges righteously *(based on Psalm 73:23-28; I Peter 2:23; 4:19)*.

C.   Encourage the disciple to put on the full armor of God so that he will stand firm in his walk with God in the midst of sufferings, tests, and trials that are sure to come *(based on Ephesians 6:10-18)*. Remind him that enduring suffering with patience finds favor with God *(based on I Peter 2:20)*. Mention that he should not be surprised or grow resentful at his suffering; rather, he should rejoice in his sufferings *(based on I Peter 1:6-9; 4:12-14)* and keep on entrusting himself to God, the faithful Creator, Who does only what is right and good in the lives of believers *(based on Romans 8:28-29; I Peter 4:19)*.

D.   Remind him that he is a soldier actively involved in spiritual warfare *(based on Ephesians 6:10-13; II Timothy 2:3-4)* and that he should remain humble before the Lord, be on the alert, and resist the devil *(based on James 4:6-7; I Peter 5:8-9)*.

E.   The disciple may also need to be reminded to continue to discipline himself for godliness *(based on I Timothy 4:7-8; II Peter 1:5-10)* and to persevere in doing good and not lose heart. Explain to him that his faithfulness to the Lord will be rewarded in due time *(I Corinthians 15:57-58; Galatians 6:9-10)*.

F.   For further guidance, study *Principles 12, 21, 23, 24, 32, 80, 95, 103-104* (*Handbook*, Pages H25-H28, H37, H40-H42).

II.   **Essential Scriptures:**

I Corinthians 15:57-58; Ephesians 6:10-18; I Timothy 4:7-8; I Peter 2:18-23; 4:12-19; II Peter 1:5-10

III.   **Cross references:**

Boxes 1, 4, 8, 14, 18

IV.   **Suggested topics for discipleship/counseling meetings:**

A.   Explain relevant portions of *Principles 12, 21, 23, 24, 32, 80, 95, 103-104* (*Handbook*, Pages H25-H28, H37, H40-H42).

B.   Explain relevant portions of **BIBLICAL PERSPECTIVE ON TESTS AND TEMPTATIONS** *(Self-Confrontation*, Pages 124-128).

C.   Explain the armor of God as described in *Ephesians 6:10-18* using appropriate portions of **PUTTING ON THE FULL ARMOR OF GOD** *(Self-Confrontation*, Pages 273-281).

D.   Prepare the committed person for possible persecution.

1.   Persecution should be expected *(John 15:18-20; II Timothy 3:12)*.

2.   Those who suffer persecution are blessed *(Matthew 5:10-12; I Peter 3:14-17)*.

3.   Bless those who persecute you — do not retaliate *(Romans 12:14-19; I Peter 3:9)*.

V.   **Key homework assignments:**

A.   Memorize the Scripture passage that will best help me in my present situation.

B.   After studying **PUTTING ON THE FULL ARMOR OF GOD** (*Self-Confrontation*, Pages 273-281), develop specific steps for putting on the full armor of God and incorporate them into the **VICTORY OVER FAILURES PLAN** worksheets (*this assignment refers to IV. C. above*).

C.   Using a comprehensive Bible concordance, list at least 20 passages that include the word "perseverance" or "long-suffering," and describe how each passage applies to my life.

NOTES FOR BOX 16

> **16**
>
> Explain how to continue to mature in God's standards for life through:
> (a) Elimination of unprofitable activities — using **MY PRESENT SCHEDULE** (BCF Form 107)
> (b) Addition of activities necessary to carry out God-given responsibilities — using **MY PROPOSED BIBLICAL SCHEDULE** (BCF Form 108)
> (c) Periodic evaluation of the plans made
> *(Principles 12, 31-32, 83, 88, 98-103, 105)***

I. **Biblical focus and guidelines:**

    A.   It is not your task to help the disciple deal with all the problems in his life *(based on Galatians 6:5; Philippians 2:12-13)*. Rather, your objective is to help him biblically face, deal with, and endure his current problems with a view to helping him become established in a pattern of righteousness that encompasses loving God and others in every area of his life *(based on Matthew 22:37-39; II Corinthians 7:1; Galatians 5:22-25; Titus 2:11-14; II Peter 1:2-11)*.

    B.   Help the disciple see the need for a disciplined life *[Principle 31 (**Handbook**, Page H28)]*. God holds him responsible for what he does today. Some planning for tomorrow may be required, but the emphasis must be on today's responsibilities *[Matthew 6:25-34; James 4:13-17 and Principle 88 (**Handbook**, Page H39)]*.

    C.   Focus must be on God's standards for continuing maturity toward Christlikeness *[Principle 12 (**Handbook**, Page H25)]*. Help the disciple/counselee evaluate the whole of his life and, if necessary, reorder every aspect of his life to conform to God's standards.

    D.   For further guidance, study *Principles 12, 31-32, 83, 88, 98-103, 105 (**Handbook**, Pages H25, H28, H38-H39, H41-H42)*.

II. **Essential Scriptures:**

    Matthew 6:25-34; Romans 13:12-14; I Corinthians 10:31; Galatians 5:22-23; Philippians 2:12-13; Colossians 3:17

III. **Cross references:**

    Boxes 1, 8, 12, 17-18

IV. **Suggested topics for discipleship/counseling meetings:**

    A.   Explain relevant portions of *Principles 12, 31-32, 83, 88, 98-103, 105 (**Handbook**, Pages H25, H28, H38-H39, H41-H42)*.

B.   Introduce the exercise described under **III. Incorporating God's standards into your life** (*Self-Confrontation,* Page 405).

C.   Encourage your disciple/counselee to persevere in the changes he has already made [*Principles 32, 103* (**Handbook**, Pages H28, H41)]. It may be appropriate at this time to tell him some of the biblical changes you, as disciplers/counselors, have been observing.

V.   Key homework assignments:

A.   Memorize the Scripture passage that will best help me in my present situation.

B.   Complete the exercise described under **III. Incorporating God's standards into your life** (*Self-Confrontation,* Page 405) (*this assignment refers to* **IV.** *B. above*).

NOTES FOR BOX 17

> 17
> Encourage ministry as a working part of the local body of believers through:
> *(Principle 41)***
> (a) Practice of spiritual gifts and cooperation with God's Spirit in bearing spiritual fruit as a faithful steward
> *(Principles 12, 39, 41, 43-44, 83, 98-105)***
> (b) Submission to the spiritual leaders
> *(Principles 116-118)***
> (c) Meeting the needs of the afflicted
> *(Principle 3)***

I.   **Biblical focus and guidelines:**

A.   You can be confident that your initial involvement in the restoration process is completed when a disciple/counselee demonstrates his commitment to be a doer of the Word by consistently carrying his own load and beginning to help others biblically *(based on Romans 15:1; Galatians 6:1-5)*.

B.   At this point, the disciple should be comforting others just as he has been comforted by God during the discipleship/counseling process *(based on II Corinthians 1:3-4)*. You should help him to become alert to the needs of others and to take the initiative in helping them *(based on Matthew 25:35-36; Romans 12:9-21; James 1:27)*.

C.   Help the disciple recognize his responsibility to become a useful member of the body of Christ in the local church *(based on Romans 12:3-8; I Corinthians 12:14-27; Hebrews 10:24-25; I Peter 4:10-11)*. Then, help him learn how to become involved in fellowship, worship, training for service, and active ministry both to unbelievers and believers *(based on Acts 2:42; Ephesians 4:12-16)*. He should seek to be trained in biblical discipleship *(based on Matthew 28:19-20; Galatians 6:1-5)*.

D.   For further guidance study *Principles 3, 12, 41, 43, 83, 98-105* (**Handbook**, Pages H23, H25, H30-H31, H38, H41-H42) and **YOUR RESPONSIBILITY AS A BIBLICAL DISCIPLER/COUNSELOR** (*Handbook*, Pages H113-H116).

II. **Essential Scriptures:**

II Corinthians 1:3-4; Galatians 6:1-5; I Peter 4:10-11

III. **Cross references:**

Boxes 1, 8, 14, 16, 18

IV. **Suggested topics for discipleship/counseling meetings:**

A.   Explain relevant portions of *Principles 3, 12, 41, 43, 83, 98-105* (**Handbook**, Pages H23, H25, H30-H31, H38, H41-H42).

B.   Explain the disciple/counselee's responsibility to become a useful member of the body of Christ in the local church *(based on Acts 2:42; Romans 12:3-8; I Corinthians 12:14-27; Ephesians 4:12-16; Hebrews 3:13; 10:24-25; I Peter 4:10-11).*

C.   Explain the importance of comforting those who are in need *(based on Romans 12:9-21; II Corinthians 1:3-5).*

V.   Key homework assignments:

A.   Memorize the Scripture passage that will best help me in my present situation.

B.   Based on *Romans 12:9-21,* make a list of those in my church who have needs and develop a plan to help them.

C.   Arrange a meeting with someone in the leadership of my church; explain how my life has changed recently and express my desire to serve in the church. Investigate together how I might minister most effectively. Make a list of ministry opportunities in which I can be involved. In the areas where I need training, make plans to become trained (for example, evangelism training).

NOTES FOR BOX 18

> 18
>
> Teach how to disciple others toward spiritual maturity and, as applicable, train how to restore those caught up in sin by:
> (a) Standing ready to give them a reason for the hope within
> (b) Exercising a spirit of gentleness
> (c) Assisting in bearing their burdens
> (d) Encouraging and stimulating them to love and good deeds
> (e) As necessary, admonishing, reproving, and disciplining
>   *(Principle 3, 105, 129-130)***

I.   **Biblical focus and guidelines:**

   A.   At this point, you should emphasize to the disciple his specific responsibility to disciple/counsel others whether or not he ever becomes involved in an organized counseling training ministry in his church *(based on Matthew 28:19-20; Galatians 6:1-5; II Timothy 2:2)*. Explain to him that he has already been discipling/ counseling others, sometimes biblically and sometimes unbiblically. Therefore, it is important to impress on him the need to prepare himself further and become involved as the Holy Spirit leads *(based on II Timothy 2:15; I Peter 3:15)*.

   B.   Teach him how to disciple others toward spiritual maturity including how to restore those caught up in sin *(based on Matthew 18:15-17; 28:19-20; Galatians 6:1-5)*. Help him to stand ready to give a reason for the hope within *(I Peter 3:15)* exercising a spirit of gentleness and assisting in bearing others' burdens *(Galatians 6:1-2; II Timothy 2:24-26)*. Teach the disciple to encourage and stimulate others to love and good deeds *(Hebrews 10:24-25)*, admonishing and reproving where necessary *(Romans 15:14)*.

   C.   Remain diligent so that you may present each disciple/counselee complete in Christ *(based on Colossians 1:28-29)*. Demonstrate your concern for each person entrusted to you by the Lord, by following-up and encouraging each one in his walk in the Lord Jesus Christ *(based on examples of the Apostles' continuing work with individuals and groups, such as seen in Philippians 1:3-11; 2:19-28; Colossians 1:3-12; I Thessalonians 2:5-12; 4:1; 5:11; I Timothy 1:5; II Timothy 1:1-14; II Peter 1:13-15)*.

   D.   For further guidance, study *Principle 3* (**Handbook**, Page H23).

II. **Essential Scriptures:**

   Matthew 18:15-17; 28:19-20; Romans 15:14; Galatians 6:1-5; II Timothy 2:2; Hebrews 10:24-25; I Peter 3:15

III. **Cross references:**

   All other boxes.

IV. **Suggested topics for discipleship/counseling meetings:**

   A.   Explain relevant portions of *Principle 3* (**Handbook**, Page H23).

B.   Explain appropriate portions of **INTRODUCTION TO COURSE II: BIBLICAL COUNSELING TRAINING** (*Self-Confrontation*, Pages 417-418).

C.   Explain appropriate portions of **BIBLICAL COUNSELING IS IN-DEPTH DISCIPLESHIP** (*Handbook*, Pages H13-H16).

D.   Explain appropriate portions of **YOUR RESPONSIBILITY AS A BIBLICAL DISCIPLER/COUNSELOR** (*Handbook*, Pages H113-H116).

E.   Explain the **BIBLICAL PRACTICES FOR FACING, DEALING WITH, AND ENDURING PROBLEMS** (*Handbook*, Pages H267-H272, BCF Form 111).

F.   Explain the need for an evangelism training course.

G.   Explain the need for the Self-Confrontation and Biblical Discipleship/Counseling courses.

V.   **Key homework assignments:**

A.   Memorize the Scripture passage that will best help me in my present situation.

B.   As I study the **BIBLICAL PRACTICES FOR FACING, DEALING WITH, AND ENDURING PROBLEMS** (*Handbook*, Pages H267-H272, BCF Form 111) develop a plan for improving my effectiveness in discipleship/counseling (*this assignment refers to* **IV. E.** *above*).

C.   Develop a plan for becoming trained for ministry in the local church.

D.   Study the Gospel of Mark and describe how Jesus discipled the Apostles.

E.   Complete an evangelism training course (*this assignment refers to* **IV. F.** *above*).

F.   Complete the Self-Confrontation Course and Biblical Discipleship/Counseling Course II (*this assignment refers to* **IV. G.** *above*).

SECTION III

ESSENTIAL PRECEPTS FOR BIBLICAL DISCIPLESHIP/COUNSELING

SECTION III

ESSENTIAL PRECEPTS FOR BIBLICAL DISCIPLESHIP/COUNSELING

INTRODUCTION

Scripture contains precepts that, when obeyed, will equip you to disciple/counsel anyone in any situation. Diligent study of the Scriptures is necessary for godly focus, conduct, and discipleship/counseling content.

Section III contains essential scriptural teaching for all aspects of your ministry as a biblical discipler/counselor. It consists of three parts: **THE DISCIPLE/COUNSELEE, THE BIBLICAL DISCIPLER/COUNSELOR,** and **THE BIBLICAL DISCIPLESHIP/COUNSELING PROCESS.** Throughout the years you spend ministering to others, this section will provide a valuable reference for your own discipleship/counseling and for training others.

SECTION III

PART 1:

THE DISCIPLE/COUNSELEE

A BIBLICAL UNDERSTANDING OF
THE DISCIPLE/COUNSELEE

> The Lord already knows what is in the heart of every man and has given you knowledge about man through His Word. Scripture provides some significant facts that are essential for understanding a disciple/counselee's problems *(based on I Kings 8:39; I Chronicles 28:9; Jeremiah 17:9-10; Hebrews 4:12)*.

I. **Those who do not know the Lord Jesus Christ as their Savior have no capability to change biblically.**

    A.   Unbelievers do not have the resources for biblical change. They lack:

        1.   The indwelling power of God in their lives *(based on John 14:17; 15:4-5; Romans 5:5; 8:9)*,

        2.   The understanding of the things of God *(I Corinthians 2:6-14, esp. verse 14)*, and

        3.   The hope to live in a manner pleasing to God *(based on Romans 8:8; Ephesians 2:12)*.

    B.   They have set their minds on the flesh, not on the Spirit, and are hostile to God *(Romans 8:5-8; Colossians 1:21)*.

    For further details concerning the condition of the unbeliever, review **YOU CAN CHANGE BIBLICALLY (PART ONE), I. If you do not already have a sincere ...** *(Self-Confrontation, Page 20)*.

    For further details concerning the resources available only to believers, review **YOU CAN CHANGE BIBLICALLY (PART TWO), I. The process of lasting biblical change begins ...** *(Self-Confrontation, Pages 32-34)*.

II. **All believers can change biblically because of the enabling they have in the Lord.**

Believers have available all that they need to change quickly and dramatically because they have the authority of the Scriptures *(John 17:17; Acts 20:32; I Thessalonians 2:13; II Timothy 3:16-17; Hebrews 4:12)*, the empowering of the Holy Spirit available to them *(based on Romans 8:9-14; Ephesians 1:13-14; 5:18)*, and the privilege of prayer to approach the throne of God in time of need *(Hebrews 4:15-16)*. Since God commands His children to walk by the Spirit, which implies His empowerment, believers are able to exhibit the fruit of the Spirit at all times *(based on Galatians 5:16, 22-25)*.

NOTE: The above paragraph is a reprint of Principle 109.
Review:
YOU CAN CHANGE BIBLICALLY (PART TWO) *(Self-Confrontation, Pages 32-34)*,
    and
THE HOLY SPIRIT EMPOWERS YOU TO SOLVE YOUR PROBLEMS *(Self-Confrontation, Pages 53-55)*.

III. **All believers undergo continuing spiritual battles and must learn to stand firm in the Lord and put on the full armor of God.**

   A. The desires of the flesh are in opposition to the Spirit *(Galatians 5:17)*.

   B. Believers are engaged in a spiritual battle *(II Corinthians 10:3-4; Ephesians 6:10-13)*.

   Review:
   BIBLICAL PERSPECTIVE ON TESTS AND TEMPTATIONS *(Self-Confrontation, Pages 124-128)*,
   GOD HAS BROKEN SATAN'S POWER *(Self-Confrontation, Pages 362-364)*,
   PUTTING ON THE FULL ARMOR OF GOD *(Self-Confrontation, Pages 373-381)*, *and*
   THE FRAMEWORK OF BIBLICAL DISCIPLESHIP/COUNSELING *"The Accused" (Handbook, Page H17)*.

IV. **Believers who are not overcoming sin in their lives are either ignorant of biblical truth or willfully practicing sin.**

   A. The disciple may be a new believer or one who has never known how to apply God's Word to his life *(based on I Corinthians 3:1-3; Hebrews 5:11-14)*.

      1. Like King Solomon, the disciple may have sought contentment through circumstances, things, or people *(based on Ecclesiastes 2:1-11)*.

      2. He may be heavily influenced by all manner of conflicting theories and philosophies from the world and false teachers *(based on Ephesians 4:13-14; Colossians 2:8-9; II Peter 2:1-3)*.

   B. The counselee may have deluded himself by being only a hearer of the Word *(based on James 1:22)*. He may not even be aware that many of his failures are described in God's Word as sins *(based on Proverbs 12:15; 14:12; 16:2, 25; 21:2)*. Remember that it is by doing God's Word that the believer gains discernment *(Hebrews 5:12-14)*.

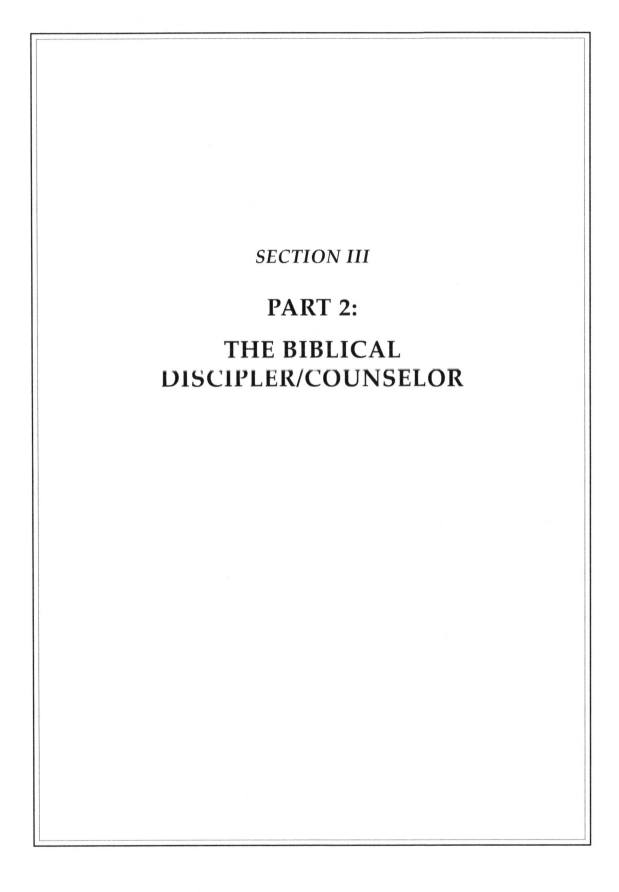

SECTION III

PART 2:

THE BIBLICAL DISCIPLER/COUNSELOR

YOUR RESPONSIBILITY AS
A BIBLICAL DISCIPLER/COUNSELOR

> The ministry of biblical discipleship/counseling involves obedience to the Lord, with a view to reconciling individuals to Him and teaching them to walk in His way. As you disciple/counsel, you must continue to judge yourself and take heed to your own walk with the Lord, remaining totally dependent on Him and His Word. You are to demonstrate tenderhearted servanthood to those whom you disciple/counsel *(based on Matthew 7:1-5; I Thessalonians 2:5-9; Galatians 6:1-5; I Peter 3:15-16).*

I.   **You have the privilege and responsibility of restoring others** *(Matthew 7:5; II Corinthians 5:18-20; Galatians 5:25; 6:1).*

    A.   No matter what age you are or how new your walk of faith may be, you are commanded to present the message of salvation through Jesus Christ and to teach believers to live God's way. For the obedient believer, discipling/counseling others is not an option *(based on Matthew 28:19-20; Galatians 6:1; I Thessalonians 5:14; I Timothy 4:6, 10-12).*

    B.   God has already taught you much about His work and His provisions as He, by the Holy Spirit, has worked in your own life. To that extent, you are responsible to disciple/counsel others *(based on Romans 15:14; II Corinthians 1:3-4).*

II. **You are to be a faithful biblical discipler/counselor.**

Recognize that God examines your heart, and that He weighs and judges your motives *(Psalm 19:14; 139:1-4, 23-24; Jeremiah 17:10).* Your ministry is to be done in a manner that is faithful to the Word of God and pleasing in His sight *(I Thessalonians 2:4; II Timothy 2:15).* This requires that you:

    A.   Maintain a fervent personal commitment to walk in a manner pleasing to the Lord *(Colossians 1:10);*

        1.   Maintain a faithful and obedient walk with the Lord *(based on Matthew 7:1-5; John 14:15; Ephesians 4:1-3; Colossians 1:9-12; 2:6-7).*

        2.   Your deeds should:

            a.   Set an example for others to follow *(based on Matthew 5:13-16; I Corinthians 11:1; I Thessalonians 1:6; I Timothy 4:12, 15-16; Hebrews 6:12; 13:7)* and

            b.   Demonstrate your commitment to the Lord Jesus Christ *(based on Mark 8:34-38; John 14:15).*

        3.   Your manner in every circumstance and with every person should exemplify the gentle and humble character of Jesus *(based on Matthew 11:29-30; Ephesians 5:1-2; Colossians 2:6; I Peter 2:21; I John 2:3-6, esp. verse 6).*

*(See Principle 111, **Handbook**, Page H44.)*

4.   Concentrate on glorifying God, not on gaining credit or praise for self *(based on Matthew 5:16; Galatians 1:10-11; Colossians 3:17, 23-24; I Thessalonians 2:3-6)*.

5.   Rely on the guidance and empowering of the Holy Spirit for your counsel and for results in the disciple's life *(based on Colossians 1:11; II Timothy 1:14; I John 2:20, 27)*. Keep in mind that you are totally inadequate in yourself, but that your adequacy is in the Lord *(II Corinthians 3:5-6)*.

6.   Continually examine (judge) yourself honestly and faithfully, and correct biblically any sinful practices in your life *(Psalm 139:23-24; Matthew 7:1-5; I Corinthians 10:12; 11:28; Galatians 6:4)*.

B.   Base your counseling solely on the Scriptures.

1.   Study God's Word diligently and remain faithful in the practice of His Word *(based on John 8:31-32; Colossians 1:9; II Timothy 2:15)* so that while discipling/counseling others, you may not delude yourself *(based on Galatians 6:1; James 1:22)*.

2.   Always point to the Lord and His Scriptures as the only standard, hope, and authority for your counsel.

a.   You are not to rely on your own (or the world's) knowledge, experience, or opinions *(Isaiah 55:8-11; Colossians 2:8; 3:16; II Timothy 3:16-17; Titus 2:1; Hebrews 4:12)*.

b.   Do not seek to be an authority in the lives of disciples/counselees or the one on whom they depend; rather your desire should be for them to submit their lives to the Lord Jesus Christ *(Proverbs 30:5; Isaiah 55:8-11; John 5:19, 30; II Peter 1:20-21)*.

C.   Be a servant to those you instruct.

Always look to the Lord Jesus Christ as the primary example of a servant-teacher *(based on I Peter 2:21)*. You are to:

1.   Demonstrate servanthood to those you disciple/counsel *(Matthew 20:25-28; John 13:13-17; I Corinthians 9:19; II Corinthians 4:5; Philippians 2:5-8)*, and exhibit a humble and gentle spirit — not a dominant or overbearing spirit — even in matters of disagreement or challenges to the counsel you give. Whether the disciple/counselee asks questions from ignorance or a desire to dispute, treat him as more important than yourself *(based on Matthew 20:25-28; John 13:13-17; I Corinthians 9:19; II Corinthians 8:3-6; Philippians 2:3-8; Colossians 4:6; I Thessalonians 2:3-9; II Timothy 2:24-25)*.

2.   Labor out of love, not out of greed *(based on I Corinthians 9:7-11; Philippians 1:9-11, 15-16, 21-26; I Thessalonians 2:5-12; I Timothy 1:5)*.

D.   Minister through biblical discipleship/counseling as a part of your daily walk with Christ. You must be prepared to minister to others in their difficulties as part of your God-given responsibilities. God calls you to build up the body of Christ, not just in the area of your giftedness or "expertise," but in all ways *(Matthew 28:19-20; I Peter 3:15)*.

III. **Your ministry of reconciliation and restoration should be directed toward both believers and unbelievers.**

Always counsel with the view that someday the disciple/counselee may be discipling/counseling others also. Have as your goal to help the disciple/counselee mature in Christ so that he too may stand ready to give others a reason for the hope that is within him *(based on Matthew 28:19-20; II Corinthians 1:3-4; II Timothy 2:2; I Peter 3:15).*

A. The counselee may be an unbeliever. In order to minister to him, you must:

1. Keep in mind that he lacks:

    a. The indwelling power of God in his life *(based on John 14:17; 15:4-5; Romans 5:5; 8:9),*

    b. The understanding of the things of God *(I Corinthians 2:6-14, esp. verse 14),* and

    c. The hope to live in a manner pleasing to God *(based on Romans 8:8; Ephesians 2:12).*

2. Help him see that the scope of his problems is beyond his limited understanding of circumstances and relationships.

    a. He is:

        1) Hopelessly separated from God *(Romans 6:23a; Ephesians 2:1-3, 11-12, Colossians 1:21);*

        2) Powerless to overcome sin's hold on his life *(Romans 5:6; 6:16);*

        3) Unable to understand the things of God *(Proverbs 14:12; I Corinthians 2:14);*

        4) Incapable of living a spiritually fruitful life *(John 15:4-6);*

        5) Guaranteed increasing heartaches, problems, and difficulties *(Proverbs 13:15; Romans 2:8-9);* and

        6) Unable to please God *(Romans 8:8; Hebrews 11:6).*

    b. His problems cannot be solved by man's devices and philosophies *(I Corinthians 3:19-20; Colossians 2:6-8).*

3. Show him the way of salvation. *Refer to Principle 1 (**Handbook**, Page H23).*

B. The disciple may be a new believer or one who has never known how to apply God's Word to his life *(based on I Corinthians 3:1-3; Hebrews 5:11-14).* In order to minister to him, you must:

1. Spend time teaching him how to study the Scriptures and train him to practice personal daily devotions and Scripture memory *(based on Psalm 1; 119:9-11).*

    *Refer to **BIBLICAL BASIS FOR DAILY DEVOTIONS AND SCRIPTURE MEMORY** (Self-Confrontation, Pages 38-40) and **FOUR PLANS FOR MEMORIZING SCRIPTURE** (Self-Confrontation, Pages 41-42).*

2. Encourage and help him become firmly established in a biblically focused local church, fellowshipping with other believers, and ministering to others *(based on Acts 2:42; Ephesians 4:13-16; II Timothy 2:22; Hebrews 3:12-13; 10:24-25).*

3. Teach him how to rely on the Word of God rather than the wisdom of man as you gently instruct him from the Scriptures in the areas about which he is confused *(based on Colossians 2:6-8; II Timothy 2:22-25; 3:16-17).*

    4.   Help him understand that his problems are being used by the Lord to show the need for change in his life *(based on Psalm 119:67, 71, 75)* and to mature him *(based on Romans 5:3-5; James 1:2-4)* and that God's plan is to use all things in the believer's life for his good, the good being to conform him to the image of God's Son *(Romans 8:28-29)*.

C.   The counselee may have deluded himself by being only a hearer of the Word *(based on James 1:22)*. He may not even be aware that many of his failures are described in God's Word as sins *(based on Proverbs 12:15; 14:12; 16:2, 25; 21:2)*. In order to minister to him, you must:

    1.   Carefully gather information (often by taking notes) regarding his specific thoughts, speech, and actions that document the contrast between the way he is living and the standard of God's Word *(based on Ephesians 5:11-12 and illustrated in Acts 5:1-10; 8:18-24)*.

    2.   Help him recognize the seriousness of his condition by describing the consequences of continued, unrepentant sin *(Proverbs 1:22-33; 13:15; 15:6; Matthew 7:24-27; Hebrews 10:26-31; James 1:22)*.

TEAM DISCIPLESHIP/COUNSELING

> Biblical teamwork facilitates using all the resources that God has provided for the ministry of biblical discipleship/ counseling. In addition, it is of great benefit, both to the disciple/counselee, and to the disciplers/counselors *(Proverbs 11:14; 15:22)*.

I. **Why disciple/counsel in teams?**

While Scripture does not prohibit one-on-one discipleship/counseling, it provides many reasons for working within a team. Having two or more other individuals to observe and help offers a number of advantages:

   A. There is wisdom and victory in a multitude of counselors *(based on Proverbs 11:14; 15:22; 24:6)*.

   B. Team members working in unity with one another are stronger and have a better return for their labor than one individual working alone *(based on Ecclesiastes 4:9-10, 12)*.

   C. Team members can sharpen one another's discipleship/counseling skills *(based on Proverbs 27:17)*.

   D. Team discipleship/counseling protects all involved against false accusations. Also, it provides objectivity and help in understanding the problem *(based on Deuteronomy 17:2-6; 19:15; Matthew 18:16)*.

   E. Ministering as a team is vital to the disciple-making process. Biblical disciple-making involves setting a godly example for the disciples to observe, participation by the disciples, evaluation of the disciples, and helping them minister as needed *(as exemplified by Jesus in training the disciples)*. Participation in actual discipleship/counseling meetings provides opportunities for less experienced members of the team to progress in their training and increase in the effectiveness of their counsel. Progressive training can be accomplished as follows:

   1. Initially, the inexperienced team member can observe and take notes during the discipleship/counseling meetings and participate in evaluation of the counseling meetings.

   2. In subsequent meetings, he can participate by contributing in small ways (e.g., he might be assigned by the lead counselor, who is also his discipler, to teach the counselee about biblical forgiveness).

   3. Gradually, his participation can be increased as he is able, while continuing to be observed and evaluated.

   4. Then, when he is ready, he can be designated to lead a team and begin training others even while being discipled.

   Refer to **UNDERSTANDING BIBLICAL INSTRUCTION OF CHILDREN** *(Self-Confrontation, Page 287)*, **VI. G. 2.**

II.   **Members of the discipleship/counseling team**

A.   *God Himself, in the Person of the Holy Spirit,* the most important member of the discipleship/counseling team. He is the guide to all that is true and right *(John 16:13).* He testifies of the Lord and teaches believers all things *(John 14:26; 15:26; I John 2:27).* He convicts men of sin and righteousness and judgment *(John 16:7-8).* He comforts and helps the afflicted and depressed *(based on II Corinthians 1:3-4; 7:6).*

The Holy Spirit accomplishes all biblical change. The human members of the discipleship/counseling team are totally dependent on the Lord's enablement to accomplish the tasks He has given them *(based on John 15:1-8; Acts 1:8; II Corinthians 3:5-6; Philippians 4:13).*

B.   *Disciples/counselees (based on I John 2:20, 27).* They are responsible to walk in a manner worthy of the Lord *(Colossians 1:9-11).*

C.   *Disciplers/counselors.* They teach, reprove, correct and train the disciples to live God's way faithfully in accordance with God's Word *(based on Romans 15:14; Galatians 6:1-5; II Timothy 2:22-24; 3:16-17; 4:2; Titus 2:1),* with love *(I Thessalonians 2:4-8).*

In forming teams, care must be taken:

1.   Not to be a stumbling block to others *(Romans 14:13, 19-21),*

2.   To avoid all forms of evil *(I Thessalonians 5:22),* and

3.   To avoid temptation *(Galatians 6:1).*

A husband and a wife may serve as a team, but care must be taken in forming teams consisting of individuals of mixed genders. It is important that an individual not spend long periods of time alone with another person of the opposite gender, other than his spouse. Therefore, one-on-one contacts between disciplers and disciples should be arranged so that they are of the same gender.

See **YOUR RESPONSIBILITY AS A BIBLICAL DISCIPLER/COUNSELOR** (**Handbook,** *Pages H113-H116).*

D.   *Local church leaders.* Even though they may not be actively involved in the meetings, they are responsible for:

1.   Equipping the saints for the work of service, to the building up of the body of Christ *(Ephesians 4:11-12);* and

2.   Shepherding (overseeing) with loving concern *(based on Hebrews 13:17; I Peter 5:1-3).*

E.   *Other members of the body of Christ (based on Romans 12:3-16; 15:14; I Corinthians 12; Galatians 6:1; Ephesians 4:12-16; I Peter 4:7-11).*

F.   *Others.* These individuals may contribute by providing information *(Deuteronomy 19:15; Proverbs 18:17).* They may be:

1.   The disciple/counselee's spouse, children, parents, or other involved family members;

2.   A single disciple/counselee's roommates;

3.   Concerned friends and individuals;

4.   Physicians, legal authorities, and other specialists; or

5.   Employers, employees, and fellow workers.

NOTE: It is important that everyone having a close relationship with the ones being discipled, particularly members of a family, be invited to become part of the discipleship/counseling team. While it is not necessary that everyone be present at all the meetings, they should be helping to restore and disciple as much as possible.

The notion that husbands and wives, for example, should be counseled separately when there is great animosity between them (or one of them does not want certain secrets to be known by the other spouse) ignores their "one-flesh" relationship and all of the advantages of team discipleship/counseling listed in the previous paragraphs. Counseling spouses separately encourages gossip and minimizes the opportunity to help the couple through difficult conversations. Because the discipler/counselors cannot observe the individuals in the midst of their difficulties with each other, the disciplers do not get accurate information to make sound judgments (based on Proverbs 18:17). Also, since the disciplers are not present during the arguments, they cannot come along side and provide help at the critical times.

III. Serving as a team

Whether in the meeting or in other discipleship times during the week, each team member has the responsibility to:

A.   Continue daily to die to self *(Luke 9:23-25)*. This means that each person should:

    1.   Give glory to the Lord for all accomplishments *(Matthew 5:16)*;

    2.   Be content with where God has placed him in the team *(based on I Corinthians 7:20; I Timothy 6:6)*; and

    3.   Press forward together to Christ's upward call *(Philippians 3:14)*, keeping his eyes fixed on Jesus *(Hebrews 12:1-2)*.

B.   Consider others as more important than himself *(Philippians 2:3-4)*. This means that each person should:

    1.   Serve the others in humility *(based on John 13:3-17; Galatians 5:13; Ephesians 6:5-8; Philippians 2:5-8)*;

    2.   Prefer the others in honor *(Romans 12:10)*; and

    3.   Build up and encourage the others *(Ephesians 4:29; I Thessalonians 5:11; I Peter 4:10)*.

C.   Communicate biblically with a view to bless co-laborers *(Ephesians 4:15, 29; Colossians 4:6)*. This means that each person should:

    1.   Use only edifying speech toward and about the others and their ministries *(Ephesians 4:29)*;

    2.   Base his counsel on biblical principles, not on personal preferences, opinions, or experiences *(based on Deuteronomy 4:2; Proverbs 30:5-6; Isaiah 55:8-11; II Peter 1:20-21)*.

    Refer to **APPLYING SCRIPTURES IN DISCIPLESHIP/COUNSELING** *(***Handbook***, Pages H125-H132).*

3.   Refrain from contradicting fellow-laborers in front of others; instead, resolve differences privately and correct miscommunications in a spirit of unity *(based on Matthew 18:15; Ephesians 4:2-3);*

4.   Not grumble or complain *(Philippians 2:14; II Timothy 2:24);*

5.   Listen to the other team members and seek understanding before speaking *(based on Proverbs 10:19; 18:2, 13; Philippians 2:3-4; James 1:19-20);*

6.   Not gossip *(Proverbs 18:8; 20:19; 26:20);*

7.   Take care not to provide counsel apart from the other team members on subjects not already discussed in previous counseling meetings; otherwise he loses the advantages of acting as a team and risks the possibility of participating in gossip and creating division on the team. If an emergency should arise, it would be best for the entire team to have a special meeting quickly.

8.   When evaluating, lovingly speak the truth *(Ephesians 4:15, 25, 29; Colossians 4:6)* and be submissive to correction *(based on Proverbs 9:9; 17:10; 27:5-6).* Even in disagreements or when correction is necessary, each team member must speak and act with gentleness *(Romans 12:18; Galatians 6:1; II Timothy 2:25-26).*

D.   Avoid the temptation to practice favoritism *(based on Proverbs 24:23; 28:21; I Corinthians 4:6-7; James 2:1-9).*

BIBLICAL HOPE AND AUTHORITY
FOR DISCIPLERS/COUNSELORS

> Your hope is from the Lord and the authority of His Word. He is your rock and salvation; He is your fortress and refuge. You are to trust in Him at all times and not lose hope because some disciples/counselees do not change. Your authority is God's Word which never changes. You are required only to present the Scriptures accurately and faithfully in love *(based on Psalm 18:2; 62:1-12; 119:160; Ezekiel 18:4, 20; 33:1-20; Romans 15:4, 13).*

I. **God will work sovereignly in the disciple/counselees' lives.**

You can rest assured that the Lord will sovereignly work in the lives of the counselees *(based on Psalm 138:8; Romans 8:28-29; I Corinthians 15:10; Philippians 1:6; 2:13; I Thessalonians 5:23-24; Hebrews 13:21).* Because all individuals are directly responsible to the Lord *(Ezekiel 18:4, 20),* you can have great confidence when you disciple/counsel them biblically.

A. You can expect God to accomplish His desire through His Word in any circumstances that disciples face *(Isaiah 55:11; I Thessalonians 2:13; Hebrews 4:12).* Therefore, you can counsel them from the Scriptures with firm confidence *(Romans 15:4).*

B. Believers have available all that they need to change quickly and dramatically because they have:

1. The authority of the Scriptures *(John 17:17; Acts 20:32; I Thessalonians 2:13; II Timothy 3:16-17; Hebrews 4:12),*

2. The empowering of the Holy Spirit available to them *(Romans 8:9-14; Ephesians 1:13-14; 5:18),* and

3. The privilege of prayer to approach the throne of God in time of need *(Hebrews 4:15-16).*

Since God commands His children to walk by the Spirit, which implies His empowerment, believers are able to exhibit the fruit of the Spirit at all times *(based on Galatians 5:16, 22-25).*

*(See Lesson 3 in the **Self-Confrontation** manual for detailed teaching on Points 1-3.)*

C. Your success as a biblical discipler/counselor depends only on your faithfulness to study, do, and present God's Word in love *(based on I Corinthians 3:6-8; 4:2; II Timothy 2:15, 24-26; Titus 2:1).*

II. **Your ministry is to be established only in the Lord and His Word.**

A. It is comforting to know that it is not necessary to have experienced the problems that disciples/counselees face, nor is it necessary to understand fully their temptations.

---

1. The Lord Jesus Christ alone is the One who was tempted in all things and understands all that disciples/counselees face *(Hebrews 4:15-16)*.

2. You can confidently counsel others in any affliction, since God comforts you in all your afflictions *(II Corinthians 1:3-4)*. It is God who is faithful in their lives *(I Corinthians 10:13; II Corinthians 1:18-22)*.

B. Disciples/counselees can gain sympathy, hope, strength, wisdom, and encouragement from the Lord and His Word *(based on Psalm 18:1-2; 39:7; 62:5; Romans 15:4-5, 13; II Corinthians 1:3-4; Philippians 2:1; Hebrews 4:15-16; James 1:5)*.

III. Your hope is to be based on pleasing God, not men.

As you help disciples/counselees, keep in mind that your ministry will be judged by God and not by whether you gain favor before men *(Galatians 1:10; Ephesians 6:6-8; Colossians 1:10; I Thessalonians 2:5-6a)*.

SECTION III

PART 3:

THE BIBLICAL DISCIPLESHIP/COUNSELING PROCESS

APPLYING SCRIPTURES IN DISCIPLESHIP/COUNSELING

> As a biblical discipler/counselor you are to rely on the Scriptures alone as your basis of authority; not on your opinions or experiences no matter how relevant they may seem *(based on Isaiah 55:8-9; II Timothy 3:16-17; Titus 2:1)*. You are to be a diligent worker who accurately handles the Word of truth *(II Timothy 2:15)*. This means first, that you need to know and obey the Scriptures *(Joshua 1:8)*, and second, that you need to know how to point disciples/counselees continually to the Word as their only authority for living *(based on Titus 1:9)*. *(Reprinted from Principle 122.)*

I. **The importance of remaining faithful to the Scriptures**

It is vital that you use **only** the Scriptures for determining first, how you live and second, how you disciple/counsel others. The Word of God is complete and adequate *(II Timothy 3:16-17)*; man's opinions are inadequate *(Isaiah 55:8-9)*. God has promised to bless His eternal Word *(Isaiah 55:11)* not your words or anyone else's.

A. Use **only** biblical terminology since the world has distorted the meaning of so many words and phrases. Do not be legalistic, but communicate clearly what is faithful to the Scriptures. For example:

1. Do not merely say "I am sorry," or "I apologize" because these are only expressions of remorse and do not include repentance and reconciliation *(based on Matthew 5:23-24; Luke 15:17-19; II Corinthians 7:9-10)*.

2. Do not speak of phobias; instead, speak of fears. Although "phobia" from the original language means "fear," the term has been distorted by the world to mean an irrational, extreme response of fear indicating that people are not responsible.

3. Do not say, "You have been conditioned to eat that way" (as though you are not fully responsible); instead, say, "You have practiced eating that way until it has become a way of life."

4. Avoid using the terms *positive* and *negative*; instead, use the terms *godly* and *ungodly*, or *righteous* and *unrighteous*, or *moral* and *immoral*. See *Titus 2:11-12*.

5. Do not use the terms *conscious* and *subconscious*; instead, use the terms *deliberate* and *without pondering*.

B. Base your counsel solely on biblical principles, not on your opinions or experiences no matter how relevant they may seem *(based on Isaiah 55:8-9; II Timothy 3:16-17; Titus 2:1; II Peter 1:3-4)*. For example:

1. Do not focus on proving your own opinions or debate to make your point *(Romans 12:16)*;

2. Do not stress your own opinion *(based on Romans 12:10; Philippians 2:3-4)*. Even when presenting your ideas, you are to do so humbly *(based on Romans 12:10, 16b)*;

3. Avoid using phrases such as "I think," "I believe," "I feel," and "I don't agree" because they focus on the speaker's authority. Also, avoid words that invite arguments. For example, when you say, "I disagree with you," you are implying, "I have an opinion and you have an opinion, and you are wrong." Your authority is to be the Scripture alone *(based on Deuteronomy 4:2; Proverbs 30:5-6; II Peter 1:20-21)*.

4. Exercise care not to present private interpretations, views, or theological positions not held generally by believers. It is important not to distract those you are discipling by presenting issues that divide *(based on Ephesians 4:3)*.

5. Be careful about giving your personal testimony.

   a. Generally, it is best to use illustrations and examples from the lives of biblical characters, rather than personal testimony, since disciples:

      1) Will see more readily God's commands, work, and direction in the lives of biblical characters and will be less tempted to look to others around them for their comfort and help. If you emphasize your personal testimony as an example of God's work in problems, the disciples/counselees may:

         a) Be tempted to see you as the "expert" and develop a dependence on you rather than on the Lord;

         b) Expect the same outcome as yours (especially if the outcome in your circumstances was just what the disciple/counselee wants in his life);

         c) Decide that their problems are far deeper and that your experience doesn't apply to them.

      2) Can find examples from Scriptures for themselves outside the discipleship/counseling meeting. Your testimony may have been a great work of God in your life, but it is either:

         a) Easy to forget, or

         b) Easy to remember and become a distraction from the Scriptures.

   b. Use your testimony to encourage the disciple, but do not present your experience as an example for the disciple to follow.

   Refer to SCRIPTURE IS YOUR AUTHORITY (Self-Confrontation, Pages 50-52).

II. How to prepare yourself for discipleship/counseling

A. As you prepare to counsel, concentrate on the study of foundational and key Scripture passages that apply to the situation so that you can explain them well. Make sure that the Bible is your primary text *(based on Isaiah 55:8-11; Colossians 3:16; II Timothy 3:16-17; Hebrews 4:12)*.

   1. Read all passages in the context of the entire biblical teaching given. Specifically, ask yourself the following as you study:

      a. What is the emphasis of the entire passage within which the verse is found? That is, what is the predominant biblical principle or command given?

      b. Is the principle in this passage consistent with the emphasis of the entire context?

      c.   Are there other verses that would support this biblical truth, or would describe it more clearly?

    2.   Identify who spoke/wrote this biblical truth and to whom it was directed. Also, ask yourself:

      a.   Is this command/principle applicable to all individuals and supported by other passages? If this passage is a parable, an illustration, or an example from a biblical character's life, is it applicable to others?

      b.   If this is a promise, is it conditional (i.e., does God require certain steps of obedience before this promise is applicable?)?

    3.   Study to understand all the words used in the passage (e.g., a verse containing the word *justification)* and determine how you will explain them. It is not necessary for you to be a theologian to do this. In studying the verses, ask yourself:

      a.   Do I need to do some research using a concordance or a Bible dictionary?

      b.   Do I need to develop my own list of "cross-references" (i.e., other verses that will expand or explain the meanings of certain words or biblical truths) for more complete understanding of this biblical truth?

B.   Develop a systematic plan for improving your understanding of how to apply Scriptures *(based on II Timothy 2:15; Titus 2:1).* Part of this preparation might include working on relevant parts of **THE BCF SELF-STUDY BIBLE COURSE IN BIBLICAL DISCIPLESHIP/COUNSELING** *(Handbook,* Pages H177-H202, BCF Form 7) over a specified period of time.

III. How to convey the Scriptures to disciples/counselees

Lay a biblical foundation for applying Scripture as the **only** source to be used in discipleship/counseling. Explain your commitment to remain entirely biblical throughout the discipleship/counseling process *(based on Titus 2:1).* Tell the disciple/counselee that, if he does not understand the biblical basis for specific things that you say, he should ask you for the biblical basis.

A.   Concentrate the teaching on one or two biblical principles at a time. Use a small number of verses that will present the teaching most clearly.

    1.   Normally, keep to one major Scripture passage when explaining a specific biblical principle. Do not jump quickly from one passage to another.

       Explain the passage thoroughly, moving as slowly as necessary to ensure that the disciple/counselee fully understands not only the principles, but also how they apply to his life.

    2.   Show him, from the information you have gathered, how his life compares with the standard of God's Word. Unless the disciple/counselee comprehends the Scriptural teaching and sees how it applies to his life, he may lose hope.

      a.   He may assume that although the Bible may apply to others, his situation is unique or his problem is far worse than you realize. He will need to see that God's Word applies specifically to the situation he is facing, and that his problem is not out of the realm of God's understanding and help *(based on I Corinthians 10:13; Hebrews 4:15-16).*

b.   It may be necessary for you to use a series of verses to stress that a particular teaching is part of the whole counsel of God. If you realize that a counselee has difficulty accepting a teaching, show him how the biblical principle you have covered is taught throughout Scripture.

B.   Ask the disciple/counselee to read the passage aloud from his Bible, unless for some reason he has difficulty reading. In this way, you are helping him develop the biblical pattern of reading the Scriptures on his own.

Make sure the disciple/counselee has found the passage in his Bible before reading it. Regardless of the individual who reads the passage aloud, it is valuable for each disciple/counselee to look at the verse for himself. Doing this will help him locate it later and eliminate confusion if he is using a translation that differs from the version being read aloud. If necessary, help him locate the passages by referring him to the table of contents in his Bible. You should encourage the disciple in every way possible to become familiar with his Bible.

C.   After the disciple has read the verse or passage, ask him to explain the biblical principle or command in his own words. When you do this, you can:

1.   Stimulate the disciple/counselee to think about what God's Word teaches about his own problem or situation. Regarding the Scripture passage, ask questions that draw attention to the biblical truths the disciple/counselee most needs at the time *(based on Ephesians 4:29)*. Using *Romans 8:28-29*, for example, ask:

a.   "What does the Lord promise to do in your life within your circumstances?"

b.   "How many circumstances or relationships does He cause to work together for good in your life?" or "Are there any circumstances that God cannot work together for good in your life, according to this passage?"

c.   "What does God say, in *verse 29*, is the good He intends to accomplish in your life?"

d.   "To whom does God promise to work all things together for good?"

e.   "What does being 'called according to His purpose' mean?"

f.   "What does loving God involve?"

2.   Observe his knowledge, interpretation, and understanding of biblical truth. Observe the focus and spiritual understanding of the disciple/counselee as he answers the questions.

3.   Explain what the verse or passage teaches based on his discussion, rather than on your assumptions about his comprehension.

NOTE: *You will not have time to have the disciple/counselee explain every passage. You must carefully select the key passages to develop.*

D.   After explaining the meaning of the passage, ask the disciple/counselee how it applies to his current situation.

E.   Continue to contrast the world's philosophies with God's truth as demonstrated by the method Jesus used when He taught. He said, *"You have heard that it was said ...,"* and contrasted the statement with, *"But I say to you ...."* Always use Scripture to explain the contrasts.

F. Use transitions when introducing each subject within the meeting. When Jesus introduced a new subject, He told his hearers why it was important for them to listen. Throughout the Scriptures, we are usually told not only what to do, but why it is good for us to do it. When you are counseling, introduce each subject by explaining why it is important for the disciple to pay careful attention to what you have to say.

G. Answer questions as follows:

1. Answer the question based on biblical principles.

    a. A good way to insure this is by broadening the answer to address the biblical principles involved, and not merely addressing an isolated, specific incident or detail.

    b. In answering questions, help the disciple to maintain a focus on the subject of confronting self. This does not mean that specific topics should never be discussed, but it is important that the general focus remain on dealing with self.

2. When you are unsure of the biblical principles that apply to any questions brought up by the disciple/counselee, tell him that you need to study the Scriptures further in order to give him a biblical answer. In so doing:

    a. You demonstrate that your commitment is to remain faithful to God's Word alone, not to give the quick or "convenient" answer that seems right at the moment, and

    b. You guard from presenting yourself as the primary resource or the authority in the individual's life and show that you have the same responsibility to study God's Word as the disciple/counselee does.

H. Do not debate (argue); let the Bible stand on its own merit. Be gentle, kind, and humble in your conduct toward the counselee, even when he seems to question, resist, or rebel against God's Word *(based on II Timothy 2:23-26)*, recognizing that the Lord through His Word and the Holy Spirit is responsible for working in the counselee's life *(based on Isaiah 55:8-11; John 16:8-11; Hebrews 4:12; I John 2:20, 27)*.

I. Homework assignments should be designed to encourage the disciple/counselee to search the Scriptures for God's instructions on how he should change. He should be taught:

1. How to conduct word studies using a Bible concordance.

    See **HOW TO USE A CONCORDANCE** *(Self-Confrontation, Supplement 5, Pages 442-443)*.

2. How to study the Scriptures during daily devotions using the **BIBLE STUDY AND APPLICATION FORMAT** *(Handbook,* Pages H211-H212, BCF Form 101) or the **VICTORY OVER FAILURES PLAN** *(Handbook,* Pages H213-H260, BCF Form 102).

    See **BIBLICAL BASIS FOR DAILY DEVOTIONS AND SCRIPTURE MEMORY** *(Self-Confrontation, Pages 38-40)*.

3.   How to memorize Scripture.

See FOUR PLANS FOR MEMORIZING SCRIPTURE (Self-Confrontation, Pages 41-42).

J.   Teach the disciple/counselee through practice how to pray biblically. Use the prayers from Scripture as your guide. Some of them are listed below.

1.   Prayers of praise to God

Matthew 6:9-10:   "Our Father who art in heaven, hallowed be Thy name. Thy kingdom come. Thy will be done, on earth as it is in heaven."

Revelation 4:11:   "Worthy art Thou, our Lord and our God, to receive glory and honor and power; for Thou didst create all things, and because of Thy will they existed, and were created."

Revelation 5:12-13:   "Worthy is the Lamb that was slain to receive power and riches and wisdom and might and honor and glory and blessing ....

"... To Him who sits on the throne, and to the Lamb, be blessing and honor and glory and dominion forever and ever."

Revelation 15:3-4:   "Great and marvelous are Thy works, O Lord God, the Almighty; righteous and true are Thy ways, Thou King of the nations.

"Who will not fear, O Lord, and glorify Thy name? For Thou alone art holy; for all the nations will come and worship before Thee, for Thy righteous acts have been revealed."

2.   Prayers for others and for one's own growth

Matthew 6:11-13:   "Give us this day our daily bread.

"And forgive us our debts, as we also have forgiven our debtors.

"And do not lead us into temptation, but deliver us from evil."

Ephesians 1:16-20:   "... giving thanks for you ...

"that the God of our Lord Jesus Christ, the Father of glory, may give to you a spirit of wisdom and of revelation in the knowledge of Him.

"... that the eyes of your heart may be enlightened, so that you may know what is the hope of His calling, what are the riches of the glory of His inheritance in the saints,

"and what is the surpassing greatness of His power toward us who believe ...

"... in accordance with the working of the strength of His might which He brought about in Christ."

Ephesians 3:16-19:   "that He would grant you, according to the riches of His glory, to be strengthened with power through His Spirit in the inner man;

"so that Christ may dwell in your hearts through faith;

"and that you, being rooted and grounded in love, may be able to comprehend with all the saints what is the breadth and length and height and depth, and to know the love of Christ which surpasses knowledge,

"that you may be filled up to all the fullness of God."

Philippians 1:9-11:   "... that your love may abound still more and more in real knowledge and all discernment

"so that you may approve the things that are excellent, in order to be sincere and blameless until the day of Christ;

"having been filled with the fruit of righteousness which comes through Jesus Christ, to the glory and praise of God."

Colossians 1:9-12:   "that you may be filled with the knowledge of His will in all spiritual wisdom and understanding,

"so that you may walk in a manner worthy of the Lord, to please Him in all respects, bearing fruit in every good work and increasing in the knowledge of God;

"strengthened with all power, according to His glorious might,

"for the attaining of all steadfastness and patience;

"joyously giving thanks to the Father, who has qualified us to share in the inheritance of the saints in light."

I Thessalonians 3:12-13: "... and may the Lord cause you to increase and abound in love for one another, and for all men ...

"so that He may establish your hearts unblamable in holiness before our God and Father at the coming of our Lord Jesus with all His saints."

II Thessalonians 1:11-12: "... that our God may count you worthy of your calling, and

"fulfill every desire for goodness and the work of faith with power

"in order that the name of our Lord Jesus may be glorified in you, and you in Him, according to the grace of our God and the Lord Jesus Christ."

Hebrews 13:20-21:   "Now the God of peace ...

"equip you in every good thing to do His will,

"working in us that which is pleasing in His sight, through Jesus Christ, to whom be the glory forever and ever. Amen."

UNDERSTANDING PROBLEMS BIBLICALLY

> Understanding biblically the disciple/counselee's problem(s) will help you avoid erroneous and arrogant conclusions about his life. Keeping a biblical focus concerning the problem will enable you to restore the disciple/counselee with greater understanding, wisdom, gentleness, and humility *(based on Proverbs 18:2, 13, 15; Galatians 6:1; Colossians 3:12-16).*

I.   **Basics of understanding the disciple/counselee's problems biblically**

Understanding the problem biblically is the first of the four essential elements in facing, dealing with, and enduring the problems of life. Before determining how best to help an individual, you must understand 1) the present spiritual state of the disciple/counselee and 2) God's standards for a believer's life.

   A.   *The present spiritual state of the disciple/counselee.*

   In order to help the disciple reach God's goal for his life, the discipler/counselor must first accurately assess the disciple's present spiritual state. For example, anyone who does not have peace and joy in his life is **not** living according to God's standards *(based on John 15:10-11; Galatians 5:22-23).*

   For a detailed explanation, see **A BIBLICAL UNDERSTANDING OF THE DISCIPLE/ COUNSELEE** *(Handbook, Pages H109-H110).*

   B.   *God's standards for life.*

   The example of Christ's perfect life must be the standard in evaluating the disciple/counselee's life *(Philippians 2:5; I Peter 2:21).* This standard provides a clear picture of God's goal for each disciple/counselee *(Romans 8:29; Philippians 2:5-8; I Peter 2:21-25).*

   A disciple who is walking in the Spirit will exhibit the character of Jesus Christ *(based on Galatians 5:22-25; Philippians 2:5-8; I Peter 2:21).* A sample list of how a believer should live is provided in *Self-Confrontation,* Pages 403-405. In addition, the **MASTER PLAN** *(Handbook,* Pages H51-H104) describes important aspects and activities in a growing Christian's life.

II. **Some procedures for gathering information**

   A.   *Gather only relevant information.*

      1.   Avoid listening to descriptions of the faults of other people *(based on Proverbs 11:9, 12; 20:19).* Instead, seek information that is relevant to the changes that must take place in the disciple/counselee's life. Often, the disciple/counselee's focus is on judging others and escaping from the circumstances that are relevant to God's plan for him *(based on Genesis 3:10-13; Matthew 7:1-5).*

2. Do not dwell on the specific details about sinful activities that might encourage sinful thinking either for the disciple or the discipler *(based on Galatians 6:1; II Timothy 2:22).*

B. *Gather information through listening well.* You must listen attentively to the information given by the disciple/counselee *(based on Proverbs 10:19; 15:28; 18:2).* Be careful that you:

1. Focus on what the disciple/counselee is saying rather than seeking to come up with your next response *(based on Proverbs 18:2, 13).*

2. Do not come to hasty conclusions (e.g., making a judgment after hearing only one side of a story involving other individuals whose side you have not heard) *(based on Proverbs 18:13, 17; 29:20; James 1:19).*

C. *Gather information from homework.* Much information can be gathered from homework. The various forms provided in the Supplement section of *Self-Confrontation* are specifically designed to help gather and organize significant information.

For further help, read ASSIGNING BIBLICAL HOMEWORK *(Handbook, Pages H147-H148).*

III. **Gathering factual information**

Your primary aim in gathering information is to accumulate facts, not opinions or presumptions *(based on Proverbs 13:10; 15:14; 18:15; II Timothy 2:23).*

A. To gather information, it may help if you ask questions that begin with *"who," "what," "where," "when," "how"* as these tend to focus on eliciting facts. For example:

1. Ask *"what"* questions to discover events related to the problem or responses of the disciple/counselee *(as seen in Mark 9:16, 33; 10:51).*

2. Ask *"who"* questions to learn about relationships in which the problem is evidenced *(as seen in Mark 3:33; 5:30; 8:27; Luke 10:29).*

3. Ask *"when"* questions to discover the times and patterns of temptations and sins. Often, the events and counselee's responses surrounding the onset of a problem that has continued to the present can provide very helpful information.

4. Ask *"where"* questions to determine the locations and circumstances involved in the problem(s) *(as seen in Genesis 3:9; Mark 14:12; John 8:10).*

5. Ask *"how"* questions to determine the process leading to the decision, circumstance, or sin *(as seen in Psalm 119:9).*

B. Ask questions to gain insight, not those that merely solicit a "yes" or "no" response *(based on Proverbs 20:5).* Ask questions that encourage the disciple/counselee to describe the patterns of sin in his life. You gain information much more slowly and laboriously if you are doing most of the talking and he is merely responding with *yes, no, sometimes, very little,* etc.

C. When asking questions to gather information, avoid asking:

1. "Why" questions, since they often produce personal opinions rather than facts. They also tend to produce defensive answers. They are generally useful only in asking rhetorical questions or in making a point *(as seen*

in Genesis 4:6; Luke 18:19). They may also be helpful when drawing out answers that are based on facts.

2. "How did that make you feel?" questions. Since no one can change his feelings by an act of his will, these questions do not generate an accurate assessment.

IV. Gathering information at the three levels of the problem

In order to gain a clear understanding of the disciple/counselee's problems, the discipler/counselor should gather information at all three levels (feeling, doing, and heart), but he should concentrate on gathering information related to deeds. Stress that while all three levels are important to evaluate, only God knows the heart completely *(I Kings 8:39; Jeremiah 17:9-10)*, and feelings are involuntary.

A. *Feeling level* — Carefully explore the feeling level of a problem because feelings are often indicators of deeper problems *(based on Psalm 38:3-10).* A person preoccupied with self tends to allow his feelings to dictate his behavior rather than live according to biblical principles *(based on Genesis 4:5-8; I Samuel 18:8-11; Mark 10:21-22).* Investigate the disciple/counselee's:

1. Physical health

    When there is a physical health problem, you can help the disciple face, deal with, and endure his spiritual problems *(based on Romans 8:28-29; II Corinthians 4:7-18)* at the same time that a primary-care physician or health specialist deals with his physical difficulties.

    a. Find out whether any medical treatment or prescribed drugs are having an effect on the disciple/counselee's behavior.

    b. Sometimes, the sin being committed will manifest itself in physical consequences *(based on Psalm 38).* Ask questions that may relate to causes of chronic sleeplessness, headaches, stomach upsets, ulcers, or lethargy *(see* **THE EFFECTS OF UNBIBLICAL THOUGHTS, SPEECH, AND ACTIONS,** *Self-Confrontation, Page 114).* It is helpful to know:

        1) When the physical symptoms started;

        2) At what times of the day the physical problems are most pronounced;

        3) With which people, and in what circumstances the symptoms are the most noticeable; and

        4) What the disciple/counselee has done to take care of the problem (try to determine if the disciple/counselee sees a connection between his physical problems and a deeper level problem, or if he is focused on relieving the physical symptoms).

    c. Even if the problem began as a result of an illness, hormonal difficulties, surgery, or severe bodily harm, a disciple may be responding to it in a sinful way. Ask additional questions to find out how he is dealing with the circumstances of his life in light of the physiological problem.

2. Description of the problem

    a. Be alert to the disciple/counselee blaming others or his circumstances for the problem. Take note of statements like:

1) "If only he would change, I would be so much happier" *(in violation of Ezekiel 18:2-4; John 15:10-11);*

2) "She made me so mad I couldn't help myself!" *(in violation of Matthew 15:18; I Corinthians 10:13);* or

3) "I am not saying I'm perfect, but compared to him my faults hardly even count" *(in violation of Matthew 7:1-5).*

   b.   Listen for feeling-oriented responses to people and circumstances. Take note of statements like:

1) "I cannot take his verbal abuse any more — I have to leave" *(denying I Corinthians 10:13; James 1:2-4);*

2) "I just can't forgive her," or, "I cannot stop my overeating binges" *(in violation of Romans 6:11-14 and denying Philippians 4:13);* or

3) "I will meet her halfway, but no one could expect me to initiate the reconciliation. I know I sinned, but so did she" *(in violation of Matthew 5:23-24).*

  3.   Expectations

   a.   A disciple/counselee may want to escape from his problems, not understanding that the very problems that he is facing will be used by God for good in his life *(based on Romans 8:28-29).* Watch for statements like "I cannot wait to get over this so I can get on with my life" *(violates James 1:2-4).*

   b.   He may depend on God's creation (i.e., events, situations, or people) instead of God Himself for peace and joy.

1) The disciple/counselee may be looking to his spouse, discipler/ counselor, medical doctor, or support group to give him feelings of acceptance and well-being *(in violation of Genesis 4:7; Psalm 118:8);* or

2) He may be looking toward the prospect of marriage, a better-paying job, or more prestige for his source of satisfaction *(in violation of Matthew 6:25-33; I Corinthians 7:20-24; Philippians 4:11-13; I Timothy 6:6).*

B.   *Doing level* — When gathering information about the disciple/counselee's problem, move quickly from the feeling level to the doing level. The disciple/ counselee may have much to say about his feelings and perceptions about the problem, but until he deals biblically with his known sinful deeds, he deludes himself and is unable to discern good and evil *(based on Hebrews 5:12-14; James 1:22-25; I John 2:9-11).* Therefore, concentrate on failures in the areas of:

  1.   Current situation — Ask questions that will:

   a.   Show the counselee's unbiblical deeds, so that you will be able to help him recognize his sin. For example:

1) "Describe a recent situation in which the problem occurred."

2) "What events led to the current situation?"

3) "What did you do when the situation occurred?"

   b.   Reveal ways that the disciple has sought to resolve the problem, such as:

1) "What have you been doing about the situation?"

2)   "With whom have you discussed the situation?"

2.   Ongoing relationships — The greatest commandment is to love God with all your heart, soul, and mind and to love your neighbor as yourself *(Matthew 22:37-38)*. Because the quality of our love for God is revealed in our relationships with others *(I John 4:19-21)*, pay particular attention to the disciple/counselee's relationships with others (family members, friends, co-workers, acquaintances in and outside the local church, etc.).

   a.   Ask questions that will reveal any ongoing problems with others, such as:

      1)   "With whom do you typically have a problem?"

      2)   "How long have your problems with one another been going on?"

      3)   "Have you done anything with one another about the problem, and if so, what have you done?"

   b.   Listen for answers that reveal unbiblical responses to others, such as:

      1)   "His life is just a mess, and I cannot handle it any longer, so I have given him the ultimatum to either get his life straightened out or get out of the house."

      2)   "Of course I shouted at the children! I cannot get their attention any other way. If you had the children I do, you would be tearing out your hair too."

3.   Current responsibilities — Because we demonstrate our love for God by obeying His commands *(John 14:15, 23-24)*, investigate how the disciple/counselee is fulfilling the responsibilities God has given him at home, church, school, job, etc.

   a.   Ask questions that reveal whether the disciple/counselee is neglecting any responsibilities he already knows to do *(based on James 4:17)*.

      1)   "What regular responsibilities are not getting done?"

      2)   "What things are you doing that hinder you from accomplishing what you know ought to be done?" *(Pay attention to evidences of an undisciplined practice of life; for example, taking on someone else's responsibilities.)*

   b.   Ask questions related to:

      1)   Time, frequency, and contents of personal and family devotions;

      2)   Scripture memory and Bible study;

      3)   Church attendance and involvement in ministry; and

      4)   Patterns of sleep, diet, and exercise.

4.   Current thought life — Ask questions regarding the disciple/counselee's current thoughts, such as:

   a.   "How have you been dwelling on this situation in your thought life?"

   b.   "What kind of thoughts did you have?"

5.   Nonverbal deeds (bodily motions, gestures, and actions)

   a.   Be alert to ways in which the disciples/counselees may be sinning against another without even saying a word *(based on Psalm 101:5; Proverbs 6:17)*. Ask questions about the look on the disciple/

counselee's face, tone of voice, clenched fists, gritting of teeth, etc. when responding to the other person.

b. Observe the disciple/counselee's responses in the meeting, especially if the other individual is present in the meeting. Look for bodily motions and gestures that evidence disagreement, anger, fear, etc.

C. *Heart level* — God is primarily concerned about the heart *(I Samuel 16:7)*; however, no human being (including a biblical discipler/counselor) can fully understand the heart *(based on I Kings 8:39; Jeremiah 17:9-10)*. But, since deeds come out of the heart *(based on Matthew 12:34; 15:18-19)*, you may gain insights about whether or not the disciple/counselee's heart is focused on pleasing God or pleasing self when you observe patterns of repetitive righteous or sinful deeds *(based on I John 3:4-10)*.

BIBLICAL HOPE FOR DISCIPLES/COUNSELEES

> Teaching disciples/counselees to appropriate the scriptural hope they have in the Lord Jesus Christ is essential in every topic you teach. You must teach them to place their hope in the goodness of God's overall work in their lives *(based on Jeremiah 29:11; Romans 8:28-29; Ephesians 2:8-9; Philippians 1:6)* and in the Lord's love for them as He uses specific trials and temptations to bring them to maturity in Christ *(based on Romans 5:3-5; James 1:2-4; I Peter 4:12-13).*

I. **Refer only to God and the Scriptures as the sole sources of hope.**

Keep the focus on the Lord and on His Word as the sole sources of their hope *(based on Psalm 33:18; 119:49; 130:5; Lamentations 3:21-25; Romans 15:4, 13; I John 3:3)* since all other foundations will fail *(based on Job 8:13; 27:8; Psalm 33:16-17; Proverbs 11:7; Ephesians 2:12; I Thessalonians 4:13).* Use God's Word as your only authority for counsel *(based on II Timothy 3:16-17)* as God's Word gives lasting hope *(based on Romans 15:4)* and will last forever *(based on I Peter 1:24-25).* Refer often to the biblical principles listed below (adapted from *Self-Confrontation*, Lesson 6).

A. *Principle 20.* Those in Christ are freed from the power and penalty of sin *(Romans 6:6-7, 14, 18, 23).*

1. Dealing with sin in a person's life is of first importance because sin affects his relationship with God. When sin is confessed and repentance takes place, the deeper problem of the heart is dealt with and biblical hope is immediate.

2. Do not minimize any sins in the lives of disciples/counselees. Showing disciples that their primary problem is a failure to obey God can bring tremendous hope because any sin can be dealt with quickly and completely. For example, a drunkard can be totally freed from slavery to alcohol after he becomes a believer. No sinner is beyond the reach of God even though he may have placed himself under the control of sin for many years *(based on Romans 5:6-10).* After becoming a believer, he can stop his drinking immediately and live victoriously by God's power *(Romans 6:6-7, 18).* This brings tremendous hope to someone who has been a drunkard for years and has tried many times to break his bondage to alcohol. Yes, he may still have strong cravings for some time to come, but he does not ever have to yield to temptation again. He is finally free and empowered by God to live in great victory.

3. As you teach disciples to face, deal with, and endure situations in their lives, they will gain much hope since there is an answer for overcoming their problems. When disciples/counselees acknowledge their sins, repent of them, and begin to walk God's way:

   a. They will be cleansed of unrighteousness *(based on I John 1:9),*

   b. They will gain further discernment of good and evil *(based on Hebrews 5:14),* and

c.   They will be privileged to help others also *(based on Matthew 7:5; Galatians 6:1, 2)*.

Be careful that you do not tempt counselees to have false hope by soothing their feelings (i.e., make them "feel better" about circumstances, events, or relationships) when they may be experiencing legitimate guilt over sin. Emotions are often God's tool to show disciples/counselees their sins. It may be important to show them that their feelings may directly result from their deeds (thoughts, speech, and actions) *(based on Genesis 4:5-6; Psalm 32:3-5; 38:3-8)*.

B.   *Principle 21*. God will not allow believers to be tested or tempted beyond what they can bear. He gives them His grace and strength to endure every test and resist every temptation so that they never have to sin *(Romans 8:35-39; I Corinthians 10:13; II Corinthians 4:7-10; 12:9-10; Philippians 4:13; Hebrews 4:15-16; II Peter 2:4-9)*.

1.   Regardless of the source of their feelings, disciples/counselees can have great hope in the fact that they can respond to circumstances God's way *(based on Genesis 4:7; I Corinthians 10:13; Philippians 4:13)*.

2.   In discussing *I Corinthians 10:13*, be careful to point out that the escape is from sin, not necessarily from the situation. Note that the situation may not go away. It may even intensify. But God says that a believer will be able not only to face and deal with any difficulty of life, but also to endure it. Enduring the difficulty means to live in victory whether or not the difficulty disappears. This is a marvelous hope. But it is also sobering, because when a believer sins, it is not because circumstances are too much for him to bear. Instead he sins because he chooses to do so. To sin is a choice.

C.   *Principle 22*. Our Lord Jesus Christ will grant mercy and provide grace to help in every need. He constantly intercedes as an advocate for believers to God the Father and fully understands their weaknesses *(Hebrews 2:18; 4:15-16; 7:25; I John 2:1)*.

Emphasize that

1.   Jesus' sympathy is not a passive entering into feelings. He understands each situation and actively works in the believer's life;

2.   God's grace is promised at the time of need *(Hebrews 4:16)*. Like a lifetime travel ticket, it is always available but applicable only when it is needed; and

3.   God's grace is promised for the person going through the trial.

D.   *Principle 23*. Trials and tests will develop and mature believers in Christ if they respond to them in God's way *(Romans 5:3-5; James 1:2-4)*. He never devises evil or harm for believers; rather His plans for them are for good *(Genesis 50:20; Deuteronomy 8:2, 5, 16; Psalm 145:17; Ecclesiastes 7:13-14; Jeremiah 29:11-13; Romans 8:28-29; James 1:13-17)*.

1.   Emphasize that every trial is an *opportunity* to become more mature *(based on James 1:2-4)*. Trials are not obstacles to spiritual growth when responded to in a biblical manner.

2.   Stress God's command to count it all joy when we undergo trials *(based on James 1:2-4)*. The disciple/counselee can choose to think, speak, and act in a joyful manner. You may need to explain that biblical joy is much deeper than what is commonly thought of as happiness. Biblical joy is

an inner contentment and satisfaction that comes from God independent of circumstances. A good example is found in *Hebrews 12:2* where the joy of sitting down at the right hand of the Father encouraged Jesus to endure the cross. *He did not enjoy going to the cross, but He had joy in what was set before Him.*

3. Stress that God works all things together for good in the believer's life *(based on Romans 8:28-29)*. Then, point out that many people have the wrong idea of what actually is good for them. They sometimes think that "good" means that circumstances and relationships work out according to the way they want them to work out. Often, they describe experiences as good or bad. In *Romans 8:29*, God identifies that the good is to be conformed to the image of His Son, Jesus Christ.

    *Refer to V. **Your tests and temptations (a review to give you hope)** (Self-Confrontation, Pages 127-128).*

4. Point out that even when people seek to harm others, God uses the situation for good *(Genesis 50:20)*. Trials not only mature the believer, but they also make him useful.

E. *Principle 24.* God's peace and joy are available to believers regardless of others, possessions, or circumstances *(Psalm 119:165; Matthew 5:3-12; John 14:27; 15:11; 16:33; 17:13; Romans 14:17; Philippians 4:4-7; I Peter 1:6-9).*

    Emphasize that God's peace and joy are not dependent on people, material goods, circumstances, or things. A believer's joy comes from his relationship with Jesus Christ and is found in keeping God's commandments *(John 15:10-11)*. Therefore, if the disciple/counselee is not content, point out that he is choosing to depend on someone or something other than the Lord for contentment *(based on John 14:27; 15:11; 16:33)*.

    *Refer to V. **Your tests and temptations (a review to give you hope)** (Self-Confrontation, Pages 127-128).*

F. *Principle 25.* Only God can change people *(Ezekiel 36:26-27; Philippians 1:6; 2:13)*, so you are not and cannot be responsible for changing them. You are accountable to God solely for your own deeds *(Jeremiah 17:10; Ezekiel 18:1-20, especially verse 20; Matthew 16:27; Romans 2:5-10; Colossians 3:23-25; I Peter 1:17)* and are to do your part in living at peace with others *(Matthew 5:23-24; Mark 11:25; Romans 12:9-21; 14:19; I Peter 3:8-9; 4:8).*

    When dealing with relationship problems, it is vital that the disciple/counselee concentrate on his own responsibilities before God and not lose hope because the other person does not change. Each person is responsible for his own sin and not for the sin of another *(based on Ezekiel 18:20)*.

G. *Principle 26.* When believers confess their sins, God forgives and cleanses them *(I John 1:9)*.

    Emphasize that even when a person fails miserably he can start afresh. God forgives and cleanses when sin is confessed *(based on I John 1:9)*.

II. **Emphasize biblical hope when discussing every topic.**

A. Continuously emphasize to the disciples that they can have lasting, meaningful changes in their lives through God's gracious provision for them:

1. Through the indwelling Holy Spirit, who will comfort *(Acts 9:31)*, teach *(I John 2:20, 27)*, help *(John 14:16, 26)*, guide *(John 16:13)*, etc.

2. Through His Word, which gives disciples/counselees all the guidance they need to change in a biblical manner *(based on II Timothy 3:16-17; Hebrews 4:12)*; and

3. Through prayer, by which they can communicate with the Lord *(based on Romans 8:26)*.

B. But remind them that they cannot overcome their problems apart from a commitment to the Lord through:

1. A sincere, personal relationship with the Lord Jesus Christ (i.e., salvation) *(based on I Corinthians 6:9-11; Ephesians 2:8-9, 12-13)*, and

2. A continuing focus to please Him by walking in His way *(based on John 15:5; Romans 12:1-2; Colossians 1:10)*.

For further help in explaining these principles, review:

YOU CAN CHANGE BIBLICALLY (PART ONE) *(Self-Confrontation, Pages 20-24)*, *and*

YOU CAN CHANGE BIBLICALLY (PART TWO) *(Self-Confrontation, Pages 32-34)*.

STRUCTURING FOR BIBLICAL CHANGE

> Structuring for biblical change is the third of the four essential elements in biblical discipleship/counseling. Biblical change starts at salvation and continues as long as a believer lives. As man puts off the practices of the old self and puts on the practices of the new self, God renews the spirit of the mind. The biblical discipler/counselor, therefore, focuses on helping the disciple establish a biblical structure of "put-offs" and "put-ons" *(based on Ephesians 4:22-24; Colossians 3:9-10).*

I. **Beginnings of biblical change**

    A.   Biblical change starts with repentance based on conviction of sin. One of the earliest priorities in the meetings should be to help the disciple/counselee recognize that he has been sinning against God, and to establish a willingness to be reconciled with God. The counselor must not depend on emotional appeals to convict the disciple of his need to change, but must rely on the Holy Spirit to bring conviction *(based on Proverbs 28:13; John 16:8).*

    B.   Biblical change requires commitment.

        1.   Commitment to the Lord Jesus Christ for salvation is foundational.

            a.   Without salvation through faith, biblical change is not possible *(based on John 15:4-5; I Corinthians 2:14-16).* Therefore, it is vital that you establish the biblical basis for the counselee's salvation.
Review:
***A BIBLICAL UNDERSTANDING OF THE DISCIPLE/COUNSELEE** (Handbook, Pages H109-H110), and*
***YOU CAN CHANGE BIBLICALLY (PART ONE)** (Self-Confrontation, Pages 20-24).*

            b.   You cannot know the hearts of counselees *(based on I Samuel 16:7; I Kings 8:39).* You can see only evidences of the heart condition based on a pattern of deeds. Lack of progress in the discipleship/counseling process may indicate that the counselee is not saved.

        2.   Commitment to please God is required in every facet of life *(based on II Corinthians 5:9-10; Colossians 1:10; 3:17).* You may need to remind the disciple/counselee of his commitment on a regular basis.

    C.   The power for lasting biblical change comes only from God *(based on John 15:5; Romans 8:3-13; Philippians 4:13).*

    D.   Wisdom for biblical change comes only from God *(based on Isaiah 55:8-9).* The disciple must:

        1.   Look to the Lord for guidance *(based on Proverbs 3:5-8);*

        2.   Ask in faith *(based on James 1:5-8);*

        3.   Depend solely on the Scripture as his authoritative guide *(based on Isaiah 55:11; II Timothy 3:16-17; I Peter 1:3-4).* Frequently remind the disciple

that he is not to look to you or any other human being as his ultimate authority. From the first meeting on, encourage him to diligently study God's Word on a regular basis *(based on Joshua 1:8; Psalm 1:2; II Timothy 2:15; 3:16-17)* and memorize Scripture *(based on Psalm 119:11, 16)*.

II. **Methodology for change**

A. Biblical change involves change at the doing and heart levels and, often, at the feeling level of a person's life. The primary focus, however, is on helping the disciple/counselee change his deeds.

Review **UNDERSTANDING PROBLEMS BIBLICALLY** *(Handbook, Pages H133-H138)*.

B. The renewal of the mind is a continuing process performed by God as we obey Him *(based on Romans 12:2; Ephesians 4:22-24; Colossians 3:9-10)*. It is our responsibility to develop biblical ways of thinking *(based on II Corinthians 10:5; Philippians 4:8)*, speaking *(based on Ephesians 4:29; 5:19-20; Colossians 3:16; 4:6)*, and acting *(Ephesians 4:28, 32; 5:3)*; but the Holy Spirit renews our minds as we do so.

C. Lasting change takes self-control, discipline, and time because it involves putting off the practices (habit patterns) of the old self, which is being corrupted, and putting on the practices (habit patterns) of the new self, which has been created in righteousness and holiness of the truth *(Ephesians 4:22-24)*. Failure to accomplish lasting, biblical change may be the result of several errors in application of "put-ons" and "put-offs."

1. *Superficial change* — A person may attempt to change superficially by selecting a convenient or easy solution. For example, a husband may buy flowers for his wife instead of asking forgiveness for sinning against her; or he may take pills to make himself feel better without following the biblical mandate related to his problem *(based on I Samuel 15:22-23; Micah 6:7-8)*.

2. *Putting off without putting on* — For example, a person may recognize that he should not get drunk and should not allow himself to be controlled by alcohol. However, to concentrate merely on quitting the consumption of alcohol without taking corresponding steps of placing one's self under the control of the Holy Spirit in everyday life only deals with the symptom. It does not deal with the cause, which is a lack of wholehearted obedience to the Lord *(based on Ecclesiastes 12:13; Matthew 22:37-39; Ephesians 5:18)*. The drunkard must not only stop drinking, he must place himself under the control of the Holy Spirit. It is important to note that most of our failures to change old patterns are due to focusing on the "put-off" without practicing a biblical "put-on."

3. *Putting on without putting off* — A person may attempt to put on a righteous practice while maintaining the basic pattern of his old life. Jesus warns against trying to put a new patch on an old garment *(Mark 2:21-22)*. A person who reforms his life by starting to attend church, studying his Bible daily, etc. without dealing with his immoral behavior is only fooling himself into thinking he is pleasing God.

4. *Not dealing with unresolved past sin* — Some believers justify not dealing with past sinful practices that affect their present lives or the lives of others by misusing the phrase *"forgetting what lies behind"* in *Philippians*

3:13. The context of *Philippians 3* is placing no confidence in self, even for past accomplishments but, instead, concentrating on the upward call in Christ Jesus. In reference to past sins, one must deal with any unresolved sin through humble confession *(based on Psalm 51; Proverbs 28:13; I John 1:9)* and thorough repentance *(based on II Corinthians 7:9-11; Ephesians 4:17-32).* As an illustration, one does not eliminate a garbage heap by sprinkling perfume on it. Adding perfume only counters the odor for a while; the basic problem remains. One must get rid of the garbage.

III. **Key considerations**

A. Place primary attention on (1) the disciple/counselee's relationship with God and others and (2) his biblically-established responsibilities.

Review **UNDERSTANDING PROBLEMS BIBLICALLY** *(Handbook, Pages H133-H138).*

B. Start with the current, known failures. Until he deals biblically with his known sinful deeds, he deludes himself and is unable to discern good and evil *(based on Hebrews 5:12-14; James 1:22-25; I John 2:9-11).*

Review **UNDERSTANDING PROBLEMS BIBLICALLY** *(Handbook, Pages H133-H138).*

C. Emphasize that for each "put-off" in Scripture often there is a corresponding "put-on" in the same passage. Be alert to disciples trying to match "put-offs" to unrelated "put-ons."

D. Concentrate on the "put-on." When the disciple focuses attention on the "put-on," his mind is not easily distracted to do wrong. When he focuses only on the "put-off," the temptation to do wrong is continually before him.

E. Point out that sins of omission, i.e., not putting on, are often overlooked. Yet sins of omission are just as serious as sins of commission *(James 4:17).*

F. Help the disciple/counselee complete a **VICTORY OVER FAILURES PLAN** *(Handbook,* Pages H213-H260, BCF Form 102) and teach him how to use it to approach all problems of life. By showing the disciple/counselee how to use the **VOFP** in dealing with just one problem, you have shown him how to face, deal with, and endure all future problems.

Review **VICTORY OVER FAILURES PLAN: GUIDELINES AND WORKSHEETS** *(Handbook, Pages H213-H260, BCF Form 102).*

G. Help the disciple/counselee identify and contend with stumbling blocks in his life as they arise.

ASSIGNING BIBLICAL HOMEWORK

> Assigning biblical homework is a means of encouraging the disciple/counselee to take purposeful action to establish the practice of obeying the Word of God in his life *(based on Matthew 7:24-25; Romans 6:12-13; Titus 2:11-12; James 1:22-25).*

I. **Assigning biblical homework is important to the disciple/counselee because applying biblical principles through completion of biblical assignments:**

   A. Blesses him *(based on James 1:22-25);*

   B. Demonstrates his commitment to the Lord *(based on Matthew 7:20-21; 21:28-31);*

   C. Helps him to discern between good and evil *(based on Hebrews 5:14);* and

   D. Helps him to look increasingly to the Lord rather than to the discipleship/counseling team for guidance and comfort *(based on John 14:26; Philippians 2:12-13; 4:13).*

II. **Biblical homework assignments are characterized by having their foundation in Scriptural commands or principles. This requires that they are:**

   A. Based on the Lord's commands in Scripture *(based on Joshua 1:8; II Timothy 3:16-17),* not the opinions of either the disciplers/counselors or the disciple/counselee *(based on Isaiah 55:8-9, 11; I Thessalonians 4:1-2);*

   B. Pleasing to the Lord *(based on II Corinthians 5:9; Ephesians 5:15-17);*

   C. Relevant to dealing with the disciple/counselee's current problems *(based on James 4:17);*

   D. Repetitive, establishing a pattern of biblical practice *(based on I Timothy 4:7; Hebrews 5:14; I John 3:7);* and

   E. Specific and measurable so that failure or success can be determined.

   For a list of sample biblical homework assignments see MASTER PLAN FOR THE MINISTRY OF BIBLICAL DISCIPLESHIP/COUNSELING (Handbook, Pages H51-H104).

III. **Failure to complete the entire assignment on a consistent, daily basis, may indicate the following:**

   A. The homework may not be biblically based.

   B. The disciple may not recognize that the homework assignment is something that God requires.

   C. Too much homework may have been assigned. Be sensitive to the disciple/counselee's schedule. A person who works 12 hours a day and supports a family may not be able to complete as much as a single person working 8 hours per day with few additional responsibilities.

D.   The disciple may have misunderstood the homework assignment (either because it was not explained clearly or because the disciple was not listening carefully). It is important that you have him write it down as you explain it and then have him repeat it aloud.

E.   The Lord may have sovereignly redirected his plans *(based on Proverbs 16:1, 3, 9)*.

F.   He may have experienced a temporary setback (e.g., sick in bed all week).

G.   He may be in the process of learning or not yet have the habits established to be totally consistent *(based on Proverbs 24:16)*.

H.   The disciple may lack commitment. If this is true, you need to:

1.   Remind him of his commitment to please God *(based on II Corinthians 5:9; Colossians 1:10)*;

2.   Exhort him to be a doer of the Word *(based on James 1:22-25)*;

3.   Investigate to see if he is truly a believer *(based on I Corinthians 2:14; John 15:5; III John 1:5)*; and

4.   Emphasize the serious consequences that could come upon a person who claims to be a believer but disobeys the Lord deliberately as a continued practice *(based on Matthew 18:15-17; I Corinthians 5:1-13; Hebrews 3:13; James 1:14-15)*.

OVERVIEW OF THE
BIBLICAL DISCIPLESHIP/COUNSELING PROCESS

After you begin to deal biblically with your sins, you have the privilege of helping others. All believers must be prepared to provide biblical counsel to family members, co-laborers, unbelieving contacts, friends, strangers, etc. either in organized local church training ministries or informal settings. An essential first step to becoming a discipler/counselor must be to learn the fundamentals of discipling/counseling others. It is important to build a solid foundation and structure that, once learned, can be adapted to a wide variety of circumstances.

The process described below provides guidelines for conducting discipleship/counseling in an established training ministry of a local body of believers. This process is structured to enhance training that will be helpful to the biblical discipler/counselor throughout all his relationships and ministry opportunities. Keep in mind that your goal should be to make disciples in whatever ministry you are involved (*based on Matthew 28:19-20; II Timothy 2:2*). Therefore, the guidelines are based on team discipleship/counseling where the lead discipler/counselor has the responsibility to disciple the assistants. To understand why discipling/counseling as a team is important, study **TEAM DISCIPLESHIP/COUNSELING** (*Handbook*, Pages H117-H120).

As you are learning the process outlined below, consider how to adapt it to your own ministry.

I. **Preparing for the discipleship/counseling process**

    A. Provide basic information to the one requesting help.

    Arrange for a series of weekly meetings with the disciple/counselee. If time permits, ask the disciple/counselee to complete a **BASIC INFORMATION ABOUT THE PROBLEM** form (*Handbook*, Page H157, BCF Form 1) and encourage him to read the **BASIS FOR BIBLICAL DISCIPLESHIP/COUNSELING** form (*Handbook*, Pages H163-H166, BCF Form 3) before meeting with the team. The completed forms will give you initial information and understanding about the disciple/counselee's problems so that you can prepare more effectively to help.

    B. Prepare individually to help the one in need.

        1. Remember that you are to minister in love as a servant of the Lord and others (*based on Philippians 1:6-11; 2:3-8; I Thessalonians 2:5-12; I Timothy 4:11-12*).

        2. Be faithful to plan and organize well so that you can minister effectively to those whom you disciple/counsel (*based on I Corinthians 14:40; I Peter 3:15*). As part of your consideration, determine what the discipleship/counseling process for this individual will require. Study **YOUR RESPONSIBILITY AS A BIBLICAL DISCIPLER/COUNSELOR** (*Handbook*, Pages H113-H116).

    C. Prepare as a discipleship/counseling team to meet with the disciple/counselee.

    Assemble a discipleship/counseling team. The makeup of the team should be determined by considering both the needs of the disciple/counselee and the training needs of the disciplers/counselors (*based on Galatians 6:1-2; II Timothy 2:2*).

1. Begin together as a team to plan for meetings with the disciple/counselee.

   a. Based on the information provided by the disciple/counselee and information that is available from God's Word regarding the disciple/counselee's problem(s), develop the first meeting plan, along with the associated scriptural references and prospective homework assignments. Record this information in appropriate sections of the **BIBLICAL DISCIPLESHIP/COUNSELING RECORD** (*Handbook*, Page H167, BCF Form 4).

      For help in developing your plan, review: **THE MASTER PLAN FOR THE MINISTRY OF BIBLICAL DISCIPLESHIP/COUNSELING** *and its explanation* (**Handbook**, *Pages H51-H104*).

   b. Begin looking ahead and develop an overall biblical plan for the entire discipleship/counseling process. In doing this, look at the training needs and abilities of each member of the team and be prepared to assign portions of the discipleship/counseling meetings as applicable and necessary. The lead discipler/counselor holds the two-fold responsibility of discipling/counseling the ones coming for help and training the other team members.

2. A designated member of the discipleship/counseling team should call the disciple/counselee to:

   a. Schedule the date, time, and location of the first meeting; and

   b. Remind him to read the **BASIS FOR BIBLICAL DISCIPLESHIP/COUNSELING** and to write down any questions he may have when he comes to the first meeting.

II. First meeting with the disciple/counselee

Conduct the meetings in a way similar to a small group Bible study that is specifically directed to deal with the problems described by the disciple/counselee. Your faithfulness as a biblical example in the first meeting sets the pattern for the entire discipleship/counseling process, so take care to maintain biblical standards from the beginning (*based on Luke 16:10; I Thessalonians 2:5-7*).

A. Final preparation

The team should meet approximately 10-15 minutes prior to the disciple/counselee's scheduled arrival to:

1. Pray for wisdom and for the Holy Spirit's strengthening and illumination of God's Word, both for the disciple/counselee and for themselves as disciplers/counselors (*based on Ephesians 1:16-19; Colossians 1:9-12; James 1:5*).

2. Review the discipleship/counseling plan for the first meeting to determine if any changes are necessary, based on any additional information gained about the disciple/counselees' situation.

3. Make final adjustments, and plan the seating in such a way that all members of the team may readily see and be able to work with one another.

B.   Conduct of the first meeting

    1.   Greet the disciple/counselee and introduce the team members.

    2.   Review the appropriate paragraphs in the **BASIS FOR BIBLICAL DISCIPLESHIP/COUNSELING** (*Handbook,* Pages H163-H166, BCF Form 3).

    3.   Gather information.

       a.   Review with the disciple/counselee the completed **BASIC INFORMATION ABOUT THE PROBLEM** form (*Handbook,* Page H157, BCF Form 1) to see if any of the information has changed or needs clarification.

       b.   Ask additional questions about the disciple/counselee's problem(s), using the **DETAILED INFORMATION RELATED TO THE PROBLEM** form (*Handbook,* Pages H159-H162, BCF Form 2) as a guide. Thoroughly check salvation and the current situation.

    4.   Help develop initial hope and recognition of personal sins.

    5.   Continue with the other topics for the meeting making sure that the disciple/counselee understands the counsel given and the Scriptures studied.

       a.   Explain the biblical basis for devotions.

       b.   Show the need for Scripture memory.

    6.   Assign homework. Have the disciple/counselee:

       a.   Write each specific homework assignment in his notebook,

       b.   Read aloud each homework assignment for verification and clarification. This will help the entire team to ascertain whether the disciple/counselee fully understands the homework before he leaves, and

       c.   Commit himself to the Lord for completion of the homework.

    7.   Assign a team member (male for male disciples/counselees and female for female disciples/counselees) to arrange for a midweek follow-up for the purpose of encouragement to complete the homework and help as necessary.

    8.   End the meeting with prayer and, as appropriate, have the disciple/counselee commit himself to the Lord in prayer to do his homework in the upcoming week.

C.   Evaluation

    After the disciple/counselee leaves, the disciplers/counselors should spend a short time reviewing and evaluating the meeting, using the **CHECKLIST FOR EVALUATING BIBLICAL DISCIPLESHIP/COUNSELING MEETINGS** (*Handbook,* Pages H205-H210, BCF Form 13). As appropriate, the lead discipler/counselor should assign areas of study to the other members of the team. End with prayer.

III. **Between meetings**

    A.   Each discipler/counselor on the team completes the **BIBLICAL DISCIPLESHIP/COUNSELING REPORT** (*Handbook,* Pages H171-H174, BCF Form 5) and also studies the Scriptures to help the disciple/counselee for the next meeting. Since both the completion and the evaluation of the **BIBLICAL DISCIPLESHIP/**

COUNSELING REPORT are part of the training process, evaluation of each report should be completed by the team leader as soon as possible.

B.   The designated discipler/counselor should communicate with the disciple/counselee during the week. The major purpose of this time is to check and encourage the disciple/counselee's progress in doing the Word. At the agreed time:

1.   Ask the disciple/counselee what portion of the homework has been completed. Especially, check on his Scripture memorization.

2.   Answer any questions about homework.

3.   Gather any needed information for future meetings but do not discuss new subjects **unless** an emergency arises. If an emergency should arise the team may need to meet with the disciple/counselee quickly.

4.   Pray with him.

5.   Encourage him to continue to do the Word.

C.   Each team member should prepare the right side of the **BIBLICAL DISCIPLESHIP/COUNSELING RECORD** for the next meeting.

For help, review: **THE MASTER PLAN FOR THE MINISTRY OF BIBLICAL DISCIPLESHIP/COUNSELING** *and its explanation (**Handbook**, Pages H51-H104).*

D.   The disciplers/counselors should meet together personally or on the telephone with completed **BIBLICAL DISCIPLESHIP/COUNSELING RECORDS** to plan for the next meeting. Normally at this meeting, the designated discipler/counselor reports the highlights of his midweek conversation with the disciple/counselee.

IV.   **Continuing the discipleship/counseling process**

A.   Preparation for ongoing meetings

As in the first meeting, the disciplers/counselors should meet approximately 15 minutes prior to the disciple/counselee's scheduled arrival for prayer and final arrangements.

B.   Conduct of ongoing meetings

1.   Greet the disciple/counselee and ask for a general statement on how the disciple/counselee has progressed since the last meeting. In particular, look for changes that may affect your counsel for the meeting at hand, such as unusual events, difficulties, and victories experienced by the disciple/counselee. Then, pray in light of the information just received.

2.   Next, check on the completion of assigned homework. It is important that you discuss the homework before continuing with any new teaching in order to determine whether you must:

a.   Clarify previous counsel, or homework assignments;

b.   Review misunderstood or forgotten biblical principles *(based on Philippians 3:1; II Peter 1:12-13);*

c.   Change your plan because of unusual or emergency situations that arose during the week *(based on Proverbs 16:1, 9; 19:21);* or

    d.   Evaluate how much new biblical truth to teach based on his practice of the biblical principles taught in the previous meeting *(based on I Corinthians 3:1-2; Hebrews 5:11-14)*.

3.   Adjust your plan based on any new information you received during the first part of the meeting. Be careful, however, that you do not change your plan solely on the basis of the disciple/counselee's desire or discomfort.

4.   Continue following your modified plan.

5.   Assign homework following the same guidelines as outlined above.

6.   End all meetings with prayer. It is often useful to ask the disciple/counselee to pray at the end of the discipleship/counseling time, so that he may thank the Lord and ask for His wisdom, strength, and help to live victoriously in the week(s) to come *(based on Philippians 4:4-7, 19; I Thessalonians 5:17; James 1:5; I Peter 5:6-7)*.

NOTE: *As you go through the discipleship/counseling process, build in a review time every three or four meetings. This will help all involved in the discipleship/counseling process to see spiritual progress through increasing practice of God's Word (based on Hebrew 5:14).*

V.   Transition meetings (near end of formal discipleship/counseling)

When it becomes evident that the disciple/counselee has begun to live consistently and faithfully according to biblical principles, prepare to end the structured discipleship/counseling phase and help him prepare to stand firm in the future by:

A.   Giving him increasing responsibility to assign his own homework based on what he has learned from God's Word through the meetings *(based on Luke 16:10)*,

B.   Assigning him the responsibility to review all that he has learned through the entire time he has been with you,

C.   Preparing him for ongoing follow-up that will help him deal with any problems quickly, and

D.   Encouraging him to enroll in a Self-Confrontation course to help him review biblical principles he has learned through the personal discipleship/counseling he has received.

VI.   On-going follow-up discipleship

Purposes of on-going discipleship:

1.   To help the disciple/counselee face, deal with, and endure problems on a continuing basis;

2.   To assist him in taking increasing responsibility to minister as part of the local body of believers; and

3.   To train him to disciple/counsel others.

Review **THE MASTER PLAN FOR THE MINISTRY OF BIBLICAL DISCIPLESHIP/ COUNSELING** *and its explanation* (**Handbook**, *Pages H51-H104*).

SECTION IV

RESOURCE HELPS AND FORMS FOR BIBLICAL DISCIPLESHIP/COUNSELING

SECTION IV

RESOURCE HELPS AND FORMS FOR BIBLICAL DISCIPLESHIP/COUNSELING

INTRODUCTION

This section includes forms for discipleship/counseling, guidelines for completion of the forms, guidelines for completing homework assignments, guidance for how to carry out discipler/counselor training responsibilities and standards of conduct for biblical disciplers/counselors.

In many informal discipleship/counseling situations, it will not be appropriate to use some of these forms; however, even then, the information on the forms provides valuable guidance for gathering information during your discipleship/counseling meeting.

An important item is the **BCF SELF-STUDY BIBLE COURSE IN BIBLICAL DISCIPLESHIP/COUNSELING.** It is designed to acquaint the prospective discipler/counselor with principles and precepts from the Old and New Testaments that apply to dealing with problems and achieving maturity in Christ. The course consists of five major sections: 1) a study of twelve key scriptural doctrines that have direct application to biblical discipleship/counseling, 2) a study of 24 Old Testament characters from a biblical discipler/counselor's perspective, 3) a biblical discipleship/ counseling perspective of poetic and prophetic books in the Old Testament, 4) a variety of discipleship/counseling topics, and 5) studies on the way that Jesus discipled.

The documents in this section appear by BCF form number. You may reproduce only the pages in this section that contain the sentence, "Permission is granted to reproduce this form for personal or ministry use." For example, in the **VICTORY OVER FAILURES PLAN: GUIDELINES AND WORKSHEETS**, only the blank forms on Pages H252-H260 have the sentence granting permission, so you may copy only those blank worksheet forms, and not the rest of the **VICTORY OVER FAILURES PLAN** guidelines.

BASIC INFORMATION ABOUT THE PROBLEM

DATE: _____

PERSONAL INFORMATION

NAME: _____ PHONE #: _____ FAX #: _____

ADDRESS: _____

OCCUPATION: _____ BUSINESS PHONE #: _____

GENDER: _____ BIRTHDATE: _____ AGE: _____ EMAIL ADDRESS: _____

MARITAL STATUS:

Single ❑   Engaged❑   Married ❑   Separated ❑   Divorced ❑   Widowed ❑

EDUCATION: Last Grade Completed (Prior to college) _____ Other Education (List type and years) _____

_____ RECOMMENDED BY: _____

NAME OF SPOUSE: _____ OCCUPATION: _____

SPOUSE'S ADDRESS (If different than yours): _____

THE BASIC PROBLEM AS YOU UNDERSTAND IT:

Briefly complete the following (please use the back if necessary):

1. PLEASE DESCRIBE THE CURRENT PROBLEM.

2. WHAT HAVE YOU DONE ABOUT IT?

3. WHAT HELP ARE YOU SEEKING?

4. WHAT LED YOU TO SEEK HELP NOW?

DETAILED INFORMATION RELATED TO THE PROBLEM

INFORMATION ABOUT SPIRITUAL LIFE

CHURCH NAME: _____

CHURCH ADDRESS: _____ PASTOR'S NAME: _____

CHURCH ATTENDANCE: Frequency of attendance _____ Times per month

WHAT ARE YOU LEARNING THROUGH THE SERMONS/MESSAGES/BIBLE STUDIES AT YOUR CHURCH?

_____

PLEASE LIST MINISTRY INVOLVEMENT: _____

CHURCH ATTENDED IN CHILDHOOD: _____

HAVE YOU BEEN BAPTIZED? Yes ❑ No ❑ WHEN? _____

IF MARRIED, RELIGIOUS BACKGROUND OF SPOUSE: _____

(ONLY IF APPLICABLE) SPOUSE'S CHURCH ATTENDANCE:

Spouse's church name _____ Frequency of attendance _____ Times per month

DO YOU PRAY TO GOD? Never ❑ Occasionally ❑ Often ❑ How often? _____

WHAT DO YOU PRAY ABOUT? _____

HAVE YOU COME TO THE PLACE IN YOUR SPIRITUAL LIFE WHERE YOU KNOW WITH CERTAINTY THAT IF YOU WERE TO DIE TONIGHT YOU WOULD GO TO HEAVEN?
Yes ❑ No ❑ Uncertain ❑

IF YES, WHAT IS YOUR BASIS FOR ANSWERING THE ABOVE QUESTION AS YOU DID? _____

_____

HAVE YOU RECEIVED JESUS CHRIST PERSONALLY AS YOUR SAVIOR?
Yes ❑ No ❑ Uncertain ❑ Don't Know What You Mean ❑

IF YES, HOW DO YOU KNOW THAT JESUS CHRIST IS YOUR SAVIOR? _____

_____

IF YOU HAVE RECEIVED CHRIST AS SAVIOR, WHAT CHANGES TOOK PLACE IN YOUR LIFE WHEN YOU BECAME A BELIEVER?_____

_____

IF YOU HAVE RECEIVED CHRIST AS SAVIOR, HAVE YOU TOLD HOUSEHOLD/FAMILY MEMBERS ABOUT RECEIVING JESUS AS SAVIOR? Yes ❑ No ❑

IF YES, WHOM HAVE YOU TOLD? _____

DO YOU READ THE BIBLE? Never ❑ Occasionally ❑ Often ❑ How often? _____

DO YOU HAVE PERSONAL DEVOTIONS? Never ❑ Occasionally ❑ Often ❑ How often? _____

DESCRIBE YOUR PERSONAL DEVOTIONS: _____

_____

DO YOU HAVE FAMILY DEVOTIONS? Never ❑ Occasionally ❑ Often ❑ How often? _____

DESCRIBE YOUR FAMILY DEVOTIONS: _____

_____

EXPLAIN ANY RECENT CHANGES IN YOUR SPIRITUAL LIFE: _____

_____

INFORMATION ABOUT PRIOR COUNSELING

HAVE YOU HAD ANY COUNSELING BEFORE?   Yes ❑   No ❑

COUNSELOR NAME(S)	DATES FROM TO	MEDICATION PRESCRIBED	OUTCOME

INFORMATION ABOUT PERSONAL HABITS AND HEALTH

APPROXIMATELY HOW MANY HOURS OF SLEEP DO YOU GET EACH NIGHT? _____

WHEN DO YOU NORMALLY: go to bed? _____ fall asleep? _____ wake up? _____ get out of bed? _____

IF THERE IS A LENGTH OF TIME BETWEEN YOUR GOING TO BED AND FALLING ASLEEP, WHAT DO YOU DO DURING THAT TIME? _____

IF THERE IS A LENGTH OF TIME BETWEEN YOUR WAKING UP AND GETTING OUT OF BED, WHAT DO YOU DO DURING THAT TIME? _____

DESCRIBE ANY RECENT CHANGES IN SLEEP HABITS: _____

STATE OF HEALTH: Very Good ❑   Good ❑   Average ❑   Declining ❑   Other ❑

DATE OF LAST MEDICAL EXAMINATION: _____ RESULTS: _____

ARE YOU PRESENTLY TAKING MEDICATION? Yes ❑ No ❑ WHAT? _____ DOSAGE? _____

FOR WHAT REASON DO YOU TAKE THIS MEDICATION? _____

HAVE YOU USED DRUGS FOR OTHER THAN MEDICAL PURPOSES? Yes ❑ No ❑ WHEN? _____
WHAT? _____ AMOUNTS/DOSAGES? _____

DO YOU DRINK ALCOHOLIC BEVERAGES? Yes ❑ No ❑ WHEN? _____ HOW MUCH? _____

MARRIAGE AND FAMILY INFORMATION

NAME OF SPOUSE: _____ ADDRESS: _____

PHONE #: _____ OCCUPATION: _____ BUSINESS PHONE #: _____

YOUR SPOUSE'S AGE: _____ EDUCATION (In years): _____ RELIGION: _____

IS SPOUSE WILLING TO COME WITH YOU? Yes ❏ No ❏ Have not asked yet ❏ Not certain ❏

ARE YOU CURRENTLY SEPARATED? Yes ❏ No ❏ Since when? _____

HAVE YOU EVER BEEN SEPARATED IN THE CURRENT MARRIAGE? Yes ❏ No ❏ No. of times _____

HAS EITHER OF YOU EVER FILED FOR DIVORCE? Yes ❏ No ❏ When? _____ Who? _____

DATE OF MARRIAGE: _____ YOUR AGES WHEN MARRIED: Husband _____ Wife _____

HOW LONG DID YOU KNOW YOUR SPOUSE BEFORE MARRIAGE? _____

LENGTH OF STEADY DATING WITH SPOUSE: _____ LENGTH OF ENGAGEMENT: _____

HAVE YOU BEEN MARRIED BEFORE? Yes ❏ No ❏

IF YES, HOW MANY TIMES? Husband _____ Wife _____

IF YOU WERE MARRIED BEFORE, HOW DID THE MARRIAGE(S) END? _____

_____

CHILDREN'S NAMES	AGES	GENDER	LIVING? Yes	No	EDUCATION IN YEARS	MARITAL STATUS	*PM
_____	_____	_____					
_____	_____	_____					
_____	_____	_____					
_____	_____	_____					

*CHECK THIS COLUMN IF CHILD IS BY PREVIOUS MARRIAGE

IF YOU WERE REARED BY ANYONE OTHER THAN YOUR OWN PARENTS, BRIEFLY EXPLAIN: _____

_____

NO. OF OLDER Brothers _____ Sisters _____ NO. OF YOUNGER Brothers _____ Sisters _____

BASIS FOR BIBLICAL DISCIPLESHIP/COUNSELING

1. **BIBLICAL DISCIPLESHIP/COUNSELING: A MINISTRY** — All believers are to minister through biblical discipleship/counseling within the body of Christ to all who have need *(based on Matthew 28:19-20; Romans 15:14; Galatians 6:1-5)*. The range of problems with which biblical disciplers/counselors deal is very wide. It includes broken marriages, parent-child relationships, depression, alcohol and drug abuse, tension, turmoil, anxiety, fear, worry, and any number of other problems that may result in mental and physical distress.

2. **TRAINING OF THE BIBLICAL DISCIPLER/COUNSELOR** — The biblical discipler/counselor is trained in the use of Scripture and its principles for biblical living. He is committed to the position that the Scriptures are the only authoritative standard for faith and conduct *(II Timothy 3:16-17)*. He does not base his knowledge on his own or others' opinions, experience, or concepts of behavior *(Isaiah 55:8-11; II Timothy 2:15; Titus 2:1)*; instead, he seeks to marshal the full range of biblical truth to bear on your need *(Hebrews 4:12)*. Throughout the discipleship/counseling process, he will hold to the essential truths of Scripture without particular theological emphasis on any practice not specifically advocated in the Scriptures *(Titus 2:1)*.

3. **A LABOR OF LOVE** — Biblical disciplers/counselors provide their time and energy as a service to God and a labor of love to individuals *(based on I Thessalonians 2:7-8; I Timothy 1:5)*. Therefore, each discipler/counselor serves without any charge or fee, or any financial arrangement, actual or implied.

4. **TEAM DISCIPLESHIP/COUNSELING: A BIBLICAL CONCEPT** — Typically, you will find that biblical disciplers/counselors work in teams since team discipleship/counseling has many biblical benefits, both for you and the disciplers/counselors *(Proverbs 11:14; 15:22; 18:17; 20:18; 24:6; Matthew 18:16)*. Normally, you will meet with a team of disciplers/counselors who will help you as you face, deal with, and endure problems in a way that leads to lasting change in your life. You are a vital member of the team as you seek to overcome the problems in your life. The most important member of the team, however, is the Lord Himself, in the Person of the Holy Spirit. It is He who will provide the hope, the enabling, and the wisdom (through God's Word) for you to deal with your problems *(John 14:26; Romans 5:3-5; 8:26-27; Ephesians 3:16)*.

5. **LASTING CHANGE AND MATURITY THROUGH BIBLICAL DISCIPLESHIP/COUNSELING** — Biblical disciplers/counselors are committed not only to help you overcome the current problem in your life but also to train you to live all your life in a manner that leads to increasing maturity in the Lord *(Psalm 119:165; Proverbs 2:6-12a; Galatians 6:1-5; I Timothy 4:7-8; I John 5:1-5)*. Thus, in the scriptural sense, biblical discipleship/counseling is a ministry that teaches you to walk in God's way even in the midst of serious problems *(based on Matthew 28:19-20; I Timothy 1:5; II Timothy 2:2)*.

6. **CONFIDENTIALITY** — A commitment to trustworthiness is an important quality of biblical disciplers/counselors *(based on I Corinthians 4:2)*. Thus, although they may talk with others about a particular situation, you may be confident that the discussions will be restricted to whatever is necessary to help you overcome your problems *(based on Proverbs 10:18-21; 15:28; 18:8; 25:11)*.

7. **MEDICAL NEEDS** — Biblical disciplers/counselors believe in considering your total health needs. If you require medical assistance, discipleship/counseling will continue at the same time, whenever possible.

8. **ELEMENTS OF BIBLICAL DISCIPLESHIP/COUNSELING** — Biblical disciplers/counselors will use their biblical training to help you overcome whatever problem is keeping you from experiencing the peace and joy that God has promised in His Word. Your disciplers/counselors will concentrate on four essential elements from Scripture:

    Biblical understanding — You must apply biblical principles to all of your difficulties, not "fix your feelings" or change your circumstances. Your disciplers/counselors, in a spirit of gentleness, will make inquiry into the various levels of your problems and help you gain a biblical understanding of your difficulties (*based on Proverbs 18:13; Isaiah 55:8-9; Mark 7:20-23; Galatians 6:1-4; Hebrews 4:12; James 1:19, 22-25; 4:17*).

    Biblical hope — In Jesus Christ you have a great High Priest who has been tempted in all things, yet without sin (*Hebrews 4:14-16*). Even though currently you may be going through a difficult test, God has promised that He will not allow any trial in your life that is beyond your endurance. He has promised to provide a way of escape from sin so that you may be able to endure the problem (*I Corinthians 10:13*). He will use every trial for your good as you respond to it in a biblical manner (*Romans 5:3-5; 8:28-29; James 1:2-4*).

    Biblical change — In Christ, you can learn how to lay aside the old selfish ways of living and put on the new ways of living in a manner worthy of the Lord (*Romans 6:11-13; Ephesians 4:20-24*). In changing biblically, you will begin to please the Lord in all respects, bearing fruit in every good work and increasing in the knowledge of God (*Colossians 1:9-12*).

    Biblical practice — It is vital that you are a doer of God's Word and not merely a hearer who forgets what kind of person he is and deludes himself. Only in becoming an effectual doer of the Word will you be blessed in what you do, and only then will you please the Lord (*Hebrews 13:20-21; James 1:22-25; I John 3:22*).

    In order to help you to become an effectual doer, we will be teaching you how to use the *Victory Over Failures Plan* booklet as a guide. This booklet provides step-by-step instructions on how to have complete and lasting victory in your life.

9. **WAITING PERIOD** — If a discipleship/counseling team is not immediately available to begin the regular process with you, we will meet with you as soon as possible on a one-time basis. During this meeting, your disciplers/counselors will provide a plan for you to follow while you are waiting for the regularly scheduled meetings. You may be encouraged to attend an ongoing Self-Confrontation course while you are awaiting discipleship/counseling; in this way, you can begin working immediately on solutions to overcome problems.

10. **LENGTH OF REGULAR MEETINGS** — Normally, the meetings will last one to one-and-a-half hours each week and will continue for approximately 12-14 weeks. Depending on the nature of the problem and on your response to the Word of God, the number of regular discipleship/counseling meetings may vary somewhat. If the disciplers/counselors do not observe definite change in the first few weeks, they will seek to identify the cause of the failure, discuss it with you, and help you to correct it.

11. **DISCIPLESHIP/COUNSELING APPOINTMENTS** — Because effective discipleship/ counseling requires consistency and faithfulness in your applying God's principles, it is important that you reserve the designated time for the regular meetings, barring unforeseen circumstances *(based on Luke 14:27-30; I Timothy 4:7).*

12. **INVOLVEMENT WITH A LOCAL BODY OF BELIEVERS** — In order to achieve lasting victory over the problems of life, it is vital that each person become established in a consistent Christian walk. The Lord has provided other believers to help in this process *(Hebrews 3:13, 10:24-25).* Therefore, it is important that biblical discipleship/ counseling meetings be accompanied by church activities that encourage discipleship, worship, and fellowship. If you do not have a church home, you are welcome to join us in our fellowship. If you are part of another church family, we ask you to seek the assistance of your church's leadership so that you may more fully receive the benefit of all the spiritual resources given to you by God. One of your pastors or other spiritual leaders may even become part of the discipleship/counseling team to provide the most effectual help for you. It is our commitment to do what will best help you walk in obedience to God's Word and thus to experience victory over your problems.

13. **MATERIALS NEEDED AND EXPECTATIONS** — You will need your Bible and writing supplies at all meetings, including the first. Be sure to bring them each time. Come with high expectations. You will receive hope and encouragement from the Scriptures even during your first meeting. From then on, as you respond God's way, you will find trustworthy and biblical answers for the difficulty that prompted you to ask for help.

BIBLICAL DISCIPLESHIP/COUNSELING RECORD

Date _____ Confidential # _____ Meeting # _____ Length of Meeting _____

Discipler/Counselor's Initials _____ Disciple/Counselee's Initials _____

Homework Assigned Last Meeting:

Proposed Homework:

Notes:

Proposed Discipleship/Counseling Topics for This Meeting:

Possible Discipleship/Counseling Topics for Future Meetings:

(Write on back as needed)

BCF Form 4

Permission is granted to reproduce this form for personal or ministry use.

USE OF THE
BIBLICAL DISCIPLESHIP/COUNSELING RECORD

Date _____ *Confidential #* _____ *Meeting #* _____ *Length of Meeting* _____

Discipler/Counselor's Initials _____ *Disciple/Counselee's Initials* _____

Homework Assigned Last Meeting:

Proposed Homework:

> Possible homework assignments for the upcoming meeting are recorded here. The primary source for these assignments is the **MASTER PLAN FOR THE MINISTRY OF BIBLICAL DISCIPLESHIP/ COUNSELING**.

Planning

Notes:

Proposed Discipleship/Counseling Topics for This Meeting:

> Start taking notes here in the first meeting. Start all subsequent meetings by reviewing homework. In the meeting, you should build upon what the disciple/counselee has already learned from his practice of the Word.

> Using the **MASTER PLAN FOR THE MINISTRY OF BIBLICAL DISCIPLESHIP/ COUNSELING** as a primary source, develop topics for biblical teaching that will lead the disciple/counselee to understand the importance of doing the above assignments to please the Lord.

> As your questions and discussion continue, record the disciple/ counselee's responses here. Biblical violations can provide information to help you determine proposed topics for future meetings.

Possible Discipleship/Counseling Topics for Future Meetings:

> Here, keep note of topics for further discipleship/ counseling.

(Write on back as needed)

BCF Form 4a

BIBLICAL DISCIPLESHIP/COUNSELING REPORT

> This form is designed to help summarize each discipleship/
> counseling meeting and prepare for the next meeting.
> It will provide a short history of your progress and
> indicate patterns of faithfulness or unfaithfulness of
> the disciple/counselee.

PLEASE NOTE: This first page is for information gathered from the first meeting only.

INITIAL EVALUATION

A. Briefly describe the disciple/counselee's state of health.

B. Describe the reason that the disciple/counselee came for help. Please describe the state of any and all relationships involved in his problem.

C. Describe the disciple/counselee's spiritual state at the onset of discipleship/ counseling.

D. Before the discipleship/counseling process began, how did the disciple/counselee utilize the following spiritual resources?

Personal devotions/Bible memory:

Family devotions:

Church attendance/involvement:

Believing family members:

BCF Form 5, Page 1

Permission is granted to reproduce this form for personal or ministry use.

On this page, briefly list the actual meeting topics, along with the disciple/counselee's corresponding responses for each meeting (this may sometimes be substantially different from the plan). Just below meeting 1, continue with subsequent meetings. Use additional copies of this page as necessary. Take note of both spoken and unspoken responses on the part of the disciple/counselee.

ACTUAL MEETING TOPICS:

DISCIPLE/COUNSELEE'S ASSOCIATED RESPONSES:

Meeting # _____ — Date _____

On this page, briefly describe the homework actually assigned at the end of the first meeting in the left column; in the right column, provide an evaluation of the disciple/counselee's accomplishment of each homework item. Just below the first meeting, continue with subsequent meetings. Use additional copies of this page as necessary.

ACTUAL HOMEWORK ASSIGNED:

HOW THE DISCIPLE/COUNSELEE COMPLETED THE HOMEWORK ITEMS:

Meeting # _____ — Date _____

SUMMARY OF
THE BIBLICAL DISCIPLESHIP/COUNSELING PROCESS

> You should keep records of discipleship/counseling meetings, both for the church leadership and for you to evaluate the disciple/counselee's progress. After you have completed the **SUMMARY**, attach it to the finished meeting-by-meeting **BIBLICAL DISCIPLESHIP/ COUNSELING REPORT**.

Date of Summary: _____

PLEASE NOTE: On this page, briefly summarize what led to the ending of regular weekly meetings.

A.   Briefly describe the reason for ending the regular weekly meetings.

B.   Describe the follow-up procedure that will take place. Please list the name of the discipler/counselor who will be conducting the follow-up of the disciple/ counselee.

C.   Describe the disciple/counselee's current spiritual state.

D.   List any concerns or further steps that should be taken by the church leadership (if any).

BCF SELF-STUDY BIBLE COURSE
IN BIBLICAL DISCIPLESHIP/COUNSELING

GENERAL OVERVIEW

Biblical discipleship/counseling that is based firmly on the Word of God has always been vital to the church's life and ministry. A commitment to the inerrancy of Scripture and to its complete sufficiency as a guide for all of life's conduct is essential for true ministry. The **BCF SELF-STUDY BIBLE COURSE IN BIBLICAL DISCIPLESHIP/ COUNSELING** has been developed to assist those who are committed to this basic belief, and desire to be biblically equipped for a discipleship/counseling ministry.

During the process of completing this study, students will learn how the principles and truths of the Old and New Testaments apply to actual practices of faith and conduct in individual and family life.

The length of time for completion of the course is completely determined by the student although 400-600 hours of study are usually required. Work toward completion of this course can begin any time during attendance at the **BIBLICAL DISCIPLESHIP/COUNSELING COURSE III**, and may continue throughout the biblical discipleship/counseling training.

This course is not to be merely an exercise on paper; rather, it is designed to be a believer's personal workbook and reference manual for discipleship/counseling. Therefore, each time that personal study in the Scriptures is required in discipling/ counseling another, it should — as much as possible — be done in conjunction with the various parts of this self-study course.

COURSE DESCRIPTION

In order to understand and apply biblical answers to the needs of each disciple/ counselee, the biblical discipler/counselor must learn certain essential truths from Scripture and be able to explain them clearly. If you desire to study the Scriptures systematically from a discipleship/counseling perspective, this **SELF-STUDY BIBLE COURSE** is a practical training guide. It consists of three major parts:

I. **Doctrinal Survey** — *A biblical study of doctrinal words as they apply to discipleship/ counseling*

You will find a comprehensive concordance or topical Bible to be especially helpful in studying each of the twelve doctrinal subjects. However, even without these reference works, your diligent study of God's Word will always prove to be profitable. As you study this portion of the course, you will begin to compile your own list and explanations of meaningful verses/passages. You can use this to help disciples/counselees recognize and gain biblical hope, see the need for biblical change, understand specific changes to be made in their lives, and complete specific homework assignments to accomplish that change in becoming doers of the Word.

II. **Old Testament Survey** — *A study of Old Testament biblical characters and books from a discipler/counselor's perspective*

This part contains two sections:

A. *Biblical Character Study* — In Section A., you will study the lives of 24 biblical characters, as though each character himself were coming to you to seek answers to the problems in his life.

B. *Study of Poetic and Prophetic Books* — In Section B., you will identify major discipleship/counseling principles from *Psalms, Proverbs, Ecclesiastes, Song of Solomon,* and the prophetic books.

III. Biblical Discipleship/Counseling Survey

Part III consists of two sections:

A. Section A asks a variety of questions that have to do with discipleship/counseling topics, principles, development of reference materials, etc.

B. Section B is a study in the Gospels, focusing on the way that Jesus Himself discipled/counseled. You will look at Jesus' understanding of man's problems, types of questions that Jesus asked, the way He helped establish hope, changes He showed individuals they must make, and homework assignments He gave to specific people.

MATERIALS NECESSARY FOR THE STUDY

You should use the following reference books for the **BCF SELF-STUDY BIBLE COURSE:**

- REQUIRED:
    - A literal translation of the Bible, such as the King James Version, the New King James Version, New American Standard Bible, or the New International Version.
    - An exhaustive concordance such as Young's or Strong's.
    - *Self-Confrontation* manual and *Handbook for the Ministry of Biblical Discipleship/Counseling.*

- RECOMMENDED, BUT NOT REQUIRED:
    - A comprehensive topical Bible such as Naves' or Zondervan's, or a chain reference Bible such as Thompson's.
    - A Bible dictionary, such as Zondervan's or Unger's.

Writing Materials

- All assignments should be typed or neatly printed, on one side only. This is to give your ministry leader room for writing corrections and helpful comments. Standard sized, white paper is recommended.

- Copies of blank format pages for the completion of applicable sections are provided in this document for your use. It is not necessary for the format pages to be photocopied, although it may be the simplest. You may hand-draw columns on your own paper.

- A binder is helpful to hold your assignments and format pages. If available, use a three-ring loose-leaf binder.

PART I — DOCTRINAL SURVEY INSTRUCTIONS

> As a biblical discipler/counselor, you will need a thorough understanding of the essential truths of the Bible that help fellow believers develop and mature into Christlikeness.

On Page 5 are twelve (12) major doctrinal subjects. Using a concordance of at least 700 pages or a topical Bible, look up each major subject (designated in capitalized, bold face letters) to find essential truths about these subjects to communicate to all disciples/counselees. The words under the headings are listed to help you find verses in your concordance/topical Bible. It is not necessary to find verses for all subheadings.

For each doctrinal area, select at least:

- Three (3) passages that provide biblical understanding;

- Three (3) passages you would use primarily to emphasize biblical hope;

- Three (3) passages you would use to help a disciple/counselee establish biblical change; and

- Three (3) passages you would use to help a disciple/counselee develop biblical practice in his life.

NOTE: Some verses may apply to more than one of the above essential elements of biblical discipleship/counseling. When this happens, determine how you would most often convey this verse/passage to others. For example, if you would present a verse/passage to help disciples recognize or grow in biblical hope, then identify the verse(s) as one of your "hope" passages, with a statement signifying that you recognize the verse(s) could be used for one or more of the other three essential elements.

Next, highlight or otherwise mark these important Scriptures in your Bible. If these are verses that you will use often, memorize them. Finally, using the form entitled **DOCTRINAL SURVEY WORKSHEET** (Page 7), write an explanation of the passage as follows:

1. In the left-hand column, list the reference or write out the verse(s), depending on how familiar the passage is to you.

2. In the center column, write out how you would explain this passage. You may either write out the explanation word-for-word or list the points you would cover, including any cross-referencing that may be necessary to complete the explanation. Always give cross-reference substantiation for any teaching points not found directly in the original passage. You might not turn to or use all these cross-references in your explanations, but you need to know that all you say is biblically based. Use the same kind of wording that you would use with a disciple/counselee.

    As you progress through the explanation, write out the questions or objections that may arise. Then, write out your response to these, listing any cross-reference passages. As you gain experience in discipleship/counseling, you may have many more questions come up about the same passage; record them, along with your biblical explanations. Thus, this column becomes a very valuable and personal reference help in your continuing ministry.

3.   In the right-hand column, if applicable, write out specific homework assignments derived from this passage.

WARNING: *Not all passages lend themselves to the development of homework assignments. This may be particularly true of "hope" verses. Please write N/A if you cannot develop or derive a homework assignment directly from the passage.*

PART I — DOCTRINAL SURVEY (CONTINUED)

WORDS FOR STUDY

1. **WORD** (of God)
   Thy Word
   Scripture(s)
   Law
   Statutes

2. **GOD**
   Father
   Lord

3. **JESUS/CHRIST**
   Son of God
   Son of man

4. **HOLY SPIRIT**
   Holy Ghost
   Spirit (of God)

5. **NEW BIRTH**
   Believe(th)
   Born (again)
     (of God)
   Dead
     (to sin)
     (in trespass)
     (in Christ)
   Faith
   Justified
   Love(d)
   New Creature
   New Man
   Newborn babes
   New Testament
   New Covenant
   Sacrifice
   Salvation, Saved

6. **PRAYER**
   Pray
   Prayed
   Praying

7. **OBEDIENCE**
   Abide
     (in Me)
     (in My Love)
     (in Him)
   Discipline(th, d)
   Endure(th, d)
   Persevere (perseverance)

8. **SIN(S)**
   Sinned (eth)
   Sinner
   Transgression
   Trespass
   Unrighteous(ness)

9. **GRACE**
   Mercy
   Trust
   Works

10. **REWARD(S)/ JUDGMENT**
    Condemnation
    Crown
      (of life)
      (of rejoicing)
      (of righteousness)
      (of glory)
    Everlasting Life
    Gift of God
    Imperishable

Judged
Resurrection
Rewarded
Throne

11. **SANCTIFICATION**
    Abundant(ly) life
    Filled
      (with the Spirit)
      (with the Holy Ghost)
      (with all knowledge)
      (with fullness of God)
      (with the fruits)
      (with joy, with peace)
    Renewed(ing)
    Sanctify(ied, ieth)
    Separate(d)

12. **CHURCH(ES)**
      (in the, of the church)
      (Church of God)
    Body (of Christ)
    Elder, Deacon
    Gifts
    Overseer
    Pastor/Shepherd
    Teacher

DOCTRINAL SURVEY WORKSHEET (GUIDELINES)

SCRIPTURE REFERENCE	WHAT YOU WOULD TELL A DISCIPLE/COUNSELEE ABOUT THIS VERSE OR PASSAGE	POSSIBLE HOMEWORK ASSIGNMENTS BASED ON THIS VERSE OR PASSAGE
Designate whether you will use this passage for understanding, hope, change, or practice (II Timothy 3:16-17). *(Identify Bible version)*	Accurately dividing the Word of Truth; speaking what is fitting for sound doctrine (II Timothy 2:15; Titus 2:1) *(Designate disciple/counselee's remarks or questions by writing all upper case or using a different color pen)*	Specific ways to help a disciple/counselee to become a doer of the Word (James 1:22-25) *(Write "N/A" in this column for Scripture passages not lending themselves to homework assignments)*
In this column, list the reference or write/type out the verse, depending on your familiarity with the passage. Also, please identify which version of the Bible you are using. Next to the reference, write "**UNDERSTANDING**," "**HOPE**," "**CHANGE**," or "**PRACTICE**," to indicate how you would most often use this Scripture in a counseling situation. Remember that this study will become your reference manual for counseling individuals, so be sure that the pages are of the greatest help to you. Do not merely shorten the work here, because you may find later that you have forgotten what should have been written down.	Here, write out how you would explain this passage to a disciple/counselee, listing all the points you would cover. List other verses as necessary, so that you have at hand the biblical basis for all the statements made here. **Complete sentences are not necessary** — just be sure that you, or anyone who reads this sheet, can understand the points you are making. IF REFERRING TO A QUESTION OR OBJECTION THAT A DISCIPLE/COUNSELEE MAY MAKE ABOUT THIS BIBLICAL PRINCIPLE OR COMMAND, WRITE OR TYPE THE HYPOTHETICAL STATEMENTS IN "ALL CAPS", AS SHOWN IN THIS PARAGRAPH, OR USE A PEN OF A DIFFERENT COLOR THAN THE REST OF THE EXPLANATION. All your responses should be substantiated by God's Word. Remember that you are not to rely on opinion or man's wisdom. In a sense, your study in frequently-used Scriptures will never end, as long as you disciple/counsel, since you will continue to gain new insights, and since a disciple/counselee may conceivably ask you a question you may not have heard before. Add any new insights or answers as you continue in ministry, to make your resource manual a more complete help for you. It may help to add the date to the beginning of a newly-added explanation, so you can see your development in the knowledge of God's Word.	In this column, write out the specific homework assignment that may be derived directly from this passage. Be sure that you write the assignment just as you would explain it to a disciple/counselee. **WARNING: Not all the passages you use will lend themselves to become the basis for specific homework items.** Do not seek to manipulate the Scriptures in order to fill in this column. If you see that a passage is not appropriate as a basis for homework assignment, simply write N/A in this column.

DOCTRINAL SURVEY WORKSHEET

SCRIPTURE REFERENCE	WHAT YOU WOULD TELL A DISCIPLE/COUNSELEE ABOUT THIS VERSE OR PASSAGE	POSSIBLE HOMEWORK ASSIGNMENTS BASED ON THIS VERSE OR PASSAGE
Designate whether you will use this passage for understanding, hope, change, or practice (II Timothy 3:16-17).	Accurately dividing the Word of Truth; speaking what is fitting for sound doctrine (II Timothy 2:15; Titus 2:1)	Specific ways to help a disciple/counselee to become a doer of the Word (James 1:22-25)
(Identify Bible version)	(Designate disciple/counselee's remarks or questions by writing all upper case or using a different color pen)	(Write "N/A" in this column for Scripture passages not lending themselves to homework assignments)

PART II — OLD TESTAMENT SURVEY

> This section of the **BCF SELF-STUDY BIBLE COURSE**
> is designed to help you: 1) learn how to plan the entire
> discipleship/counseling process, 2) disciple/counsel
> individuals regardless of the circumstances in which
> they find themselves, and 3) learn major discipleship/
> counseling principles from the prophetic and poetic
> books of the Bible.

Section A.   Biblical Character Study

In this section of the **SELF-STUDY COURSE**, you will study characters of the Old Testament according to the format beginning on the page 10 of this study. Based only on the information you have from the Scriptures about these biblical characters, you will be determining their discipleship/counseling needs, and will develop a plan, as if these individuals were coming to you for help with their respective problems. You may use the entire Bible to complete the study. Please be careful to deal with these Old Testament characters just as you would in helping a disciple today.

This portion of the **SELF-STUDY COURSE** is designed to help you develop plans for the complete discipleship/counseling process. For many of the biblical characters, you will notice that God counseled them directly. Be sure to include God's counsel as part of the plan you will develop. Because Scripture does not give us every detail of God's dealing with an individual, however, it will be your responsibility to develop the rest of the plan.

In studying how to disciple/counsel the biblical characters, do not invent situations. Use only the facts given in the Bible.

You will notice that 12 of the biblical characters listed are marked with an asterisk. Study of these individuals is required. In addition, you must select and study six (6) other Old Testament characters of your choice, from the list that follows.

© Biblical Counseling Foundation

BIBLICAL CHARACTER LIST

* **Adam**	Rahab	Zimri
Eve	Gideon	Omri
Cain	Jeptha	* **King Ahab**
Noah	* **Samson**	Jonah
* **Abraham**	Ruth	Jehu
* **Sarah**	Samuel	Joash
Isaac	* **Saul**	* **Hezekiah**
Rebekah	* **David**	Josiah
Esau	Eli	Nebuchadnezzar
Joseph	Nathan	Ezra
* **Moses**	* **Absalom**	Zerubbabel
Aaron	Nabal	Nehemiah
Pharaoh	Abigail	* **Esther**
Balaam	Solomon	Mordecai
Aaron's sons	Elijah	Haman
Miriam	Elisha	* **Job**
Joshua	Namaan	Eliphaz
Caleb	King Rehoboam	Bildad
Nadab	King Asa	Zophar
Korah	King Jehoshaphat	Elihu

BIBLICAL CHARACTER STUDY FORMAT

1.   Name of Character: _____

      Meaning of His/Her Name: _____

2.   List all the biblical references and major facts about this character, in both the
      Old and New Testaments. Do not begin your study of the facts here; merely list
      the facts.

SCRIPTURE REFERENCE	MAJOR FACTS

© Biblical Counseling Foundation

BIBLICAL CHARACTER STUDY FORMAT (CONTINUED)

3.   In answering this question, study the problem levels of this biblical character. You must designate below what you consider the "Early Life" and "Later Life" of this individual.

PERIOD OF LIFE	FEELING LEVEL What this biblical character perceived as the problem (Genesis 4:7)	DOING LEVEL Unbiblical thoughts, speech, and actions (James 1:22-25)	HEART LEVEL The motivation, the revealed intentions (Matthew 15:18)
Early Life Designate what you consider "early life" period: _____ _____			
Later Life Designate what you consider "later life" period: _____			

Permission is granted to reproduce this form for personal or ministry use.

BIBLICAL CHARACTER STUDY FORMAT (CONTINUED)

4.   As you answer this question, identify the significant incidents that occurred in the life of this biblical character, and study according to the format below:

THE INCIDENT OR PROBLEM THAT OCCURRED (WITH SCRIPTURE REFERENCE)	GOD'S COMMAND OR THE APPLICABLE SCRIPTURAL PRINCIPLE	THE INDIVIDUAL'S RESPONSE TO GOD'S COMMAND OR PRINCIPLE	THE RESULTS OF THE OBEDIENCE OR DISOBEDIENCE OF THIS INDIVIDUAL

© Biblical Counseling Foundation
Permission is granted to reproduce this form for personal or ministry use.

BIBLICAL CHARACTER STUDY FORMAT (CONTINUED)

5.   From the facts available, describe how you would disciple/counsel this biblical character. You may use the New Testament as well as the Old Testament as your resource for discipleship/counseling. Please list all applicable Scripture references next to the principle or counsel you would give.

TELL HOW YOU WOULD HELP ESTABLISH HOPE:

_____

_____

_____

_____

_____

_____

_____

_____

WHAT CHANGES NEED TO BE ESTABLISHED IN THE LIFE OF
THIS BIBLICAL CHARACTER?

_____

_____

_____

_____

_____

_____

_____

_____

_____

WHAT SPECIFIC HOMEWORK WOULD YOU ASSIGN TO HELP ESTABLISH
THE CHANGE?

_____

_____

_____

_____

_____

_____

_____

_____

_____

Permission is granted to reproduce this form for personal or ministry use.

BIBLICAL CHARACTER STUDY FORMAT (CONTINUED)

6.   If you were going to use this biblical character as an example or illustration of a godly or sinful pattern of life, what characteristic would you say typified his life? You do not need to answer in complete sentences — just a few words will do.

_____

_____

7.   In counseling this biblical character, list the topics you would discuss over the entire discipleship/ counseling process, based on the pattern observed in question 6 above. Please do not use complete sentences; merely list the discipleship/counseling topics, in as few words as possible.

MEETING NUMBER	DISCIPLESHIP/COUNSELING TOPICS (MEETING PLAN) AND ASSOCIATED SCRIPTURE REFERENCES	ASSOCIATED SPECIFIC HOMEWORK ASSIGNMENTS

© Biblical Counseling Foundation

Permission is granted to reproduce this form for personal or ministry use.

PART II — OLD TESTAMENT SURVEY (CONTINUED)

Section B.   Discipleship/counseling Principles: Poetic and Prophetic Books

For the Old Testament books listed below, you must study and list major biblical principles for living or discipling/counseling others. As you study *Psalms, Proverbs,* and *Ecclesiastes,* identify at least one important biblical discipleship/counseling principle for each chapter. For each of the other books listed, you need only list as many principles as will fit on one-half to one page, typewritten. Complete this section using the **DISCIPLESHIP/COUNSELING PRINCIPLES: POETIC AND PROPHETIC BOOKS** sheet on the next page. Do not write directly on the blank format sheet, so that you may make copies of as many sheets as you need. Please be sure to use a separate format sheet for each of the books.

Psalms	Lamentations	Obadiah	Haggai
Proverbs	Ezekiel	Jonah	Zechariah
Ecclesiastes	Daniel	Micah	Malachi
Song of Solomon	Hosea	Nahum	
Isaiah	Joel	Habakkuk	
Jeremiah	Amos	Zephaniah	

DISCIPLESHIP/COUNSELING PRINCIPLES:
POETIC AND PROPHETIC BOOKS

Book Studied: _____

CHAPTER: VERSE/PASSAGE Neatly write or type significant passages	DISCIPLESHIP/COUNSELING PRINCIPLE Write only the major discipleship/ counseling principle

PART III — BIBLICAL DISCIPLESHIP/COUNSELING SURVEY

> In this part of the **SELF-STUDY COURSE**, you will examine discipleship/counseling topics and complete overview studies to help your disciples/counselees. For study and reference purposes, you will find much help through an exhaustive concordance, your *Self-Confrontation* manual, and the *Handbook*.

Section A. Discipleship/Counseling Topics and Principles

1. List important biblical principles, with their accompanying Scripture references, for you as a biblical discipler/counselor to remember a) during a typical meeting and b) in your ministry. You may also attach biblical principles from this *Handbook*, Section I to keep as references. To help you develop the biblical principles, keep in mind your:

   a. Attitude toward the disciple/counselee, the other team members, and others involved in the problem;

   b. Conduct before the Lord and others;

   c. Source and the reasons for the hope within you;

   d. Speech, both casually and while teaching or discipling/counseling;

   e. Thoughts; and

   f. Standard for successful biblical discipleship/counseling.

2. Write or refer to biblical principles related to gaining a biblical understanding of a disciple/counselee's problem. Pay particular attention to:

   a. The types of questions to ask disciples/counselees and others involved in the problem(s);

   b. The importance of listening, and what to listen for;

   c. What areas to avoid when seeking information. Here, also be careful to tell why you should avoid seeking details or information in these areas; and

   d. How to evaluate biblically the information you gain through the questions and listening.

   Refer to **UNDERSTANDING PROBLEMS BIBLICALLY** *(Handbook, Pages H133-H138).*

3. Write biblical principles related to helping disciples recognize, gain, and mature in biblical hope. Especially study the Scriptures to teach disciples:

   a. What constitutes biblical hope,

   b. How to avoid false hope, and

   c. The importance of dealing with sin as part of gaining and maturing in biblical hope.

4. List biblical principles related to assigning homework. When developing the biblical principles, deal with:

   a. The importance of homework in establishing a biblical pattern of life,

   b. The characteristics of biblically-based homework, and

   c. What to do when the disciple fails to complete the homework assigned.

5. List at least ten (10) significant homework assignments, along with their supporting Scriptures, and give examples of situations when you would assign them. Also, tell what scriptural practices each of these homework assignments will help establish. Use the **SIGNIFICANT HOMEWORK ASSIGNMENTS** format on the next page to help you answer this question.

6. As a biblical discipler/counselor, your ministry is not merely to help the disciple deal with his current problems but to help him become established and to mature in a new victorious pattern of life. Thus, you must learn to recognize the scriptural patterns necessary in the lives of all individuals, regardless of the problem(s) they face. Develop a list of topics you would discuss with a disciple, from the beginning to the end of the discipleship/counseling process, regardless of the problem that he may present to you. List the discipleship/counseling topics in the order of use, as much as possible, using the **MASTER PLAN FOR THE MINISTRY OF BIBLICAL DISCIPLESHIP/COUNSELING** and its explanation (*Handbook*, Pages H51-H104).

7. In question 6, you outlined a biblical plan for the entire discipleship/counseling process. Within the process, you may need to address the following problems with disciples/counselees. Outline counseling approaches to the subjects marked with an asterisk below along with five (5) additional subjects. Especially describe in detail the plan you would follow before you would deal with each of the subjects. Using the **DEALING WITH SPECIFIC PROBLEMS** format on Page 20 of this form, describe what you would tell a disciple/counselee about:

* "Addictions"	* Daydreams/ Fantasies	* Gifts (spiritual)	Peace
Adultery	* Depression	Gossip	* Reconciliation
* Anger	Desire (wants vs. needs)	* Grief	Repentance
Anxiety, Worry	Discipline/Reproof	* Guilt	Self, Selfishness
Arguing	Divorce	Homosexuality	* Sin in others
Assurance (of salvation)	Drunkenness	Hope	Speech, Tongue
Bitterness/ Resentment	Doubt	Husband	* Spouse/child abuse
* Bizarre behavior	Envy, Jealousy	* Inadequacy	Suffering
Blessing	Faith	Joy	* Suicide
* Change	* Fear	Laziness	Trials/Testing
Child/Children	* Feelings	Love	Wife
Conscience	* Forgiveness	Lust	Work/Labor
Coveting	Fornication	Lying	* Worry
		* Marriage	

8. Describe an uncooperative (uncommitted) counselee. At what point in the discipleship/counseling process can you tell that a counselee is uncommitted? How should you proceed?

9. Describe the biblical process of church discipline, as it ought to occur in a local church.

SIGNIFICANT HOMEWORK ASSIGNMENTS
(based on Psalm 119 and Matthew 28:20)

SPECIFIC HOMEWORK ASSIGNMENT THAT IS OF SIGNIFICANT BENEFIT IN THE DEVELOPMENT OF SCRIPTURAL PRACTICES (based on Psalm 119:5)	SCRIPTURAL BASIS FOR THIS ASSIGNMENT (based on James 1:22-25)	SPECIFIC INSTANCES AND CIRCUMSTANCES IN WHICH YOU WOULD ASSIGN THIS HOMEWORK (based on 1 Corinthians 10:13; Hebrews 4:15-16; James 5:13-20)	THE BENEFIT OR USEFULNESS OF THIS ASSIGNMENT IN A DISCIPLE/COUNSELEE'S LIFE (based on 1 Timothy 4:7-8)

DEALING WITH SPECIFIC PROBLEMS
(based on Ephesians 4:22-32)

Problem Area Addressed: _____

SCRIPTURE REFERENCES THAT APPLY TO THIS PROBLEM AREA (List references and give a brief synopsis of the passages)	WHAT YOU WOULD TELL A DISCIPLE/ COUNSELEE TO HELP HIM HAVE HOPE WITHIN THIS PROBLEM	WHAT YOU WOULD TELL A DISCIPLE/COUNSELEE TO HELP HIM CHANGE BIBLICALLY	SPECIFIC HOMEWORK ASSIGNMENTS TO ESTABLISH A BIBLICAL PATTERN OF RIGHTEOUSNESS

PART III — BIBLICAL DISCIPLESHIP/COUNSELING SURVEY (CONT'D.)

Section B. Jesus' Discipleship/Counseling Method and Example

In order to answer the following questions, you need to research the Gospels and portions of other New Testament books to study Jesus' teachings and life. In particular, look for ways in which Jesus discipled/counseled. Remember always to list Scripture references and examples when answering the questions. Listed directly below you will find a listing of the passages that will be of help to you in answering the questions.

```
┌─────────────────────────────────────────────────┐
│          HELPFUL RESEARCH PASSAGES:               │
│                                                   │
│   The Gospels          I Corinthians 11:24-25     │
│   Acts 1:5, 7-8        II Corinthians 12:9        │
│        8:4-16          Revelation 1:8, 11, 17-20  │
│        11:16                    2:1-3:22          │
│        22:7-21                  22:7, 12-20       │
│        23:11                                      │
│        26:14-18                                   │
└─────────────────────────────────────────────────┘
```

Because Jesus, as God, already knew what was in the heart of man (*Mark 2:8; John 2:24-25*), He did not need to gather information as humans do. Nevertheless, He asked questions and listened to the answers, in order to show the individuals He taught, rebuked, and counseled what was true about them and their lives. When you disciple/counsel, you must follow Jesus' example in giving counsel appropriate to the need, so that both you and the disciple/counselee gain an understanding of the problem and of God's answers. From your research through the passages listed above, answer the following:

1.   When Jesus developed within individuals a godly understanding of their problems,

   a.   What kinds of questions did He ask to elicit informational responses from them?

   _____

   _____

   b.   What questions did He ask rhetorically (to make a point) or to cause people to think?

   _____

   _____

   _____

2.   Using the **QUESTIONS JESUS ASKED** format on the next page, give examples of events and incidents when Jesus asked questions:

   a.   To develop an overall view of individuals' lives (more general or extensive questions, covering the broad spectrum of life).

   b.   To focus on one problem area in the lives of different people (more probing or intensive questions designed to reveal information about specific circumstances and responses, and a recognition of specific sins).

QUESTIONS JESUS ASKED
STUDYING JESUS' LIFE AND EXAMPLE TO GAIN UNDERSTANDING OF PROBLEMS

SCRIPTURE REFERENCE AND BRIEF SYNOPSIS OF THE EVENT OR CIRCUMSTANCE	WHAT JESUS ASKED THE PERSON OR GROUP	TYPE OF QUESTION (Overall/Extensive, or Probing/Intensive?)	THE INDIVIDUAL'S (OR GROUP'S) RESPONSE TO JESUS' QUESTION	WHAT YOU LEARNED ABOUT THE SPIRITUAL CONDITION OF THE INDIVIDUAL OR GROUP FROM THIS PASSAGE

PART III — BIBLICAL DISCIPLESHIP/COUNSELING SURVEY (CONT'D.)

Section B. Jesus Discipleship/Counseling Method and Example (Cont'd.)

3. Using the **HOW JESUS OFFERED HOPE** format on Page 24 of this form, list five (5) specific ways that Jesus gave hope to individuals.

4. Using the **HOW JESUS DEALT WITH SIN** format on Page 25 of this form, list what Jesus said and did regarding the sins of:

    a. Religious and political leaders in Israel,

    b. His disciples, and

    c. Any other individuals with whom He dealt.

5. Using the **ASSIGNMENTS JESUS GAVE** format on Page 26 of this form, list five specific homework assignments that Jesus gave, citing Scriptural references and examples.

HOW JESUS OFFERED HOPE
(based on John 4:13–14; John 17)

SCRIPTURE REFERENCE WITH A BRIEF SYNOPSIS OF THE EVENT OR CIRCUMSTANCE	WHAT JESUS SAID TO GIVE HOPE TO THE PERSON OR GROUP PRESENT	THE DIFFERENCE BETWEEN THE HOPE THAT JESUS GAVE AND THE HOPE THAT OTHERS OFFERED TO THIS INDIVIDUAL OR GROUP	THE RESPONSE OF THE PERSON OR GROUP, AND ANY RESULTS IN LIVES THAT YOU NOTICED FROM THIS PASSAGE

HOW JESUS DEALT WITH SIN

SCRIPTURE REFERENCE AND BRIEF SYNOPSIS OF THE EVENT OR CIRCUMSTANCE	THE CHANGES JESUS TOLD THIS INDIVIDUAL OR GROUP THAT THEY NEEDED TO MAKE	THIS INDIVIDUAL'S OR GROUP'S RESPONSE	THE RESULT AND JESUS' RESPONSE

ASSIGNMENTS JESUS GAVE
(based on John 14:15)

SCRIPTURE REFERENCE AND BRIEF SYNOPSIS OF THE EVENT OR CIRCUMSTANCE	THE ASSIGNMENT GIVEN BY JESUS *Also write out the possible implications of the assignment given*	THE INDIVIDUAL'S OR GROUP'S RESPONSE	THE RESULT AND JESUS' RESPONSE *Also list evident changes in lives, as described by the Scripture passage*

© Biblical Counseling Foundation

TELEPHONE/EMERGENCY
BIBLICAL DISCIPLESHIP/COUNSELING RECORD

Date _____ *Time Discipleship/Counseling Took Place* _____ *Length of Conversation* _____

Name of Discipler/Counselor Reporting _____ *Initials of Person Discipled/Counseled* _____

Evident Emotional State of Disciple/Counselee _____

Disciple/Counselee's Reason for Calling _____

Conversation Notes:

Scriptures Given to Disciple/Counselee:

Possible Problems to Investigate:
(As observed in this conversation)

Outcome of the Conversation:

(Write on back as needed)

BCF Form 11

CHECKLIST FOR EVALUATING
BIBLICAL DISCIPLESHIP/COUNSELING MEETINGS

Confidential #: _____ Date: _____ Meetings # _____ to # _____ Your Initials: _____

Discipleship/Counseling Team (Last Names): _____ _____ _____

Please scan the following pages and place a check (✔) in the boxes by the discipleship/counseling areas that need correcting, and in the blank lines, briefly list how the corrections will be made. Since this form is designed to be used for six meetings, it may be helpful for you to use different styles of writing or different colors of ink for each meeting when you make any notes.

Meeting # : I. **EXAMINING/JUDGING YOURSELVES AS DISCIPLERS/COUNSELORS IN THE FOLLOWING AREAS:**

A. **Lack of Scriptural knowledge in dealing with this particular problem**

How could you tell? _____

What will you do to correct this? _____

B. **Lack of adequate discipleship/counseling training in conducting this meeting**

How could you tell? _____

What will you do to correct this? _____

C. **Failure in teamwork**

1. **In the meeting:**

   a. Not reinforcing one another's biblical counsel *(Philippians 2:1-3)*

   b. Not focusing on biblical principles as your authority *(Isaiah 55:8-11)*

   c. Not listening before speaking *(Proverbs 18:2, 13)*

   How were any of the above displayed? _____

   How will it be corrected? _____

2. **In the planning/evaluation times:**

   a. Not heeding biblical counsel of fellow counselors *(Philippians 2:3-4)*

   b. Basing planning/evaluation on opinions, and not on the Scriptures *(Titus 2:1)*

   c. Not listening before speaking *(Proverbs 18:2, 13)*

   d. When evaluating or correcting, not speaking the truth in love *(Ephesians 4:15)*

   How were any of the above displayed? _____

   How will it be corrected? _____

D. **Unbiblical conduct toward disciple/counselee**

1. **In your speech**

   a. Giving unbiblical counsel *(Titus 2:1)*

   b. Arguing with the disciple/counselee *(II Timothy 2:23-26)*

   c. Using harsh, demeaning, authoritarian or otherwise unloving words or tone of voice *(I Corinthians 13:4-8a; Ephesians 4:15, 29; Colossians 4:6a)*

   d. Demonstrating love with hypocrisy toward (i.e., attempting to manipulate) the disciple/counselee by:

BCF Form 13, Page 1

Meeting # :

1) Merely soothing the disciple/counselee's feelings *(Proverbs 27:6)*

2) Appealing to an authority other than the Scriptures (e.g., yourself, authors, speakers, etc.) *(Proverbs 14:12; 16:25; Isaiah 55:8-11)*

3) Giving the disciple/counselee suggestions, forms, or opinions rather than biblical principles and commandments *(Proverbs 14:12)*

How were any of the above displayed? _____

How will you correct this? _____

e.   Giving false hope by:

1) Not calling sin sin (e.g., calling sins "mistakes") *(based on Jeremiah 23:16-18; I John 1:8)*

2) Accepting superficial changes as a substitute for biblical restructuring of relationships and responsibilities *(Micah 6:7-8)*

f.   Spoon-feeding the "answers" to the disciple/counselee without giving him an opportunity to implement the scriptural solutions *(Galatians 6:2, 5)*

How did you do any of the above? _____

What will you do instead? _____

2.   **In your actions**

a.   Taking over the counselee's responsibilities for him by:

1) "Fixing" the situation (i.e., changing or removing the very circumstance that God may be using in the life of the disciple/counselee to get his attention) *(Romans 8:28-29; James 1:2-4)*

2) Doing the disciple/counselee's responsibilities for him (e.g., the responsibility of asking for help from spouse, parents, roommates, pastor, personal physician, etc.) *(Galatians 6:5)*

b.   Not dealing with sin when necessary by:

1) Allowing continued blameshifting, gossip, or excuses *(Ezekiel 18:20; Matthew 7:5)*

2) Holding back from dealing with sin in the disciple/counselee's life *(Galatians 6:1; Romans 15:14)*

3) Not being faithful to begin the process of church discipline, when necessary *(Matthew 18:15-18)*

How did you do any of the above? _____

What will you do instead? _____

3.   **In your thought life**

a.   Making assumptions regarding the disciple/counselee's commitment, actions, or motives *(Proverbs 18:2, 13, 17)*

b.   Merely commiserating with the disciple/counselee *(Proverbs 27:6)*

c.   Agreeing with the disciple/counselee's unbiblical/inaccurate view of the problem *(based on Isaiah 5:20-21; Matthew 7:5)*

How did you become alert to the above? _____

How will you correct this? _____

Meeting # :

II.   **EXAMINING THE DISCIPLE/COUNSELEE'S RESPONSES AND DOING OF THE WORD THROUGH THE UNDERSTANDING GAINED FROM THIS MEETING:**

A.   **Lack of understanding** *(Matthew 13:23)*

1.   **Of biblical solutions (i.e., commands or principles)**

2.   **Of discipler/counselors' explanations**

3.   **Of homework assignments**

How were any of the above displayed? _____

How will you help the disciple/counselee correct the lack of understanding?

_____

B.   **Lack of commitment**

1.   **For salvation** *(I Corinthians 2:14)*

2.   **To please the Lord, as evidenced by**

a.   Arguing with clear biblical commands *(Proverbs 9:7-9)*

b.   Verbally claiming to be committed to the Lord, but continuing in sinful patterns, such as

1)   Arguing/bickering *(II Timothy 2:23-26)*

2)   Blameshifting *(e.g., Genesis 3:12-13)*

3)   Disorderly pattern of life *(II Thessalonians 3:6)*

4)   Attempting to manipulate the disciplers/counselors (e.g., seeking to have the counselors choose sides) *(Romans 12:9)*

5)   Continued failure to deal biblically with his specific problem *(I Corinthians 6:9)*

6)   Not doing homework *(James 1:22; 4:17)*

7)   Minimizing sin *(I John 1:8)*

8)   Other evidences, as seen from consultation with the **MASTER PLAN** and its explanation *(Handbook, Pages H51-H104)*. Please specify what you noticed:

_____

_____

_____

How were any of the above displayed? _____

How will it be corrected? _____

III.   **EVALUATING THE MEETING BASED ON THE FOUR ESSENTIAL ELEMENTS OF EVERY DISCIPLESHIP/COUNSELING TOPIC:**

A.   **Failing to gather information/gain understanding of the problem** *(Proverbs 18:2, 13, 17, 19)*

1.   **At all levels of the problem:**

a.   At the feeling level *(Genesis 4:6-7)*

b.   At the doing level (thoughts, speech and action) *(Matthew 7:16; James 1:22-25)*

Meeting # :

c.   At the heart level *(Matthew 15:18)*

How did you determine your failure to gather information at all levels?

_____

What will you do to gather the needed information?

_____

2.   **By not listening to the disciple/counselee** *(Proverbs 18:2)*

3.   **By not asking questions designed to gain information:**

a.   About all areas of life that may be affected by this problem (Extensive questioning).

b.   About specific incidents or sinful actions that relate to the problem area (Intensive questioning).

B.   **Failing to help the disciple/counselee have hope through God's Word:**

1.   **In God's solutions** *(II Timothy 3:16-17)*

2.   **For specific problem areas** *(Ephesians 4:22-24)*

3.   **By not helping the disciple/counselee recognize personal sin** *(Hebrews 4:12)*

4.   **By not establishing or strengthening commitment** *(Colossians 1:10)*

5.   **By not teaching the "how to's" of doing the Word** *(Colossians 3:23-24; James 1:22-25)*

What specifically did you fail to do? _____

How will you correct it? _____

C.   **Failing to explain the need for change or to establish changes in the following areas:**

1.   **Commitment**

a.   For salvation *(Ephesians 2:1-5, 8-10, 12)*

b.   Of focus of life to please God *(II Corinthians 5:9; Colossians 1:10)*

2.   **Put-offs and Put-ons** *(Ephesians 4:22-24)*

3.   **Judging self** *(Matthew 7:1-5; Galatians 6:1, 4)*

a.   In relationships *(Matthew 22:37-39; I John 2:9-11)*

b.   In responsibilities *(Galatians 6:4; II Thessalonians 3:10-12)*

4.   **Forgiveness** *(Mark 11:25-26)*

5.   **Reconciliation** *(Matthew 5:23-24)*

6.   **Discipline of thought life** *(Philippians 4:8-9)*

7.   **Biblical communication** *(Ephesians 4:15, 29-32; Colossians 4:6)*

Meeting # :

8. Denying self *(Luke 9:23-25)*

9. Considering others as more important than self — being a blessing *(Romans 12:9-21; Philippians 2:3-4)*

10. Dealing with specific problem areas *(Ephesians 4:22-32; Revelation 2:4-5)*

D. Failure in clearly explaining or assigning the appropriate practice of the Word by not giving homework that was:

1. God-directed *(I Samuel 15:22)*

2. Biblical *(Joshua 1:8)*

3. Designed to affect thought patterns *(II Corinthians 10:5; Philippians 4:8-9)*

4. Designed to affect physical actions *(Colossians 3:23-24)*

5. Designed to affect speech *(Ephesians 4:15, 29; Colossians 4:6)*

6. Specific *(e.g., Matthew 19:21)*

7. Measurable *(Luke 16:10)*

8. Repetitive where biblical habits need to be formed *(Hebrews 5:14)*

Which homework assignments failed to meet the above standards?

_____

_____

What assignments will you give to the disciple/counselee to correct the unbiblical homework given?

_____

_____

Are there any other items that must be dealt with?

_____

_____

    BCF Form 13, Page 5

BIBLE STUDY AND APPLICATION FORMAT

(based on II Timothy 3:16-17)

Biblical Reference	Teaching	Reproof	Correction	Training in Righteousness
	What is the commandment or principle?	How have I failed to live by it?	What do I need to do?	What is my specific plan — how will I do it?

GUIDELINES:
BIBLE STUDY AND APPLICATION FORMAT

> Because all Scripture is God-breathed, it is completely sufficient to teach, reprove, correct, and train you in godly living so that you may be fully equipped for every good work *(II Timothy 3:16-17)*.

I. **Purposes of the BIBLE STUDY AND APPLICATION FORMAT**

   A. To give you a format for studying the Scriptures that will assist you in being obedient to God's Word. The **BIBLE STUDY AND APPLICATION FORMAT** is a tool to help you be an effective doer of the Word and is based on *II Timothy 3:16-17:*

   > *"All Scripture is inspired by God and profitable for **teaching**, for **reproof**, for **correction**, for **training in righteousness**; that the man of God may be adequate, equipped for every good work"* *(II Timothy 3:16-17, New American Standard Version, emphasis added).*

   B. To help you:

   1. Judge yourself in the light of Scripture *(based on Psalm 119:9-11, 139:23-24; Matthew 7:1-5; Hebrews 4:12)*,

   2. Develop specific biblical plans which will become patterns of godly living in your life *(based on Luke 11:28; John 13:17; Hebrews 5:13-14; James 1:22-25)*.

   C. To help you identify specific biblical principles that will help you face, deal with, and endure the problems you encounter *(based on Psalm 25:4-5; 94:12; 119:99, 104, 130; Proverbs 6:23)*.

II. **Procedures for completing the BIBLE STUDY AND APPLICATION FORMAT**

   A. In the **Biblical Reference** column, list the Scripture verse or passage. (Consider memorizing this portion of God's Word as part of your growth in Jesus Christ.)

   B. In the **Teaching** column, write the commandment or principle that this passage emphasizes. As you thoroughly study the passage, you will be more accurate in your understanding and application of the principles or commandments you see.

   C. In the **Reproof** column, list your specific deeds (i.e., your thoughts, speech, and actions) that reveal your failure to obey God's principles or commandments listed in the **Teaching** column. Be as thorough and specific as possible.

   D. In the **Correction** column, list specific biblical changes you need to make in order to correct the failures listed in the **Reproof** column. This list may include reconciling or making restitution.

   E. In the **Training in Righteousness** column, develop a plan listing the specific biblical steps you will take in order to carry out the changes listed in the **Correction** column. Keep in mind that these changes should become patterns of life to help you continue in your spiritual growth and maturity.

BCF

VICTORY OVER FAILURES PLAN:
GUIDELINES AND WORKSHEETS

VICTORY OVER FAILURES PLAN:
GUIDELINES AND WORKSHEETS

This booklet is published by the Biblical Counseling Foundation, Inc., a non profit, non stock corporation founded in 1974 and incorporated in the Commonwealth of Virginia, USA, in 1977.

ISBN 978-1-60536-037-9

First printing, September, 2004
Second printing, January, 2005
Third printing, August, 2007
Fourth printing, January, 2009
Fifth printing, January, 2010
Sixth printing, July, 2010
Seventh printing, March, 2011
Eighth printing, July, 2012
Ninth printing, September, 2016
Tenth printing, August, 2018

Biblical Counseling Foundation
42550 Aegean Street
Indio, CA 92203-9617, USA

760.347.4608 telephone
760.775.5751 fax
orders@bcfministries.org e-mail for orders
admin@bcfministries.org e-mail for other
877.933.9333 (in USA) telephone for orders only
http://www.bcfministries.org webpage for orders and information

TABLE OF CONTENTS

> *SPECIAL NOTE FOR PAGE NUMBERING:* Since this **VICTORY OVER FAILURES PLAN** occurs in numerous BCF training materials, all the page numbers referenced will refer to the numbers at the bottom of the page.

INTRODUCTION
TO THE VICTORY OVER FAILURES PLAN

> You can never truly understand or help others, even in your own family, unless you first look thoroughly into your own life and deal with your own sins without compromise, excuses, or evasion *(based on Matthew 7:1-5; II Corinthians 1:3-5).*

Overview

The **VICTORY OVER FAILURES PLAN** is a biblically based tool that can help you overcome any difficulty of life with the full expectation of complete and lasting victory. To live victoriously in a lasting, fruitful way, we first need to see how we have failed to live God's way, hence the phrase "victory over failures." By victory over "failures" we don't mean failures at business or failures in school. We mean having victory over failures to love biblically (what God calls sin) that keep us from having a joyful, vibrant, growing relationship with the Lord. Part of the process involves putting off the old manner of life and putting on new, righteous practices in their place *(Ephesians 4:22-24).* The **VICTORY OVER FAILURES PLAN** describes how to do that in very practical ways and gives you a format you can follow.

This booklet is a companion to the Biblical Counseling Foundation's *Self-Confrontation* manual. It can be used independently from the Self-Confrontation Course, but is best understood and applied along with the course. The Self-Confrontation Course is designed to lead you through a personal life application study of God's Word using the *Self-Confrontation* manual as a reference. This life application study focuses on how to live sacrificially for God and for others, rather than living for self. It presents biblical principles that are fundamental to living the kind of victorious, contented life God intended for you, regardless of the circumstances.

This booklet explains these and other biblical principles about how to have lasting change in your life. It asks you to identify a problem area in your life that you can then work on, applying the principles from God's Word in the power of the Holy Spirit. The objective is to help you to rely wholly on the Scriptures and the work of the Holy Spirit Himself, rather than to rely on the superficial remedies of the world, or on your own strength. There are vast contrasts between God's way of dealing with problems and the world's way *(Isaiah 55:8-11).* Only through applying God's principles can you expect lasting change. As you walk according to the biblical principles written in your **VICTORY OVER FAILURES PLAN**, you will develop Christlike character in your life. The changes will be enduring and meaningful, and you will be a faithful, fruitful vessel in God's hands.

The booklet starts with an explanation of why you should develop a *written* plan. Then, it describes the materials you will need, the purposes of the plan, foundations for biblical change, biblical hope for change, and the process for putting the plan together. The **VICTORY OVER FAILURES PLAN** is not just a one-time exercise, but is an organized, biblical approach that you can use to deal with tests, temptations, and sin throughout your life. You can also use it in helping others with their problems.

Why develop a written plan?

Problems in life are not unusual, but many believers, even those who have known Christ for years, have not learned how to deal biblically with difficult problems as part of the process of sanctification. They may experience grave difficulties at home or at work, disappointments with others, financial losses, health problems, etc. For most of their lives, many believers fluctuate between living in victory and living in defeat.

The Scriptures tell us that believers will always undergo spiritual battles *(John 16:33; Galatians 5:17)*. It is also true that God has given us victory in the Lord Jesus Christ *(Romans 8:28-38)*. Sadly, many have not learned how to live victoriously in the empowerment of the Holy Spirit. Often in ignorance, they continue to respond to problems the same way they responded as unbelievers. Therefore, it is vital that all believers learn how to face, deal with, and endure problems as they progress through life. Each believer needs a simple, organized way of evaluating the situation according to God's truth and developing a plan that, if followed, will bring complete and lasting change. This **VICTORY OVER FAILURES PLAN** has been developed to help believers become established in living God's way.

You might ask the question, "Why should I actually have a plan written out to deal with a difficulty in my life?" One reason is found in a careful study of *I Corinthians 10:12-14*. In this passage, *verse 13* provides great hope that God will not allow a temptation or trial in your life that is more than you can handle. The previous verse, *I Corinthians 10:12*, warns that we must take heed (to our spiritual walk), or we might fall into sin. Isn't it interesting that in the very passage where God gives us a great promise of His sovereignty, He also tells us not to be presumptuous or arrogant about our ability to withstand temptation on our own? He tells us to "be careful" or "be prepared." The verb "take heed" has the idea of being watchful on a continuing basis in anticipation of a future event. It is the same word that Jesus used when He warned the disciples to stay alert in anticipation of His return. In the same way, we need to be alert to when we might be tempted and to be prepared to respond the way the Lord commands. Then in *I Corinthians 10:14*, we are told, "therefore" (referring back to *verse 13*), to "flee idolatry." In other words, in light of God's providing us with the way to endure trials, He tells us not to hesitate when tempted, but take immediate and decisive action. The **VICTORY OVER FAILURES PLAN** will help you to be prepared to take decisive, godly action when temptations come. Many temptations can be anticipated, especially where we have been tempted previously, and have yielded and sinned. Many times, we even put ourselves in the path of temptation unnecessarily. Making biblical plans ahead of time will help you to remember what to do when you face temptation, and will be an indication of your commitment before God to handle trials His way, in the power of the Holy Spirit.

You may ask yourself, "Will I need to make written plans all my life?" After you have become established in overcoming temptations through the development and practice of biblical plans, you will become more able to think through how to deal with sins in your life. This is because the **VICTORY OVER FAILURES PLAN** has become part of your life. Then it will only be occasionally that you might need to write out a **VICTORY OVER FAILURES PLAN** for complicated matters.

Materials needed to develop your plan

The Bible

It is important that you use a literal translation of the Bible. While a paraphrase of the Bible may be useful as an expansion or supplemental study tool, it is important to memorize and understand the Bible in its most literal form. Because paraphrases are not translations, but interpretations, they may focus on man's insights rather than God's truth at certain points. When you study for your own benefit or to minister to others, it is important that you remain faithful to God's Word.

As you study this booklet, you will find that the biblical principles and precepts presented are substantiated with Scripture references which you are encouraged to look up as you progress. The Scripture references are listed in the order they are found in the Bible, not necessarily in the order of importance or clarity.

Whenever you see italicized parentheses with references to Scripture verses, each of the references listed directly substantiate the previous statement fully. Whenever you see the words *"based on"* before the list of references, the truth of the previous statement cannot be understood from a single reference, but can be seen from a study of all the referenced verses put together.

The *Self-Confrontation* manual

You will find it helpful to use the *Self-Confrontation* manual as a supplementary reference. It is designed to guide you through a set of biblical principles that are fundamental to living the kind of victorious, contented life God intended for us, regardless of the circumstances. The manual will always direct you to God's Word, not to man's opinion. In a sense, it is like a topical concordance. It contains many biblical references that cover both the fundamentals of the Christian life as well as how to deal with specific problem areas. For additional help, the guidelines in the next section refer at times to portions of the *Self-Confrontation* manual.

Purposes of the VICTORY OVER FAILURES PLAN

Based on biblical principles, the **VICTORY OVER FAILURES PLAN** guides you to victory even in the midst of any trial, test, or temptation of life. The **PLAN** has four purposes, and there are worksheets related to the purposes as shown below:

A. To help you learn how to examine yourself biblically *(Psalm 139:23-24; Matthew 7:1-5; I Corinthians 11:31; Galatians 6:4);*

   Applies to Worksheets 1 and 2 on Pages 40 and 41

B. To help you recognize specific biblical "put-offs" and "put-ons" for daily living *(for example: Ephesians 4:22-32; Colossians 3:5-17);*

   Applies to Worksheet 3 on Page 42

C. To help you develop and act upon specific plans for biblical change *(based on Titus 2:11-14; James 1:22-25);* and

   Applies to Worksheets 4-6 on Pages 43-48

D. To help you make your specific biblical changes part of your daily walk in every area of your life *(based on Romans 6:12-13; Colossians 2:6; 3:2-17; II Timothy 3:16-17; I Peter 1:14-16).*

   Applies to the entire plan

NOTE: While these guidelines are useful for dealing with isolated sins that are only committed rarely, the most valuable use of the VICTORY OVER FAILURES PLAN is for dealing with sinful patterns where there has not been consistent victory.

Your relationship with Jesus Christ — the basic foundation for biblical change

The *Self-Confrontation* manual provides an extensive scriptural study of how you can have victory in the midst of difficult trials, tests, and temptations. The next several sections provide a brief overview of some of the foundational biblical principles you should know before developing your **VICTORY OVER FAILURES PLAN**. So, before you start on the worksheets, take some time to read through these principles. At a minimum, read in your Bible the passages referenced in **boldface** print below.

A.   In order to change biblically, you must first recognize your inability to overcome life's problems in your own strength or by your own wisdom. Biblical change is only possible when you become a child of God.

   1.   If you do not know Jesus Christ as your Lord and Savior, you have no capability to change biblically because you do not have:

      a.   The indwelling power of the Holy Spirit (*based on John 14:17;* ***Romans 5:5b***, *8:9),*

      b.   The understanding of the things of God (*I Corinthians 2:6-14, esp. verse 14*), and

      c.   The hope to live in a manner pleasing to God (*based on* ***Romans 8:8**; Ephesians 2:12).*

      NOTE: You may be able to make some changes in your life here and there, but the changes will be superficial and temporary if you do not have a personal relationship with God.

   2.   To become God's child you must:

      a.   Repent of your sin (***Mark 1:15**; Luke 13:3; II Corinthians 7:10; II Peter 3:9).* In *Luke 13:3,* Jesus says that unless a person repents, he shall perish. Repentance is very important since it is an admission that you have been going against God's purposes, that you are sorry for opposing God, and you are turning around to go God's way.

      b.   Wholeheartedly believe that the blood of Jesus Christ which was shed on the cross is the only means for receiving forgiveness for your sins (***Romans** 3:23-25; 5:8;* ***6:23**; Ephesians 1:7; Colossians 1:19-23; I Timothy 2:5; I Peter 1:18-19)* and likewise, that Christ died for your sins according to the Scriptures, and that He was buried, and that He was raised on the third day according to the Scriptures (*I Corinthians 15:3-4).*

      c.   Sincerely receive the Lord Jesus Christ into your life (***John 1:12**; I John 5:12).* In *John 1:12,* receiving and believing are synonyms. This leads to a deeper understanding of the biblical truth about belief. Jesus said in *John 17:3, "And this is eternal life, that they may know Thee, the only true God, and Jesus Christ whom Thou hast sent."* Receiving Jesus Christ is not merely believing in Christ intellectually; it includes committing yourself to an intimate, vital relationship with Him.

      d.   Confess Jesus as Lord (*John 5:24; Romans 10:8-13).* Notice in ***Romans 10:9-10*** that salvation includes both believing in the heart and confessing with the mouth Jesus as Lord. This is a public declaration that Jesus is Lord. The word "Lord" means master. You are to submit to Him as your master or head.

Salvation is by grace through faith, not by works *(Ephesians 2:8-9)*; but believers are God's workmanship, created in Christ Jesus for good works *(Ephesians 2:10)*. As a new creation *(II Corinthians 5:17)*, you intend to live in faithful and loving obedience to God *(I John 2:3-6)*.

B.   If you are already a believer:

1.   Your purpose for change must be to please God, not self.

  a.   You are to worship and serve God *(Luke 4:8)*, pleasing Him in all respects *(II Corinthians 5:9; **Colossians 1:10**)*. As a responsible member of God's family, you are to give glory to God in all things *(I Corinthians 10:31; Colossians 3:17)*.

  b.   Instead of living for yourself, you are to die to self, take up your cross daily, and follow Christ *(Matthew 10:38; **Luke 9:23**; I Corinthians 15:31)*. You are to lose your life for the Lord's sake *(Matthew 10:39; Luke 9:24)*. This change in allegiance is demonstrated by practical expressions of loving God *(Matthew 22:37-38; John 14:15, 21; I John 5:3)* and loving others *(Matthew 22:39; I Corinthians 13:4-8a; Philippians 2:1-4; I John 4:7-8, 11, 20)*.

  c.   Therefore, your purpose for change is not to escape your situation so that you may feel better, but rather live for the Lord whether or not your circumstances change *(based on **Romans 14:7-8**; I Corinthians 7:20-24; II Corinthians 5:15; Philippians 1:21; James 1:2-4)*.

2.   To change biblically, your focus must be to walk by the Holy Spirit. This involves:

  a.   Trusting in the Holy Spirit for the power to live according to His way. God's Spirit is within you *(John 14:16-17; Romans 8:9)*, always available to teach you God's truths *(John 14:26, 16:13; I Corinthians 2:10-13)*, to strengthen you *(Romans 8:11)*, to intercede for you *(Romans 8:26-27)*, to help you discern between truth and error *(based on I John 2:18-27)*, and to develop Christlike character in your life *(Galatians 5:16-17, 22-23)*. This includes responding to the Holy Spirit's conviction by:

    1)   Admitting your failures to love in God's way *(based on Matthew 7:1-5; **Revelation 2:4-5**)* and

    2)   Confessing all sins to the Lord *(**I John 1:9**)* and practicing biblical forgiveness *(Matthew 6:12, 14; **Mark 11:25**; Ephesians 4:32)* and reconciliation *(**Matthew 5:23-24**)*.

  b.   Studying the Scriptures as your sole standard and authority for life *(based on Psalm 19:7-11; 119:105; **Isaiah 55:8-9, 11**)*. God's Word is completely sufficient for discernment *(Hebrews 4:12; II Peter 1:2-4)*, hope *(Romans 15:4)*, and counsel in any situation *(II Timothy 3:16-17)*. Two daily disciplines that will help you immensely to understand and apply the Word are daily devotions and Scripture memory.

    1)   Daily devotions are vital to your spiritual development. They include time spent each day in prayer, study of God's Word, and biblical self-evaluation *(based on **Psalm 1:1-4**, 119:9-11; I Corinthians 11:31; I Thessalonians 5:17; II Timothy 2:15; I Peter 2:2)*.

> 2) Memorization of Scripture follows the example of the Lord Jesus Christ *(Matthew 4:1-10)*; and will help you keep your way pure *(Psalm 119:9-11)*.

c. Loving God and others by obeying God's Word. Biblical change in you, sovereignly begun, sustained, and to be completed by God *(Philippians 1:6)*, is always linked to your obedience to God's Word *(Hebrews 5:14; James 1:22-25)*. Your obedience to His Word is a grateful response to God's love that is revealed in Christ Jesus *(John 14:15, 21, 23-24; I John 5:3; II John 1:6)*; it is not to be dependent on circumstances *(Acts 5:28-29; II Timothy 3:1-17)*, your fleshly desires (feelings) *(Galatians 5:17, 24; I Peter 4:2)*, or other people *(Ezekiel 18:20; I Peter 3:8-17)*.

d. Praying. You are to be devoted to prayer, according to God's will, and to bring everything and everyone unceasingly before the Lord in prayer *(Luke 18:1; Ephesians 6:18; I Thessalonians 5:17; I Timothy 2:1; I John 5:14-15)*.

Biblical hope for change

The hope that God has provided for you is not merely a wish. Neither is it dependent on other people, things, or circumstances for its validity. Instead, biblical hope is an application of your faith that supplies a confident expectation in God's fulfillment of His promises. Coupled with faith and love, hope is part of the abiding characteristics in a believer's life *(based on Romans 5:1-5; I Corinthians 13:13; II Corinthians 1:3-11; Colossians 1:3-6; I Thessalonians 1:2-3; I Timothy 1:1; Hebrews 6:17-20; I Peter 1:3)*.

The only lasting hope is promised in the Scriptures. Listed below are seven reasons that the believer has great hope. **NOTE:** *The following Biblical Principles are from the* **Self-Confrontation** *manual.*

A. Those in Christ are freed from the power and penalty of sin *(Romans 6:6-7, 14, 18, 23)*.

NOTE: You might be wondering why dealing with your own sin is a matter of hope for you, and not discouragement. Dealing with your sin should give you great hope because:

1. *You can deal with sin very quickly. It does not take years of therapy;*

2. *It is not dependent on whether others change. You can have peace and joy if your relationship with God is right, even in the most difficult circumstances; and*

3. *It is God's method for restoring relationships with Him and others.*

This is why it is so important to start your plan by identifying your own failures to live God's way (your sin). You don't deal with your problems by focusing on the sin of others or on your circumstances.

B. God will not allow believers to be tested or tempted beyond what they can bear. He gives you His grace and strength to endure every test and resist every temptation so that you never have to sin *(Romans 8:35-39; I Corinthians 10:13; II Corinthians 4:7-10; 12:9-10; Philippians 4:13; Hebrews 4:15-16; II Peter 2:4-9)*.

C. Our Lord Jesus Christ will grant mercy and provide grace to help in every need. He constantly intercedes as an advocate for you to God the Father and fully understands your weaknesses *(Hebrews 2:18; 4:15-16; 7:25; I John 2:1)*.

D. Trials and tests will develop and mature you in Christ if you respond to them in God's way *(Romans 5:3-5; **James 1:2-4**)*. He never devises evil or harm for you; rather His plans for you are for your good; God's good for you is to conform you to the image of Jesus *(**Genesis 50:20**; Deuteronomy 8:2, 5, 16; Psalm 145:17; Ecclesiastes 7:13-14; Jeremiah 29:11-13; **Romans 8:28-29**; James 1:13-17)*.

E. God's peace and joy are available to believers regardless of other people, material goods, things, or circumstances in your life *(Psalm 119:165; Matthew 5:3-12; **John 14:27**; **15:11**; **16:33**; **17:13**; Romans 14:17; Philippians 4:4-7; I Peter 1:6-9)*.

F. Only God can change people *(Ezekiel 36:26-27; Philippians 1:6; 2:13)*, so you are not responsible for changing them. You are accountable to God solely for your own deeds *(Jeremiah 17:10; **Ezekiel 18:1-20, especially verse 20**; Matthew 16:27; Romans 2:5-10; Colossians 3:23-25; I Peter 1:17)* and are to do your part in living at peace with others *(Matthew 5:23-24; Mark 11:25; Romans 12:9-21; 14:19; I Peter 3:8-9; 4:8)*.

G. When you confess your sins, God forgives and cleanses you *(**I John 1:9**)*.

The biblical process for change

A. While the new self has been put on at salvation, the old manner of life must be decisively put off and new righteous practices must be put on *(Ephesians 4:22, 24)*.

B. For each "put-off" in the Bible, there is usually a "put-on" and often it is in the same passage *(for examples, see **Ephesians 4:25-32**)*.

C. Lasting change takes self-control, discipline, work, and time because it involves putting off the practices (habit patterns) of the old self, which is corrupted, and putting on the practices (habit patterns) of the new self, which has been created in righteousness and holiness of the truth *(based on Ephesians 4:22-24; **I Timothy 4:7-8**)*.

D. When you focus your attention on the "put-on," your mind is not easily distracted to do wrong. When you focus your attention only on the "put-off," the temptation to do wrong is always before you *(based on **Galatians 5:16**; II Timothy 2:22)*.

*NOTE: Later, when you develop your **VICTORY OVER FAILURES PLAN**, you will identify biblical "put-offs" and "put-ons" that relate directly to your problem area.*

GUIDELINES
FOR COMPLETING THE
VICTORY OVER FAILURES PLAN

GUIDELINES FOR COMPLETING
THE VICTORY OVER FAILURES PLAN

Description of the Problem

Complete *Worksheet 1.* For your use, a blank worksheet is located on Page 40. *NOTE: You may make copies of all the worksheets at the end of this booklet.*

A. Under the "**Ongoing problem area**" section, write down the problem area that is of greatest hindrance to your walk with God *(Hebrews 12:1-2)*. To make the selection, use the following guidelines:

1. Focus on dealing with a problem that is ongoing, not on one that you experience only occasionally. You may wish to review **WHERE TO FIND BIBLICAL REFERENCES TO SPECIFIC PROBLEM AREAS** located on the next page. It contains a list of problem areas with references to relevant sections of the *Self-Confrontation* manual. Also listed are some key passages of Scripture to help determine possible areas of failure.

2. Seek the Lord's wisdom in determining the problem area to choose. Concentrate on an area in your life that requires the most immediate change, even though it may be difficult. The Lord is primarily concerned about your commitment to Him, not how much you can accomplish easily. So, choose the pattern that the Lord is convicting you to develop. To do this, ask yourself, "In what ways do I continue to show that I fail to love God and others?" *(based on Matthew 22:37-40; John 13:34-35; 14:15, 20-21; I Corinthians 13:4-8a)*. Ask the Holy Spirit to bring to your mind the specific ways you have sinned against the Lord and others.

   One of your tendencies with sinful habits may be to identify only those areas you want to change. However, when you seek to change some area of your life according to your own perceptions, you may focus on something that seems easy to do or that appeals to self-centered accomplishments (for example, overcoming fear of flying motivated by pride).

B. Under the "**Short description of the problem**" section, summarize the problem in one or two paragraphs. See Page 14 for a sample of a description written by a fictitious person who is angry and bitter toward a co-worker. Subsequent samples represent how he might complete a **VICTORY OVER FAILURES PLAN** based on these guidelines.

(GUIDELINES FOR COMPLETING THE VICTORY OVER FAILURES PLAN continue on Page 15.)

WHERE TO FIND BIBLICAL REFERENCES
TO SPECIFIC PROBLEM AREAS

Some key passages of Scripture to help determine possible problem areas:

Proverbs Chapters 15 and 18

Romans Chapters 12 - 14

I Corinthians 13:4-8a

Ephesians 4:22 - 6:9

Colossians Chapter 3

I Peter 2:11 - 3:17

A sample set of problem areas:

Scripture references containing biblical principles, "put-offs," and "put-ons" for these problem areas can be found in the indicated lessons of the *Self-Confrontation* manual and the *Biblical Principles for Discipleship/Counseling* booklet. In some of the referenced lessons, the problem area may not be specifically listed, but the biblical principles and biblical references will apply.

Contentment, lack of — Lesson 6

Envy, jealousy, covetousness, greed — Lessons 9 and 10

Self-belittlement — Lessons 9 and 10

Self-exaltation — Lessons 9 and 10

Self-pity — Lessons 9 and 10

Stealing (covetousness) — Lessons 9 and 10

Grief focused on self — Lessons 9, 10, 20 and 21

Eating problems (overeating; starving self, called "anorexia;" or binging on food and purging self, called "bulimia") — Lessons 9, 10, 20, and 21

Lust — Lessons 9, 10, 20-21

Stewardship problems (body, time, material goods, abilities) — Lesson 10

Anger — Lesson 11

Bitterness — Lesson 11

Unforgiveness — Lesson 12

Reconciliation problems — Lessons 12 and 13

Relationship problems (marriage, relative, acquaintances, etc.) — Lessons 12-17, 20 and 21

Communication, sinful (lying, slander, arguing, cursing) — Lesson 13

Marriage problems — Lessons 14 and 15

Parent-child problems — Lessons 16 and 17

Depression (despair, lack of fulfillment of responsibilities, total inactivity) — Lesson 18

Fear (including "panic attacks") — Lesson 19

Worry (anxiety) — Lesson 19

Drug abuse — Lessons 20 and 21

Drunkenness — Lessons 20 and 21

Gambling — Lessons 20 and 21

Satanic influences — Lessons 20 and 21

Sexual sins (adultery, fornication, homosexuality, pornography) — Lessons 20 and 21

Sample Worksheet 1: Description of the Problem

Ongoing problem area:

Anger and bitterness toward my co-worker

This portion should be the identification of the ongoing difficulty that is of greatest hindrance to your walk with God *(Hebrews 12:1-2).*

Short description of the problem:

I have a very bad relationship with my co-worker at the office. We argue about almost everything. He criticizes my work all the time. He blames me for mistakes that I don't make and lies to the boss about me. I get so bitter that I can't concentrate on my work, and the situation gets worse. I am about to lose my job because of our arguments over responsibilities of projects that our boss has assigned. My co-worker takes the easy jobs and leaves the hard ones for me. I would like to quit, but I need the money. So I just get more angry and bitter.

NOTE: In order to make this description more accurate, please read the explanation for how to complete a list of specific failures (Pages 15-17). You will see an evaluation of this sample worksheet on Page 18.

Lists of Specific Failures to Live Biblically

Complete *Worksheet 2*. A blank worksheet is located on Page 41.

In order to determine how God intends for you to change, you must first describe clearly *what* needs to be changed in your life. This worksheet helps you learn to judge yourself biblically.

On *Worksheet 2*, list your unbiblical deeds related to the problem area you selected. For some problem areas, the unbiblical deeds may involve offenses to specific people. For others, it may involve sins only against God. Keep in mind that offenses against others are also sins against God.

Once you have worked through the plan with one person, you may find that there are others you have sinned against. You will need to use a separate sheet for each person you have offended in order to avoid confusion.

Keep in mind that you should list only your own failures, not another person's *(Matthew 7:5)*. God tells us to concentrate on our own sins first. Otherwise, we cannot even understand the other person's life accurately. We do not see clearly how to deal with our brother's sins until we have first dealt with our own sins.

A. Under the "**List of speech and actions related to the ongoing problem area**" section, write your sinful speech and actions (not your thoughts) committed against the person you have identified.

 NOTE: If the problem involves sins only against the Lord, you would only fill out the bottom of the worksheet.

B. Under the "**List of thoughts, speech, and actions against the Lord alone**" section, list your unbiblical thoughts, speech, and actions committed only before the Lord. These are failures that do not involve other people (for example, sinful thoughts — even about others, or sins of grumbling, shouting, or using curse words when you are alone, stomping your feet or slamming doors while no one else is around, not spending time in daily devotions, lusting, drug abuse when you are alone, etc.).

 NOTE: Thoughts are not included in the first list since sinful thoughts are only committed against the Lord. However, if thoughts are communicated to the one offended, through speech or actions, these must be added to the first list.

C. In making your list, be sure it meets the following criteria:

 1. **Be specific.** Write exactly how you demonstrated your failures in each situation.

 a. It is very important to be specific. Change takes place in specific ways, i.e., specific changes in thoughts, speech, and actions. Change does not take place in generalities. For example, you would not just say "I was angry." Rather, you would list the specific ways in which you have demonstrated your anger. List specific unbiblical thoughts (such as grumbling inside self, devising sarcastic responses, etc.), speech (including the tone and volume of your voice), and actions (including looks, gestures, etc.). These are the things you can change.

 b. Following are examples of the wrong and right ways to describe failures.

1) *Wrong description:* "I get *angry* with my co-worker often." This is too general. Change is demonstrated only by acting in specific ways.

2) *Correct description:* "I think about getting revenge" (thoughts); or "I speak loudly frequently to my co-worker with a harsh tone of voice" (speech); or "I glared at my co-worker, then stomped out of the room, slamming the door behind me" (actions).

c. When developing your specific list, you should take into account the following:

1) Do not include specific details about sinful thoughts that may present a stumbling block to you or others to whom you may need to show the list. It is enough to list the kinds of thoughts (e.g., grumbling, arguing, reviling). Keeping a written record of exact words can serve as a reminder to keep you thinking those sinful thoughts.

2) Do not list emotions (i.e., feelings) because God does not hold you responsible for how you feel; in addition, you cannot change your feelings by a direct act of your will. Feelings, in themselves, are not sinful, since nowhere in the Scriptures does God command you to change them.

3) It may at times be difficult for you to determine whether some activities are sinful, where the deed is not specifically named as sin in the Scriptures (e.g., modes of dress, certain items ingested, companions, activities, etc.). In these situations, ask yourself the following questions:

a) Is this profitable (in other words, does this contribute toward the development of godly traits or help to accomplish biblical responsibilities in my life or in the lives of others) *(I Corinthians 6:12, 10:23a)*?

b) Does this bring me under its power or am I controlled by it in any way *(I Corinthians 6:12)*?

c) Is this an area of spiritual weakness (a stumbling block) in my life *(Matthew 5:29-30, 18:8-9)*?

d) Could this lead another believer in Christ to stumble *(Romans 14:13; I Corinthians 8:9-13)*?

e) Does this edify (build up) others or, stated in another way, is this the biblically loving thing to do *(Romans 14:19; I Corinthians 10:23-24)*?

f) Does this glorify God *(Matthew 5:16; I Corinthians 10:31)*?

2. **Be thorough.** For each situation in which you know you failed to love biblically, it is important to consider thoughts, speech, and actions. Remember that it is possible to sin in many ways in a very short period of time. For example, if you had an argument with another person, within seconds you might have:

a. Reviled and grumbled about the person in your mind (thoughts),

b. Shouted at the person, used a harsh tone of voice, called him/her tearing down names (speech),

c. Given hard looks, thrown objects, and slammed doors (actions).

3. **Do not shift blame.** When making your list, take care not to place blame on anyone else for your failures *(based on Ezekiel 18:20; Matthew 7:5)*. Do not write such statements as "I slammed the door in my wife's face when she yelled at me." Instead say, "I slammed the door in my wife's face." Regardless of what the other person did, it is not an excuse for your sins. It is important that you do not use the list of your own sins as a way of pointing blame at the other person.

4. **Do not minimize sin.** In listing your failures, take care not to minimize away your sin *(based on Proverbs 28:13; Ezekiel 18:20; I John 1:5-9)*. Do not write such statements as "I told a little lie, but I was tired and couldn't think of anything better to say." Instead say, "I lied."

The next page provides an evaluation of the *Sample Worksheet 1: Description of the Problem* from Page 14. Note the blameshfiting, etc. Then, notice that the sample of *Worksheet 2* (on Page 19) is specific and thorough, and does not shift blame nor minimize sin.

NOTE: It is important to repent and confess all sins to God as soon as you recognize them as sins (I John 1:8-10); however, before going to be reconciled with another human being, you must be careful to take proper precautions so that you do not place a stumbling block before the person you have offended. If you are not careful, even the way you approach reconciliation could be a stumbling block to them. It may be helpful to develop a biblical plan for change first. Putting the plan into effect is a practical way of demonstrating to the one you have offended how serious you are in your intention to change and not repeat the offense. A "Forgiveness/ Reconciliation" Plan is described later in these guidelines.

(GUIDELINES FOR COMPLETING THE VICTORY OVER FAILURES PLAN continue on Page 20.)

Evaluation — Sample Worksheet 1:
Description of the Problem

Ongoing problem area:

Anger and bitterness toward my co-worker

This portion should be the identification of the ongoing difficulty that is of greatest hindrance to your walk with God *(Hebrews 12:1-2).*

Short description of the problem: *Blameshifting; justifying own sin*

I have a very bad relationship with my co-worker at the office. We argue about almost everything. He criticizes my work all the time. He blames me for mistakes that I don't make and lies to the boss about me. I get so bitter that I can't concentrate on my work, and the situation gets worse. I am about to lose my job because of our arguments over responsibilities of projects that our boss has assigned. My co-worker takes the easy jobs and leaves the hard ones for me. I would like to quit, but I need the money. So I just get more angry and bitter.

Not thorough   *Not specific*   *Blameshifting*   *Not specific; not thorough*

© Biblical Counseling Foundation

Sample Worksheet 2:
Lists of Specific Failures to Live Biblically

List of speech and actions related to the ongoing problem area:

1. Often, I speak to my co-worker in an angry way. I speak with a loud voice using condemning and accusing words.

2. I argue with my co-worker every day, and I often speak with a harsh tone of voice and say tearing down words to my co-worker.

3. I gossip about my co-worker to others in the office saying tearing down things, and I complain to my family members about my situation at work.

List of thoughts, speech, and actions against the Lord alone:

1. I have bitter, vengeful thoughts toward my co-worker, not only at the office, but in many other places.

2. When I pray, I grumble and complain to the Lord about my situation at work.

3. When on my way home from work, I think and speak to myself about sharp, tearing down statements I might make to my co-worker.

"Put-offs" and "Put-ons"

Complete *Worksheet 3*. A blank worksheet is located on Page 42.

This foundational worksheet is designed to help you learn how to find the biblical "put-offs" and "put-ons" associated with your personal problem. To complete *Worksheet 3*, follow the steps below:

A.   At the top of your worksheet in the space titled, "Ongoing problem area," copy what you wrote as your ongoing problem area from your ***Worksheet 1: Description of the Problem***, which you completed earlier.

B.   Complete the first column of ***Worksheet 3*** by copying each item from your ***Worksheet 2: Lists of Specific Failures to Live Biblically*** which you have completed. ***NOTE:*** *Be sure to leave a little empty space between each failure in the first column so that you can relate the corresponding entries in the second and third columns to the appropriate failure.*

NOTE: The reason you need to wait until now to copy the information into the first column is to make sure your list conforms to all the guidelines for completing Worksheet 2. This will save you from starting Worksheet 3 repeatedly.

C.   Complete the second and third columns of ***Worksheet 3***.

1.   Search the Scriptures for the appropriate biblical words to write in the second and third columns. The purpose of the second and third columns is to describe the failures listed in the first column using biblical terms. The "put-off" (in the second column) is the biblical term given to the failure (listed in the first column); the "put-on" (in the third column) is the phrase in the Scriptures that corresponds to the "put-off" in the second column.

It may be helpful to use a concordance. Other sources, such as the *Biblical Principles for Discipleship/Counseling* booklet or the ***Self-Confrontation*** manual, may also be helpful to find the related passages.

You may also find key passages of Scripture listed in **WHERE TO FIND BIBLICAL REFERENCES TO SPECIFIC PROBLEM AREAS** in this booklet on Page 13 to be helpful.

2.   List the "put-offs" along with the associated Scripture references in the second column, and list the "put-ons" along with the associated Scripture references in the third column. To make sure that you base each entry in the second and third columns only on Scripture passages, it is important that you place the Scripture reference next to each "put-off" and "put-on."

Generally, each pair of "put-offs" and "put-ons" is in the same Scripture passage. You may find a "put-off" without a related "put-on" in the same passage, such as *"You shall not bear false witness" (Exodus 20:16)*. In this case, find another passage that contains the same "put-off" along with an associated "put-on" such as *Ephesians 4:25* that designates a "put-on" of "speaking truth." You also may find "put-ons" without related "put-offs." Again, search for other passages where the "put-ons" and "put-offs" correspond to one another.

(GUIDELINES FOR COMPLETING THE VICTORY OVER FAILURES PLAN continue on Page 23.)

Sample Worksheet 3: "Put-offs" and "Put-ons"

Ongoing problem area *Anger and bitterness toward my co-worker* Page 1 of 2

(1) My specific unbiblical deeds (thoughts, speech, and actions) *(based on Matthew 7:1-5; 15:18)*	(2) "Put-off" and biblical reference(s) *(Ephesians 4:22; Colossians 3:5-9)*	(3) "Put-on" and biblical reference(s) *(Ephesians 4:24; Colossians 3:10-17)*
Often, I speak to my co-worker in an angry way. I speak with a loud voice using condemning and accusing words.	Bitterness, wrath, anger, clamor, malice (Ephesians 4:31)	Kindness, tender-heartedness, and forgiveness (Ephesians 4:32)
	Anger (James 1:19)	Quick to hear, slow to speak, slow to anger (James 1:19)
	Unwholesome words (Ephesians 4:29)	Words good for edification according to the need of the moment that they may give grace to those who hear (Ephesians 4:29)
	Harsh words (Proverbs 15:1)	Gentle words (Proverbs 15:1)
	Hot temper (Proverbs 15:18)	Slow to anger (patience) (Proverbs 15:18)
	Evil speech (Proverbs 15:28)	Pondering before answering (Proverbs 15:28)
I argue with my co-worker every day, and I often speak with a harsh tone of voice and say tearing down words to my co-worker.	Bitterness, wrath, anger, clamor, malice (Ephesians 4:31)	Kindness, tender-heartedness, and forgiveness (Ephesians 4:32)
	Anger (James 1:19)	Quick to hear, slow to speak, slow to anger (James 1:19)
	Unwholesome words (Ephesians 4:29)	Words good for edification according to the need of the moment that they may give grace to those who hear (Ephesians 4:29)
	Harsh words (Proverbs 15:1)	Gentle words (Proverbs 15:1)
	Hot temper (Proverbs 15:18)	Slow to anger (patience) (Proverbs 15:18)
	Evil speech (Proverbs 15:28)	Pondering before answering (Proverbs 15:28)
	Quarrels (arguments) (II Timothy 2:23-24)	Kindness, patience, gentleness (II Timothy 2:24-25)

Sample Worksheet 3: "Put-offs" and "Put-ons"

Ongoing problem area *Anger and bitterness toward my co-worker* Page 2 of 2

(1) My specific unbiblical deeds (thoughts, speech, and actions) *(based on Matthew 7:1-5; 15:18)*	(2) "Put-off" and biblical reference(s) *(Ephesians 4:22; Colossians 3:5-9)*	(3) "Put-on" and biblical reference(s) *(Ephesians 4:24; Colossians 3:10-17)*
I gossip about my co-worker to others in the office saying tearing down things, and I complain to my family members about my situation at work.	*Talebearing (gossip) (Proverbs 11:13)* *Unwholesome words (Ephesians 4:29* *Evil speech (Proverbs 15:28)*	*Concealing a matter (keeping a secret) (Proverbs 11:13)* *Words good for edification according to the need of the moment that they may give grace to those who hear (Ephesians 4:29)* *Pondering before answering (Proverbs 15:28)*
I have bitter, vengeful thoughts toward my co-worker, not only at the office, but in many other places.	*Bitterness, wrath, anger, clamor, malice (Ephesians 4:31)*	*Kindness, tender-heartedness, and forgiveness (Ephesians 4:32)*
When I pray, I grumble and complain to the Lord about my situation at work.	*Grumbling and disputing (Philippians 2:14)*	*Holding fast the Word of God and rejoicing (Philippians 2:16, 18)*
When on my way home from work, I think and speak to myself about sharp, tearing down statements I might make to my co-worker.	*Unwholesome words (Ephesians 4:29)*	*Words good for edification according to the need of the moment that they may give grace to those who hear (Ephesians 4:29)*

© Biblical Counseling Foundation

Upon completion of *Worksheet 3: "Put-offs" and "Put-ons,"* you may need to develop up to three kinds of plans in parallel with one another. They are, the *"Daily Practices" Plan*, the *"Overcoming Temptations" Plan*, and the *"Forgiveness/Reconciliation" Plan*.

The purpose of the *"Daily Practices" Plan* is to help you put off a particular ongoing pattern of unrighteous behavior and to put on the appropriate biblical pattern of righteous deeds instead. It includes changes that must be made throughout the day.

The purpose of the *"Overcoming Temptations" Plan* is to help you to respond in a godly manner to situations where you have been tempted and have fallen repeatedly. It is for you to use only at the time the temptation occurs, but it is prepared in advance of the temptation so that you will be better prepared to deal with the temptation when it occurs.

The purpose of the *"Forgiveness/Reconciliation" Plan* is to help you deal with relationships that are not reconciled.

Development of each of these plans is described next.

(GUIDELINES FOR COMPLETING THE VICTORY OVER FAILURES PLAN continue on Page 24.)

"Daily Practices" Plan

Complete *Worksheet 4.* A blank worksheet is located on Pages 43-44.

Remember, the purpose of the *"Daily Practices" Plan* is to help you put off a particular ongoing pattern of unrighteous behavior and to put on the appropriate biblical pattern of righteous deeds instead. It includes changes that must be made throughout the day.

NOTE: You do not need to develop a separate plan for each person against whom you have sinned, as long as your pattern of sin is the same as on your lists of sins against the others.

A. Complete the two items in the top portion of the page (based on what you entered into *Worksheet 3: "Put-offs"* and *"Put-ons"*).

    1. Under "**Sin pattern that I need to change**," list the "put-offs" from the second column of *Worksheet 3* that relate to the pattern causing the greatest hindrance to victory in your walk with God. Remember, even though you list only one major pattern (such as anger) for the plan, you also need to write down the "put-offs" that demonstrate the pattern you list (such as bitterness, wrath, clamor, malice, unwholesome words, harsh words, etc.). *NOTE: Later, you may need to make additional plans for the other "put-off" patterns (such as worry or fear).*

    2. Under "**Righteous pattern to be established**," list the "put-ons" from the third column of *Worksheet 3* that relate to the "put-offs" you selected from the second column of *Worksheet 3*.

B. Complete the section titled, "**My plan to live righteously**." In this section, specify what you will do to practice the righteous pattern starting with when you awaken in the morning and proceeding through the entire day. Since the basic problem is habitual, it reveals itself in many ways throughout each day.

*NOTE: A very important portion of this section is a detailed description of your plans for daily devotions and Scripture memory. Devotions (time spent each day in prayer, study of God's Word, and biblical self evaluation) and Scripture memory are vital to your spiritual development. Daily devotions should be times that help you learn to be devoted to the Lord. Your relationship with God is more important than any other relationship, and you can depend upon Him to guide you in every way. (The biblical basis for daily devotions and Scripture memory is provided in the **Self-Confrontation** manual, Pages 38-40.)*

It is important to recognize that devotional time spent in God's Word and memorizing God's Word should directly relate to the very areas in your life where God has your attention.

It is best to memorize at times other than during your devotional time. This can be done in combination with your daily devotions. Memorizing a verse that relates to your devotional times will help you keep your mind focused on God's Word throughout the day. The best way to do this is to write the verse down on a card that you can put in your pocket. Then, take advantage of free moments during the day to review memory verses. You will be making wise use of the empty times, which are when temptations often arise due to undisciplined thinking.

C. See the sample on Pages 26-27.

D.   Implement your plan. This will include:

1.   Conviction and sorrow to the point of repentance *(II Corinthians 7:9)*. This is not an intellectual exercise. You must commit yourself to change from a pattern of disobedience to God (which demonstrates your lack of love for Him) to a new pattern of godliness.

2.   Self-control and discipline. Old habits are difficult to put off, and putting on new habits often feels unnatural initially.

3.   Acknowledging and repenting when you fail. This involves confession of your sins, placing yourself back under the control of the Holy Spirit, changing your plan, if appropriate, and starting again to implement your plan.

(GUIDELINES FOR COMPLETING THE VICTORY OVER FAILURES PLAN continue on Page 28.)

Sample Worksheet 4: "Daily Practices" Plan

My plan not to repeat this sin and, instead, to respond biblically
(James 1:22-25)

Page __1__ of __2__

Sin pattern that I need to change *(as seen from the second column of Worksheet 3):*

ANGER: *bitterness, wrath, clamor, malice, unwholesome words, harsh words, hot temper, evil speech, quarrelling, tale bearing (gossiping), grumbling, disputing*

Righteous pattern to be established *(as seen from the third column of Worksheet 3):* *Kindness, tender-heartedness, forgiveness, quick to hear, slow to speak, slow to anger, edifying words that give grace to my co-worker according to the need of the moment, gentle words, patience, pondering before answering, concealing a matter (keeping a secret), holding fast the Word of God, rejoicing*

My plan to live righteously:

A. *When rising from bed:*

    1. Thank the Lord for His grace, mercy, and comfort, and express my desire to please Him today.

    2. Thank God for the privilege of ministering to my co-worker and ask the Lord for guidance throughout the day.

    3. Ask the Lord to reveal to me, as I go through the day, areas of my conduct that are sinful and in need of change.

B. *During morning devotions:*

    1. In my study of God's Word:

        a. Using a concordance, keep listing additional Scripture verses relating to kindness, tender-heartedness, forgiveness, quick to hear, slow to speak, slow to anger, edifying words that give grace to my co-worker according to the need of the moment, gentle words, patience, pondering before answering, concealing a matter (keeping a secret), holding fast the Word of God, rejoicing. Concentrate especially on the verses that show me practical changes to make. Then, incorporate into this plan what I should apply to my life in relationship with my co-worker based on key verses.

        b. On my list of verses I have looked up, put an asterisk by the verses I should memorize.

    2. In my prayer time:

Sample Worksheet 4: "Daily Practices" Plan (Continued)

My plan not to repeat this sin and, instead, to respond biblically
(James 1:22-25)

My plan to live righteously *(continued)*:

    a. Pray about what I just studied and acknowledge my dependence upon the Lord for wisdom and strength to apply what I learned.

    b. Pray about the items on my prayer list that relate to my co-worker.

C. In my Scripture memory:

    1. Write down my Scripture memory verses on cards (from my list that relates to the problem).

    2. From my list, memorize at least one new Scripture verse a week and daily review the verses I have already learned.

    3. Carry the memory verse cards with me everywhere I go and review them often during the day, especially when I do not have responsibilities that fully occupy my mind.

D. During breakfast and preparation for work:

    1. Thank the Lord for the current situation regarding my co-worker.

    2. Ask the Lord to reveal to me the opportunities to show kindness and tenderheartedness toward my co-worker, especially as they show me areas of my life in which the Lord is maturing me.

    3. Ask for the Lord's help in dealing with my speech around others.

E. At work:

    1. When opportunities arise, show kindness and tenderheartedness toward my co-worker.

    2. Offer help to my co-worker when he is having difficulty accomplishing his tasks.

F. Evening devotions:

    1. Review the day's activities with the Lord.

    2. Review the next day's schedule and modify plans as appropriate.

"Overcoming Temptations" Plan

Complete *Worksheet 5.* A blank worksheet is located on Pages 45-46.

Remember that the purpose of the ***"Overcoming Temptations" Plan*** is to help you to respond in a godly manner to situations where you have been tempted and have fallen repeatedly. It is for you to use only at the time the temptation occurs, but it is prepared in advance of the temptation so that you will be better prepared to deal with the temptation when it occurs. The plan is then practiced at the time of the temptation.

A.   Complete the first section of the form titled, *Worksheet 5: "Overcoming Temptations" Plan.*

     1.   Under "**Type of situation in which I previously have been tempted and sinned**," describe the type of situation in which you have been repeatedly tempted and have not had victory (for example, suppose you have a weekly appointment at a location that requires you to travel through heavy traffic congestion. Suppose that in the past, you have demonstrated anger each week by reviling others, honking the horn impatiently, and forcing your way ahead of others). Normally, these types of temptations are associated with the major pattern written at the top of *Worksheet 4: "Daily Practices" Plan.*

     2.   Under "**Ways in which I sinned in this situation**," list the deeds from the first column of *Worksheet 3* that are associated with the type of situation you selected.

     3.   Under "**Righteous pattern to be established**," list the godly traits from the third column of *Worksheet 3* that you recognize need to be developed in your life.

B.   Complete the section titled, "**My plan to respond righteously the next time a similar temptation arises**." Write a specific plan that you will implement when you are tempted. To help you write a biblical plan, review the following guidance:

     1.   Deal with yourself first (*based on Matthew 7:5*).

         a.   Immediately ask for God's help (*I Thessalonians 5:17; Hebrews 4:15-16; James 1:5*).

         b.   Repent and confess to God any sinful thoughts you dwelt upon, even for a short period of time (*I John 1:9*).

         c.   Prayerfully review the biblical basis for hope in the situation.

             1)   Recite *Romans 8:28-29* and remind yourself that God causes all things to work together for good to those who love Him and are called according to His purpose. Pray accordingly.

             2)   Recite *I Corinthians 10:13* and remind yourself that God will not allow you to be tested or tempted beyond what you can bear. Pray accordingly.

             3)   Recite *James 1:2-4* and remind yourself that regardless of your feelings or circumstances, the situation is an opportunity for further spiritual maturity. Pray accordingly.

             4)   Recite *Philippians 4:13* and remind yourself that you can do all things through Christ who gives you strength. Pray accordingly.

             5)   Recite *Ezekiel 18:20* and remind yourself that you are not responsible for changing the hearts of others. Pray accordingly.

      d.   Thank God for the opportunity to serve Him and trust Him for wisdom to deal victoriously with the present situation, no matter how intense the temptation *(Ephesians 5:20; I Thessalonians 5:18)*.

      e.   Review the Scripture passages you have memorized that relate to the type of sin *(based on Psalm 119:9, 11)*. Include verses showing hope and giving practical guidance for how to change.

      f.   Write the specific thoughts, speech, and/or actions you will change based on the "put-offs" in the second column and the corresponding "put-ons" in the third column. Recognize that in most cases, thinking, speaking, and acting biblically are almost simultaneous, or within a very short time period.

2.   After dealing with yourself, when others are involved:

      a.   Listen to all sides first; make no prejudgments *(based on Proverbs 18:2, 17; James 1:19)*. Ask questions to get the facts and to gain understanding, not opinions *(based on Proverbs 13:10; 18:13, 15; II Timothy 2:23)*.

      b.   Formulate and state your evaluation carefully and slowly *(based on Proverbs 18:13; James 1:19)*, while

          1)   Judging yourself first *(Matthew 7:1-5)*.

          2)   Evaluating the observable deeds (speech and actions) of others, not their apparent motives *(based on I Samuel 16:7; Jeremiah 17:9-10)*.

      c.   Describe the situation and the biblical solution — speak at the appropriate time and only with words that edify *(Ephesians 4:29)*; speak the truth (i.e., biblical truth) in love with a gentle and humble spirit *(based on Proverbs 15:1; Ephesians 4:1-3, 15; I Peter 3:8-9)*.

      d.   Act in a way that demonstrates your love for the other person(s) who are present.

      e.   Then, deal with the deeds of others. Seek ways to edify others by serving them, not yourself, in this situation *(Romans 14:19; Ephesians 4:29; Philippians 2:3-4)*. Bless the people who are involved *(I Peter 3:8-9)*. Focus on restoration, not condemnation *(Galatians 6:1; II Timothy 2:24-26)* nor revenge *(Romans 12:19)*.

C.   See the sample *"Overcoming Temptations" Plan* on Pages 30-31.

D.   Implement your plan. This will include:

1.   Conviction and sorrow to the point of repentance *(II Corinthians 7:9)*. This is not an intellectual exercise. You must commit yourself to change from a pattern of disobedience to God (which demonstrates your lack of love for Him) to a new pattern of godliness.

2.   Self-control and discipline. Old habits are difficult to put off, and putting on new habits often feels unnatural initially.

3.   Acknowledging and repenting when you fail. This involves confession of your sins, placing yourself back under the control of the Holy Spirit, changing your plan, if appropriate, and starting again to implement your plan.

(GUIDELINES FOR COMPLETING THE VICTORY OVER FAILURES PLAN continue on Page 32.)

Sample Worksheet 5: "Overcoming Temptations" Plan

*My plan not to repeat this sin and, instead, to respond biblically
at the time of temptation (II Timothy 2:22)*

Page __1__ of __2__

Type of situation in which I previously have been tempted and sinned:
When my co-worker loads his work onto me

Ways in which I sinned in this situation *(as seen from the first column of* **Worksheet 3**):
I spoke in an angry way, with a loud, harsh tone of voice using condemning and accusing words. I quarrelled with my co-worker and said tearing down words to him.

Righteous pattern to be established *(as seen from the third column of* **Worksheet 3**):
Kindness, tender-heartedness, forgiveness, quick to hear, slow to speak, slow to anger, edifying words that give grace to the hearer according to the need of the moment, gentle words, patience, pondering before answering

---

My plan to respond righteously the next time a similar temptation arises:

A. *Deal with myself first. I will:*

   1. *Immediately, ask for God's help.*

   2. *Repent and confess to God any sinful thoughts that I purposely dwelt on.*

   3. *Review the biblical basis for hope in the situation.*

      a. *Recite Romans 8:28-29 and thank God for using this trial for my good.*

      b. *Recite I Corinthians 10:13 and thank God for giving me the strength to resist this temptation.*

      c. *Recite James 1:2-4 and thank God that this situation is an opportunity for further spiritual maturity.*

      d. *Recite Philippians 4:13 and remind myself that I can do all things through Christ Who gives me strength since my adequacy is from God and not from any natural inner strength.*

      e. *Recite Ezekiel 18:20 and thank God that it is not my responsibility to change my co-worker.*

   4. *Thank God for the opportunity to serve Him and trust Him for wisdom and grace to deal victoriously with the present situation.*

   5. *Review verses I have memorized that relate to anger.*

B. *Deal with my co-worker:*

   1. *Listen to him attentively and ask questions about the work to gain understanding.*

   2. *Repeat back what he said to make sure I understand and that he knows I've listened to him.*

Sample Worksheet 5: "Overcoming Temptation" Plan (Continued)

My plan not to repeat this sin and, instead, to respond biblically at the time of temptation (II Timothy 2:22)

My plan to respond righteously the next time a similar temptation arises (continued):

3. If the work is really his to do, and it is too much for him, tell him I will ask our supervisor how best to redistribute the responsibilities and help him accordingly so we can accomplish the work together.

4. If he needs to do the work himself, tell him that I am willing to help him as appropriate.

C. Return to my daily tasks rather than dwell on evil thoughts.

D. When temptations arise in my thought life about my co-worker:

1. Pray for my co-worker, and ask the Lord to remind me of ways to bless him.

2. Actively turn my thoughts to blessing.

3. If necessary, make a list (or add to the existing list) of ways to bless my co-worker, using Romans 12:9-21 as a guideline.

"Forgiveness/Reconciliation" Plan

Complete *Worksheets 6a* and *6b*. Blank worksheets are located on Pages 47, and 48.

In order to be reconciled with someone, first develop a *"Forgiveness/Reconciliation" Plan* (based on **Matthew 18:21-35**; **Luke 17:3-10**; *Romans 12:18*). **NOTE**: *Important Scripture passages to study are written in **boldface** print.*

The purpose of this plan is to help you deal with relationships that are not reconciled, with emphasis on long standing broken relationships or ones in which there is a serious rift. In these cases, you will want to be especially prepared to be reconciled in a godly way by writing out what you will do. This will help you to think through how to be reconciled with that other person in a biblical manner.

Depending on your situation, you may need to include in the plan:

- Steps you will take to *demonstrate* forgiveness. Jesus said in **Mark 11:25** that we need to forgive and demonstrate forgiveness whether or not the offender requests forgiveness. Remember that your forgiveness of another is much bigger than just your relationship with the other person. Your forgiveness of others is essential to unbroken fellowship with your heavenly Father (*Matthew 6:12-15*). *Worksheet 6a: My Plan for Demonstrating Forgiveness* will help you develop this part of your plan.

- Steps you will take and the words you will use for *asking* forgiveness. *Worksheet 6b: My Plan for Asking Forgiveness* will help you develop this part of your plan.

To complete your *"Forgiveness/Reconciliation" Plan*, follow the steps below:

A. Complete *Worksheet 6a: My Plan for Demonstrating Forgiveness*.

1. Complete the first section of *Worksheet 6a: My Plan for Demonstrating Forgiveness* by listing the name of the person you need to forgive, and the offenses you need to forgive at the top of the page. (See the sample on Page 34.)

2. Complete the section titled "**Steps I will take:**" The sub-points in this section are aspects of biblical forgiveness presented in Lesson 12 of the *Self-Confrontation* manual.

As God in Christ has forgiven us (*Ephesians 4:32*; *Colossians 3:13*), we are:

a. Not to dwell on the offense suffered (*based on* **Isaiah 38:17**). We are not to keep account of any wrongs suffered (*I Corinthians 13:5*). We should not dwell on the evil done to us, but consider how to give a blessing instead (*based on I Peter 3:9*).

b. Not to remind the forgiven person of his sin in an accusing manner (*based on* **Hebrews 10:17**). There may be times when you will need to remind the person of his sin even after you have forgiven him. For example, if that individual develops a pattern of repeating the sin, you are to exhort that person to repent. But the difference now is that you are to make your appeal in a spirit of gentleness, not in an accusing manner (*based on Galatians 6:1*).

c.   Not to gossip to others about the offense suffered *(II Corinthians 12:20).* You may need to bring up someone's sins to others but only with the focus on helping the person who is sinning, not to tear him down. For example, parents often need to discuss the sins of their children between themselves first in order to determine how to discipline them.

d.   To remove all reminders of the offense that are stumbling blocks, as much as it is physically possible *(based on Matthew 18:7-9).*

e.   To restore fellowship with the forgiven person, as far as is biblically possible *(based on **Romans 12:18**; II Corinthians 2:6-8).* Even if the person has not come to ask forgiveness, you must still forgive and stand ready to grant forgiveness if asked.

NOTE: *None of the steps listed above is based on how a person feels. Forgiveness is an act of the will. We are to discipline ourselves to obey God, not act according to our feelings.*

Also, when you forgive someone, it is important to distinguish between forgiveness and the release of consequences. Forgiveness is an act of obedience to the Lord (Luke 17:3-10) that gives the offender what he needs rather than what he deserves (based on Psalm 103:10; Romans 5:8). Consequences, on the other hand, are meant to encourage the offender to change his way (based on Psalm 119:67, 71). For example, a parent may have to allow his child to suffer the consequences of his sin even though the parent has already forgiven the child.

(See the sample on Page 34.)

(GUIDELINES FOR COMPLETING THE VICTORY OVER FAILURES PLAN continue on Page 35.)

Sample Worksheet 6a:
My Plan for Demonstrating Forgiveness

Name of person I need to forgive::

My co-worker

Offenses I need to forgive:

His yelling at me

His saying unwholesome words to me

Steps I will take:

A.   Not to dwell on the offense suffered:

When temptations to dwell on an offense come, I will concentrate on how to bless my co-worker; and how I can resolve the difficulties between us, rather than focus only on the differences.

B.   Not to remind the forgiven person of his sin in an accusing manner:

If I must remind my co-worker of a sin that I have forgiven, I will first take any log out of my own eye, formulate how I can show him how to overcome the sinful pattern, find out if he is open to my help, and then, lovingly and gently provide counsel.

C.   Not to gossip to others about the offense suffered:

I will not speak to anyone else about my co-worker's past sins. I will concentrate on only saying building up things about him.

D.   To remove all reminders of the offense that are stumbling blocks:

If applicable

E.   To restore fellowship with the forgiven person, as far as is biblically possible:

I will honor and respect my co-worker. I will remove stumbling blocks from him by not glaring at him, not speaking loudly with unwholesome words, and not using a harsh tone of voice. I will come alongside and help him, and I will look for opportunities to bless him.

B.   Complete *Worksheet 6b: My Plan for Asking Forgiveness.*

1.   Complete the first section of *Worksheet 6b: My Plan for Asking Forgiveness* by:

a.   Listing the name of the person of whom you need to ask forgiveness under "**Person of whom I need to ask forgiveness.**"

b.   Listing the offenses for which you need to ask forgiveness under "**Offenses for which I need to ask forgiveness.**"

(See the sample on Page 37.)

2.   Complete the second section of *6b: My Plan for Asking Forgiveness.* When you have sinned against another, you need to reconcile with that person. Even when you are in prayer and remember that your brother has something against you, your first priority is to be reconciled with that person as quickly as possible *(Matthew 5:23-24)*. This is part of preserving the unity of the Spirit *(Ephesians 4:3)*. If you do not know for sure, but think it is possible that fellowship with that person may be broken, go anyway to determine whether you may have committed an offense unknowingly. *NOTE: You may be tempted to wait for a more convenient time. God says not to wait. However, you must be careful to take the proper steps or you could become a stumbling block to the other person.*

When reconciling, you should:

a.   Make restitution whenever appropriate *(based on Leviticus 5:15-18; 6:2-5; Numbers 5:5-8; Proverbs 6:30-31; Luke 19:8)*. Under "**A. Restitution I need to make to the person offended**" in *Worksheet 6b*, list how you plan to make restitution if appropriate.

b.   Demonstrate repentance *(Psalm 51:12-13; Matthew 3:8; Acts 26:20)* by writing and implementing a plan for change. Therefore, under "**B. Specific steps I will take to put off the old pattern of sin and put on the new righteous deeds (thoughts, speech, and actions),**" write your plan for change. Include in this section a description of the specific steps you are taking to put off the old pattern of sin and to put on the new pattern of righteousness based on your *"Daily Practices" Plan* and your *"Overcoming Temptations" Plan.*

c.   Ask forgiveness. Under "**C. Words I will use when asking forgiveness,**" write words to use when asking forgiveness. You should include:

1)   Admission and confession of sin against God and the offended person *(James 5:16; I John 1:9)*.

2)   An expression of repentance which includes:

a)   An expression of sorrow for the sin *(Psalm 51:16-17; II Corinthians 7:9-10; James 4:8-10),*

b)   An intention not to repeat the sin,

c)   The specific steps you are taking to change.

(See the sample on Page 37.)

C.   Prepare yourself for various responses from the other person and plan how to respond biblically. Make sure you communicate your serious intent to change and to be reconciled. Write out what you would do and say if the other person replies:

---

1. "Oh, that's all right" or "Don't worry about it" or "People do that all the time." You might say, "Even though what I did may not have bothered you, I realize that my actions toward you were unloving, contrary to Scripture, and not pleasing to God. Since my desire is to be a Christlike person and to love you God's way, I ask for your forgiveness."

2. "I won't forgive you." You might respond with, "I am deeply sorry that I have so offended you, and greatly regret my unloving actions. I have made a commitment to the Lord to bless you, and will be praying that our relationship can soon be restored."

3. "I'll forgive you but I won't forget it." You might say, "I sincerely regret being part of such a painful memory in your life. My behavior was very unloving and I am committing to you and to the Lord to act in a biblically loving way toward you in the future. I appreciate that you are willing to forgive me."

   As you work on your relationship with the person, you may be privileged to show the person what the Bible says about forgiveness. God does not say the person has to forget the offense. God says that the person simply must not bring it up in an accusing manner in the future. The person may never forget the painful memory, but the person can still forgive.

D. After completing your plan, go in the following manner to each individual against whom you have sinned:

1. At a time when the other person is not busy or occupied, ask if you may talk with him about your failure in the relationship. If that time is not appropriate for the other person, ask if you may set an appropriate time to meet with him and confess the failures that you have committed against him (based on Proverbs 25:11; Philippians 2:4).

2. When you meet with the one you sinned against, confess your sin (James 5:16) and ask for forgiveness according to your plan.

Conclusion

Diligent application of these guidelines in developing and applying a plan for victory over one problem in your life has enormous rewards. You need not fear that some future situation might overwhelm you. Using the same procedures, you can have confidence that you can face, deal with, and endure any difficult situation that may confront you in the future.

Also, you should have confidence that you can guide others including your family members and those you are discipling to victory over any failures they might experience.

Sample Worksheet 6b: My Plan for Asking Forgiveness

Person of whom I need to ask forgiveness:
My co-worker

Offenses for which I need to ask forgiveness:
I spoke to my co-worker in an angry way, with a loud voice using condemning and accusing words. I argued with him and spoke with a harsh tone of voice, and said tearing down words to him. I gossiped about my co-worker to others in the office saying tearing down things.

Steps I will take and words I will use when asking forgiveness:

A. Restitution I need to make to the person offended:
I must confess to each person to whom I gossiped, and establish a plan to avoid future gossip and only speak the truth in love regarding my co-worker.

B. Specific steps I will take to put off the old pattern of sin and put on the new righteous deeds (thoughts, speech, and actions):
Pray for my co-worker every day, whenever he comes to mind, and when situations come up that involve us both.

Speak only those things that give honor and respect to him; respond with a soft and gentle voice and only after carefully thinking about how to answer.

C. Words I will use when asking forgiveness:
I recognize that I have sinned against the Lord and you by speaking to you in an angry way, with a loud voice using condemning and accusing words. I further sinned by arguing with you and speaking with a harsh tone of voice, and saying tearing down words. I also gossiped about you to others in the office saying tearing down things. I am sorry for having offended the Lord and you. It is my intention never again to repeat this offense against you. By God's grace I will change by speaking only those things that show honor and respect to you. I will respond to you with a soft and gentle voice and only after carefully thinking about how to answer. I will focus on helping you in whatever way I should. I would also appreciate your pointing out to me if I sin in this way again. I have asked the Lord to forgive me, and I want you to know that I desire your forgiveness as well. Will you please forgive me?

VICTORY OVER FAILURES PLAN
BLANK WORKSHEETS

Worksheet 1: Description of the Problem

Ongoing problem area:

_____

_____

This portion should be the identification of the ongoing difficulty that is of greatest hindrance to your walk with God *(Hebrews 12:1-2).*

Short description of the problem:

_____
_____
_____
_____
_____
_____
_____
_____
_____
_____
_____
_____
_____
_____
_____
_____
_____
_____
_____
_____
_____
_____
_____
_____
_____

Worksheet 2:
Lists of Specific Failures to Live Biblically

List of speech and actions related to the ongoing problem area:

_____
_____
_____
_____
_____
_____
_____
_____
_____
_____
_____
_____
_____
_____
_____
_____
_____

List of thoughts, speech, and actions against the Lord alone:

_____
_____
_____
_____
_____
_____
_____
_____
_____
_____
_____
_____
_____

Worksheet 3: "Put-offs" and "Put-ons"

Ongoing problem area _____ Page _____ of_____

(1) My specific unbiblical deeds (thoughts, speech, and actions) *(based on Matthew 7:1-5; 15:18)*	(2) "Put-off" and biblical reference(s) *(Ephesians 4:22; Colossians 3:5-9)*	(3) "Put-on" and biblical reference(s) *(Ephesians 4:24; Colossians 3:10-17)*

© Biblical Counseling Foundation

Permission is granted to reproduce this form for personal or ministry use.

Worksheet 4: "Daily Practices" Plan

My plan not to repeat this sin and, instead, to respond biblically
(James 1:22-25)

Page _____ of _____

Sin pattern that I need to change *(as seen from the second column of Worksheet 3):*

_____

_____

Righteous pattern to be established *(as seen from the third column of Worksheet 3):*

_____

_____

_____

_____

My plan to live righteously:

_____

_____

_____

_____

_____

_____

_____

_____

_____

_____

_____

_____

_____

_____

_____

_____

_____

_____

_____

_____

_____

Worksheet 4: "Daily Practices" Plan (Continued)

My plan not to repeat this sin and, instead, to respond biblically
(James 1:22-25)

Page _____ of _____

My plan to live righteously *(continued):*

_____
_____
_____
_____
_____
_____
_____
_____
_____
_____
_____
_____
_____
_____
_____
_____
_____
_____
_____
_____
_____
_____
_____
_____
_____
_____
_____
_____
_____
_____
_____

Worksheet 5: "Overcoming Temptations" Plan

*My plan not to repeat this sin and, instead, to respond biblically
at the time of temptation (II Timothy 2:22)*

Page _____ of _____

Type of situation in which I previously have been tempted and sinned:

_____

Ways in which I sinned in this situation *(as seen from the first column of **Worksheet** 3):*

_____

_____

_____

Righteous pattern to be established *(as seen from the third column of **Worksheet** 3):*

_____

_____

My plan to respond righteously the next time a similar temptation arises:

_____

_____

_____

_____

_____

_____

_____

_____

_____

_____

_____

_____

_____

_____

_____

_____

_____

_____

_____

_____

Worksheet 5: "Overcoming Temptations" Plan (Continued)

My plan not to repeat this sin and, instead, to respond biblically
at the time of temptation (II Timothy 2:22)

Page _____ of _____

My plan to respond righteously the next time a similar temptation arises (continued):

_____
_____
_____
_____
_____
_____
_____
_____
_____
_____
_____
_____
_____
_____
_____
_____
_____
_____
_____
_____
_____
_____
_____
_____
_____
_____
_____
_____
_____
_____
_____
_____
_____
_____
_____

Worksheet 6a:
My Plan for Demonstrating Forgiveness

Name of person I need to forgive::

_____

Offenses I need to forgive:

_____

_____

_____

Steps I will take:

A.   Not to dwell on the offense suffered:

_____

_____

_____

B.   Not to remind the forgiven person of his sin in an accusing manner:

_____

_____

_____

_____

C.   Not to gossip to others about the offense suffered:

_____

_____

_____

_____

D.   To remove all reminders of the offense that are stumbling blocks:

_____

_____

_____

E.   To restore fellowship with the forgiven person, as far as is biblically possible:

_____

_____

_____

Worksheet 6b: My Plan for Asking Forgiveness

Person of whom I need to ask forgiveness:

_____

Offenses for which I need to ask forgiveness:

_____

_____

_____

_____

Steps I will take and words I will use when asking forgiveness:

A.   Restitution I need to make to the person offended:

_____

_____

B.   Specific steps I will take to put off the old pattern of sin and put on the new righteous deeds (thoughts, speech, and actions):

_____

_____

_____

_____

_____

C.   Words I will use when asking forgiveness:

_____

_____

_____

_____

_____

_____

_____

_____

_____

_____

INITIATING BIBLICAL RECONCILIATION
(BY CONDUCTING A FAMILY MEETING)

> Individuals and families must have a plan, based on biblical principles, to resolve problems and failures in communication. If you will obey God's Word in biblical communication and problem solving, you will be lifted up. However, if you do not obey God's Word, whether through ignorance or willful disobedience, you invite disaster *(based on Genesis 4:7; Proverbs 14:12; 16:20; Colossians 3:25; Hebrews 12:5-6; James 1:25, 4:17).*

I. **Overall purposes for family meetings**

   A. To provide people (individuals, couples, families, roommates, co-workers, etc.) a structured environment to communicate biblically *(based on Ephesians 4:15-32);*

   B. To help restore poor relationships and to initiate a pattern of forgiveness and reconciliation between individuals *(based on Matthew 5:23-24; Mark 11:25-26; Romans 12:14, 18; 14:13, 19; Ephesians 4:32);*

   C. To provide a method for finding biblical solutions to disagreements and to maintain unity in relationships *(based on Psalm 133:1; I Corinthians 1:10; Ephesians 4:1-3; Philippians 2:1-4; James 1:5);* and

   D. To develop the habit of making daily decisions in a biblical fashion (for example: scheduling time, making financial decisions, determining personal or family responsibilities, developing biblical goals, etc.) *(based on Proverbs 16:1, 9; Ephesians 5:15-17).*

II. **Prerequisites to conducting the first family meeting**

   A. Judge yourself first *(based on Matthew 7:1-5; I Corinthians 11:31).* Complete the **VICTORY OVER FAILURES PLAN** (BCF Form 102) relating to the members who will be involved in the meetings.

   B. Ask the other individual(s) who are part of your family (or group) to work with you in developing a method for communicating lovingly with one another. Explain your commitment to build up all the others and to learn to speak with them in such a way that focuses on overcoming problems instead of attacking the participants *(based on Ephesians 4:15, 29, 31-32; Colossians 4:6; II Timothy 2:24-25).*

   As necessary, review **BIBLICAL COMMUNICATION** *(Self-Confrontation, Pages 225-227).*

   C. Demonstrate forgiveness of other meeting participants even if they have not asked for forgiveness.

Refer to **FORGIVENESS (FORGIVING OTHERS AS GOD HAS FORGIVEN YOU)** *(Self-Confrontation, Pages 196-198) and Worksheet 6a of the* **VICTORY OVER FAILURES PLAN: GUIDELINES AND WORKSHEETS** *(BCF Form 102).*

D. Thoroughly explain to each individual how to conduct a family meeting before beginning:

1. Review the purposes for having a meeting (see above, **I. Overall purposes for family meetings**).

2. Review the following biblical principles for conducting a family meeting:

    a. Base everything on God's Word, since Scripture is the authority for all faith and conduct *(Romans 15:4; II Timothy 3:16-17; Hebrews 4:12);*

    b. Be truthful *(Ephesians 4:15, 25);*

    c. Be loving and kind in your speech, avoiding talk that produces quarrels *(based on Proverbs 15:1; Ephesians 4:15; 5:4; Colossians 4:6; II Timothy 2:23-24);*

    d. Do not use unwholesome words but use only those words that edify (build up) others *(based on Romans 14:19; Ephesians 4:29);*

    e. Do not argue or be contentious *(II Timothy 2:23-24; Titus 3:9; James 4:1-2);*

    f. Work on changing yourself, not on changing others *(based on Ezekiel 18:20; Matthew 7:1-5);*

    g. Be forgiving *(Matthew 6:14-15; Ephesians 4:32; Colossians 3:12-13);* and

    h. Treat others at the meeting just as you desire to be treated *(Matthew 7:12).*

III. Procedures for the family meeting

A. One person is chosen to conduct the time together, and another is delegated to act as the recorder. In a marriage situation, the husband is to be the leader *(based on Ephesians 5:21-6:9; I Timothy 3:4-5).*

1. The meeting opens and closes with prayer *(based on Colossians 4:2; I Thessalonians 5:17; James 1:5).*

2. Since participants study the Bible during the meeting in order to discover God's will concerning questions and decisions, everyone is encouraged to bring a Bible. For those who do not bring one, have extras on the table for their use *(based on Joshua 1:8; Psalm 19:7-11; II Timothy 2:15, 3:16-17; Hebrews 4:12; II Peter 1:3-4).*

B. Select and agree on the time of day, length of each meeting, and number of times during the week to conduct the family meeting *(Ephesians 5:15-16).* The recommended meeting time is one hour or less to avoid fatigue and to encourage everyone to remain focused on the important matters *(based on Proverbs 10:19a; 15:23; 25:11-12).*

C. Select a place conducive to serious and effective communication, without interruption.

1. Choose a room with as few distractions as possible.

2. If available, select a table that provides adequate seating and is large enough for open Bibles and note taking. A table serves as a means for joining people together to meet purposefully.

3. Walking to the meeting table allows cooling of tempers *(based on Proverbs 14:17, 29; 15:28)*. When one is seated, it is also harder to walk away.

4. The meeting table will soon become a symbol of hope, as problems are faced and dealt with there on a regular basis and in a biblical manner.

D. Formulate a plan to deal with unbiblical behavior.

1. Select a silent signal (such as raising a hand or standing up) to indicate that someone's behavior is unbiblical in the opinion of one or more persons. A silent signal is best because it is less likely to incite anger *(based on Proverbs 15:1; Ecclesiastes 9:17; James 1:19)*.

2. If the one whose behavior is in question repents, confesses, and begins again to speak and act biblically, the meeting resumes. If not, biblical communication has ended and so has the meeting.

3. The meeting may resume at another time, either:

    a. That day, as soon as the person who has acted unbiblically recognizes and confesses his sin to the Lord *(I John 1:9)* and to others *(James 5:16)*; or

    b. At the next designated time for a meeting.

E. The initial meeting involves specific activities.

1. At the first meeting, read *Ephesians 4:17-32* and *I Corinthians 13:4-8a*.

2. If each person has not done so, take time to make as complete a list as possible of sinful words and actions committed against others at the meeting *(Matthew 7:1, 5)*. Each person then confesses his sinful speech and actions committed against those individuals *(based on James 5:16)*.

3. The wife (or the designated recorder) keeps a written record of the major points discussed at the meeting (suggestion: keep a separate column for each person's responses, which could be confession of one's own sins, an offer of help to another, quoting of a memory verse, etc.). At the conclusion of the meeting, the recorder reads aloud the decisions and commitments made by the group or individuals in the group. After the meeting record is read, each person is invited to suggest any changes that would help clarify any part of the written record. Appropriate written adjustments are then entered into the record.

    In later meetings, the family meeting record helps each person recall the results of earlier meetings. The record also serves as a reminder to pray about specific matters and to give thanks to the Lord for the changes He is making in the lives of meeting participants.

F. Be specific when confessing sins to one another *(Matthew 5:23-24; James 5:16)*.

1. The husband (or the designated leader) should be the first to confess his sins committed against others present, with the wife confessing next, then the children. (If the meeting participants are non-family members, the order of confessing sins should be decided by mutual agreement).

NOTE: Confessing sins at the meeting must be voluntary. No one should force another to confess his sins since convicting and prompting is the Holy Spirit's responsibility (John 14:26; 16:8). The willingness to deal with his own sins is each person's responsibility (Ezekiel 18:20). Since each person is individually responsible for his own sinful behavior (Deuteronomy 24:16), no blameshifting is to be allowed during the meeting (based on Genesis 3:12-13, 19; Romans 14:12).

2. After three or four productive meetings, any member may invite other members to remind him of sins that he may have overlooked *(based on Proverbs 27:6, 17; Matthew 7:1-5; Galatians 6:1-2; Ephesians 4:15-16).*

   a. It is especially important that all aspects of biblical love and Christ-honoring communication be maintained by those who are bringing up overlooked sins in another's life *(based on Romans 13:8-10; I Corinthians 13:4-8a; Ephesians 4:29; Colossians 4:6).*

   b. After being reminded of his overlooked sins, each person is provided an opportunity to confess only his own sinful deeds that he has committed against others *(based on Matthew 5:23-24; Mark 11:25-26).*

   To review how to confess your sins to those you have sinned against, refer to:

   Worksheet 6b of **VICTORY OVER FAILURES PLAN: GUIDELINES AND WORKSHEETS** *(BCF Form 102) and*

   RECONCILIATION (REMOVING ALL HINDRANCES TO UNITY AND PEACE) *(Self-Confrontation, Pages 199-201) under* **II. Confession.**

G. Be steadfast *(I Corinthians 15:58).*

   1. Remain faithful to develop Christ-honoring maturity *(based on Galatians 6:9; Ephesians 4:15-16; Hebrews 5:11-14).*

   2. Work to defeat the problem *(based on II Corinthians 7:11-12),* not the other person(s) *(Romans 12:18-19; 14:19).*

   3. When asked, the entire family (or group) participating in the meeting can help each person locate the biblical "put-offs" and "put-ons" listed in the Scriptures along with the biblical basis for a specific plan to change *(Galatians 6:1-2).* This will encourage thorough study of the Scriptures and will challenge growth among those participating in the meeting *(based on Proverbs 27:17; II Timothy 2:15; Hebrews 10:24).*

   4. Recognize that not all problems can be solved in just a few meetings. For multiple problems, develop an agenda and schedule your work together over a period of time *(Ephesians 5:15-16).*

H. After the pattern for reconciliation has begun among those at the meeting, the resolution of conflicts, the establishment of goals, and the process of making biblical decisions may continue. The ultimate objective is for the family meeting to be used to develop biblical communication with one another as a pattern of life.

MY PRESENT SCHEDULE

	MONDAY	TUESDAY	WEDNESDAY	THURSDAY	FRIDAY	SATURDAY	SUNDAY
6:00 a.m.							
7:00							
8:00							
9:00							
10:00							
11:00							
12:00 Noon							
1:00 p.m.							
2:00							
3:00							
4:00							
5:00							
6:00							
7:00							
8:00							
9:00							
10:00							
11:00							

Record activities and responsibilities that you have done this week (or in a typical week). Review GOD'S STANDARDS FOR YOU (Self-Confrontation, Page 405) under III. Incorporating God's standards into your life.

BCF Form 107

Permission is granted to reproduce this form for personal or ministry use.

MY PROPOSED BIBLICAL SCHEDULE (*Proverbs 16:9; Ephesians 5:15-16*)

	MONDAY	TUESDAY	WEDNESDAY	THURSDAY	FRIDAY	SATURDAY	SUNDAY
6:00 a.m.							
7:00							
8:00							
9:00							
10:00							
11:00							
12:00 Noon							
1:00 p.m.							
2:00							
3:00							
4:00							
5:00							
6:00							
7:00							
8:00							
9:00							
10:00							
11:00							

Schedule the above week in a biblical manner. Diligently maintain your schedule, remembering that God is sovereignly in control of any unforeseen events that may occur. Review GOD'S STANDARDS FOR YOU (Self-Confrontation, Page 405) under III. Incorporating God's standards into your life.

© Biblical Counseling Foundation

BIBLICAL PRACTICES

FOR FACING, DEALING WITH,

AND ENDURING PROBLEMS

Adapted from the

MASTER PLAN FOR THE

MINISTRY OF BIBLICAL DISCIPLESHIP/COUNSELING

**A Resource of the
Biblical Counseling Foundation**

B C F

HOW TO USE
THE BIBLICAL PRACTICES CHART

> The **BIBLICAL PRACTICES** chart is designed to help you face, deal with, and endure every trial and test as part of your progressive maturing in Jesus Christ.

I.   **Purposes of the BIBLICAL PRACTICES chart.**

    A.   The **BIBLICAL PRACTICES** chart has been prepared to assist you in evaluating problems according to biblical principles and constructing a personal but completely biblical plan for living that will lead to peace and joy in spite of all circumstances, conditions, or responses of others. The **BIBLICAL PRACTICES** chart will guide you in dealing with major hindrances to spiritual growth. When used in conjunction with the *Self-Confrontation* manual, the chart will supply the key biblical procedures contained in God's Word to help you face, deal with, and endure problems, be an overcomer, and enjoy abundant life in Christ Jesus.

    B.   Specifically, the **BIBLICAL PRACTICES** chart is designed to:

        1.   Increase your effectiveness in applying Scripture when dealing with problems.

        2.   Provide you with guidance in investigating, identifying, facing, dealing with, and enduring situations and problems in light of God's Word. Whether the problem seems simple or complicated, you can utilize the chart to evaluate how you think, speak, and act. The perceived problems (e.g., fear, depression, worry, anxiety, marital problems, anger, substance abuse) are usually only symptoms of deeper spiritual problems.

        3.   Direct you to specific biblical principles that encourage continuing spiritual growth as you begin to become a doer of the Word. In using the **BIBLICAL PRACTICES** chart, you will learn how to deal with your problems in a systematic manner and become a more effective doer of the Word.

    C.   The **BIBLICAL PRACTICES** chart focuses on biblical principles and, as such, is not meant to be used rigidly or legalistically. You should not assume that every item on the chart must be dealt with in the sequence given. Under the Holy Spirit's sovereign direction, you must deal with problems according to the demands of each situation in your life.

II. **Overview of the BIBLICAL PRACTICES chart.**

    A.   The **BIBLICAL PRACTICES** chart consists of three pages that describe specific areas of progressive spiritual growth in the life of a disciple of Christ, especially in relationship to facing dealing with, and enduring the trials and tests of life. Each successive page reflects increasing depth in faith and practice. The three pages are entitled and described as follows:

                     © Biblical Counseling Foundation

1. **The Foundation for Biblical Discipleship/Counseling**

    The first page of the **BIBLICAL PRACTICES** chart, containing, Boxes 1-8, focuses on establishing a basic foundation for facing, dealing with, and enduring all problems while growing as a disciple of the Lord Jesus Christ. Primary emphasis is on:

    a. Gathering information that will provide a biblical understanding of the problems,

    b. Developing initial hope and recognition of personal sins, and

    c. Dealing with your relationship with the Lord.

2. **Biblical Reconciliation with God and Man**

    The second page of the **BIBLICAL PRACTICES** chart, containing Boxes 9-14, describes how to establish a biblical structure for change. The primary tool, the **VICTORY OVER FAILURES PLAN**, is a biblically based tool that can help the you apply God's Word in the power of the Holy Spirit, so that you may overcome any difficulty of life with the full expectation of complete and lasting victory. It explains the specific steps necessary to develop biblical plans for living God's way beginning with helping you to identify a problem area in your life to work on. Part of the process involves putting off the old manner of life and putting on new, righteous practices in their place *(Ephesians 4:22-24)*. The **VICTORY OVER FAILURES PLAN** describes how to do that in very practical ways and gives you a format you can follow. Very important steps of change on this page are to forgive others, reconcile relationships, and respond biblically in the current situation.

3. **The Maturing Disciple of Jesus Christ**

    The third page of the **BIBLICAL PRACTICES** chart, containing Boxes 15-18, provides guidelines for practicing the plans established previously and persevering daily as a faithful servant of God. It describes the believer who is reordering his entire life to conform to what God commands and is beginning to minister to others, thus fulfilling the Great Commission to make disciples.

The Foundation for Biblical Discipleship

BIBLICAL PRACTICES FOR FACING AND DEALING WITH PROBLEMS — FIRST PAGE

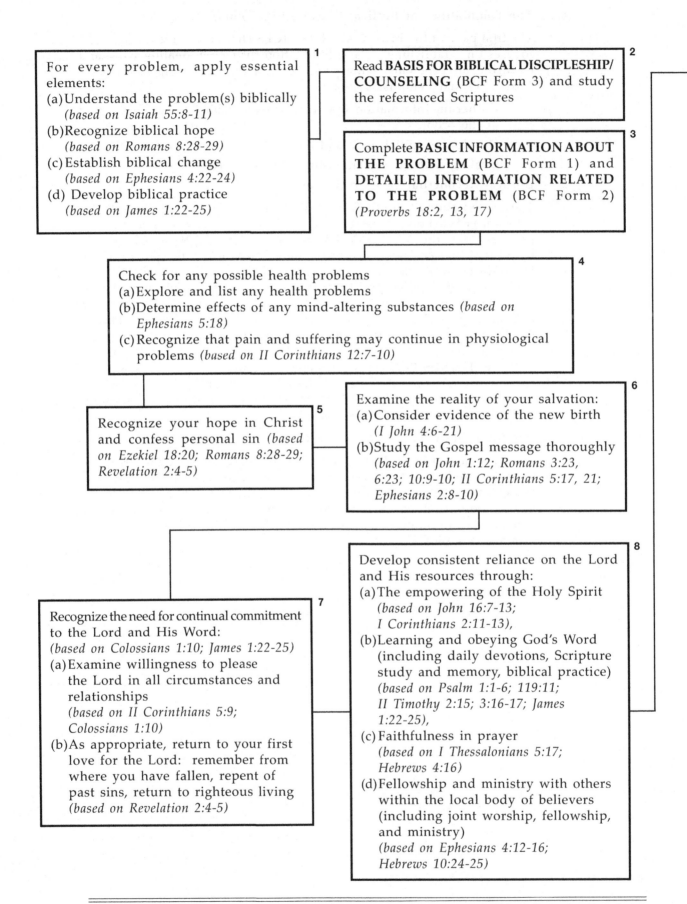

1 For every problem, apply essential elements:
(a) Understand the problem(s) biblically *(based on Isaiah 55:8-11)*
(b) Recognize biblical hope *(based on Romans 8:28-29)*
(c) Establish biblical change *(based on Ephesians 4:22-24)*
(d) Develop biblical practice *(based on James 1:22-25)*

2 Read **BASIS FOR BIBLICAL DISCIPLESHIP/ COUNSELING** (BCF Form 3) and study the referenced Scriptures

3 Complete **BASIC INFORMATION ABOUT THE PROBLEM** (BCF Form 1) and **DETAILED INFORMATION RELATED TO THE PROBLEM** (BCF Form 2) *(Proverbs 18:2, 13, 17)*

4 Check for any possible health problems
(a) Explore and list any health problems
(b) Determine effects of any mind-altering substances *(based on Ephesians 5:18)*
(c) Recognize that pain and suffering may continue in physiological problems *(based on II Corinthians 12:7-10)*

5 Recognize your hope in Christ and confess personal sin *(based on Ezekiel 18:20; Romans 8:28-29; Revelation 2:4-5)*

6 Examine the reality of your salvation:
(a) Consider evidence of the new birth *(I John 4:6-21)*
(b) Study the Gospel message thoroughly *(based on John 1:12; Romans 3:23, 6:23; 10:9-10; II Corinthians 5:17, 21; Ephesians 2:8-10)*

7 Recognize the need for continual commitment to the Lord and His Word: *(based on Colossians 1:10; James 1:22-25)*
(a) Examine willingness to please the Lord in all circumstances and relationships *(based on II Corinthians 5:9; Colossians 1:10)*
(b) As appropriate, return to your first love for the Lord: remember from where you have fallen, repent of past sins, return to righteous living *(based on Revelation 2:4-5)*

8 Develop consistent reliance on the Lord and His resources through:
(a) The empowering of the Holy Spirit *(based on John 16:7-13; I Corinthians 2:11-13)*,
(b) Learning and obeying God's Word (including daily devotions, Scripture study and memory, biblical practice) *(based on Psalm 1:1-6; 119:11; II Timothy 2:15; 3:16-17; James 1:22-25)*,
(c) Faithfulness in prayer *(based on I Thessalonians 5:17; Hebrews 4:16)*
(d) Fellowship and ministry with others within the local body of believers (including joint worship, fellowship, and ministry) *(based on Ephesians 4:12-16; Hebrews 10:24-25)*

9
Judge self through the development of personal failures lists (e.g., keeping account of wrongs suffered, inflicting wrongs, or neglecting to demonstrate biblical love toward God and others). [See explanation for *Worksheet 2: Lists of Specific Failures to Live Biblically*, **VICTORY OVER FAILURES PLAN** (BCF Form 102).]
(based on Matthew 7:1-5; 22:37-39; I Corinthians 13:4-8a; Revelation 2:4-5)

10
Repent and confess these sins to the Lord, demonstrated by asking for His forgiveness and showing the fruit of repentance
(based on Acts 26:20; I John 1:9)

11
Based on sins listed on *Worksheet 2: Lists of Specific Failures to Live Biblically*, identify "put-offs" of your sinful practices and "put-ons" of new righteous practices using *Worksheet 3: "Put-offs" and "Put-ons."*
(based on Ephesians 4:22-32, Colossians 3:1-4:6)

12
Develop biblical plans for living (*Worksheet 4: "Daily Practices" Plan* and *Worksheet 5: "Overcoming Temptations" Plan.*)
(based on Matthew 7:24-27; Ephesians 4:1, 17; James 1:22-25)

13
Restore unreconciled relationships and develop biblical relationships by:
(a) Forgiving others biblically using *Worksheet 6a: My Plan for Demonstrating Forgiveness*
   (Mark 11:25-26; Luke 17:3-4; Ephesians 4:31-32)
(b) Being reconciled in accordance with biblical principles of communication using *Worksheet 6b: My Plan for Asking Forgiveness*
   (based on Matthew 5:23-24; 18:15-17)

14
Treat others biblically by:
(a) Not retaliating when wronged
(b) Seeking ways to bless them
(c) Eliminating stumbling blocks
(based on Matthew 5:3-12; Romans 12:9-21; 14:13-21; I Peter 3:8-17)

The Maturing Disciple of Jesus Christ
BIBLICAL PRACTICES FOR FACING AND DEALING WITH PROBLEMS — THIRD PAGE

15

Stand firm in the midst of sufferings, tests, and trials and put on the full armor of God
(based on Ephesians 6:10-17; James 1:2-4; II Peter 1:5-10)

16

Continue to mature in God's standards for life through:
(a) Elimination of unprofitable activities — using **MY PRESENT SCHEDULE** (BCF Form 107)
(b) Addition of activities necessary to carry out God-given responsibilities — using **MY PROPOSED BIBLICAL SCHEDULE** (BCF Form 108)
(c) Periodic evaluation of the plans made
(based on Matthew 6:25-34; Ephesians 5:16)

17

Minister as a working part of the local body of believers through:
(a) Practice of spiritual gifts and cooperation with God's Spirit in bearing spiritual fruit as a faithful steward
(based on Romans 12:4-6; I Corinthians 4:1-2)
(b) Submission to the spiritual leaders *(based on Hebrews 13:17)*
(c) Showing how to determine and meet the needs of the afflicted *(based on II Corinthians 1:3-4; Galatians 6:1-5)*

18

Disciple others toward spiritual maturity and, as applicable, restore those caught up in sin by:
(a) Standing ready to give them a reason for the hope within *(based on I Peter 3:15)*
(b) Exercising a spirit of gentleness *(based on Galatians 6:1; II Timothy 2:25a)*
(c) Assisting in bearing their burdens *(based on Galatians 6:2)*
(d) Encouraging and stimulating them to love and good deeds *(Hebrews 10:24)*
(e) As necessary, admonishing, reproving, and disciplining *(based on Matthew 18:15-17; Romans 15:14; II Timothy 2:24-26)*

STANDARDS OF CONDUCT AND CODE OF ETHICS FOR BIBLICAL DISCIPLERS/COUNSELORS

ARTICLE I — STANDARDS FOR DISCIPLESHIP/COUNSELING BIBLICALLY

The biblical discipler/counselor performs his service as part of the ministry of the Christian church, embracing thereby the values of historic Christianity. He upholds and supports the common bond of fellowship, faith and unity as prescribed in the Scriptures and seeks to establish a relationship between the disciple/counselee and a loving God within the framework of the church. Certification of biblical disciplers/counselors by their pastors is contingent upon continued good standing in a church subscribing to the **STATEMENT OF FAITH FOR THE MINISTRY OF COUNSELING/DISCIPLESHIP** (BCF Form 210). One so certified will always seek approval, recognition, and oversight by the spiritual leadership of his church.

The biblical discipler/counselor, in serving God, will seek the best interest of the disciple/counselee, the church, and the general public by teaching, exhorting, admonishing, encouraging, and helping others on the basis and authority of Scripture. He does not base this ministry on his own concepts of behavior, but seeks only to marshal the full range of biblical truth into focus on the disciple/counselee's need.

The biblical discipler/counselor, in the practice of the discipleship/counseling ministry, holds to the essential truths of biblical faith and conduct without theological emphasis on any practice not specifically advocated in the Scriptures.

The biblical discipler/counselor is committed to maintain the standards and principles as described in this document and to seek to enhance the total ministry of the church and the public good.

A. The biblical discipler/counselor does not represent himself as having qualifications, affiliations, or experience that he does not possess. He does not use his knowledge, experience, or position for personal recognition, benefit or gain, nor does he allow or use his ministry for unethical and unbiblical purposes.

B. The biblical discipler/counselor provides his service as a ministry of the Christian church or a faith group.

   1. He does not make exploitive representation of his services in any type of unseemly listing or advertising. He does not make claims orally, or in writing, that are inaccurate or unbecoming.

   2. He does not practice privately apart from the church or other recognized ecclesiastical service or educational organization which bears the endorsement of his church. He acts within the scope of the church in the performance of his regular or specialized ministerial duties.

   3. Because of his personal concern, he provides his time, resources, and energy as a ministering service to the church or faith group as well as to the individual or family in need. Recipients or beneficiaries of his services are not subject to any charge or fee, or any financial requirement, actual or implied.

   4. He encourages the disciple/counselee to maintain a strong church involvement and will emphasize the need for continued authoritative biblical faith, instruction, and conduct.

C. The biblical discipler/counselor recognizes the total health needs of the disciple/counselee.

1. He accepts that the general practice of medicine and nutrition is an essential ministry to the physical body based on a systematic and scientifically developed body of knowledge. The ministry to the mind, the spirit, and the soul is based on the unalterable and completely sufficient Word of God.

2. He recognizes the need in some instances for early medical evaluations to determine whether the disciple/counselee's behavior may result partially from organic dysfunction.

3. He recognizes that there are occasional circumstances, such as extreme pain or physical safety, where medication which may alter behavior is required, but will seek to help a disciple/counselee refrain from taking substances that lead to dependence or that substantially affect or alter the mind or behavior.

D. The biblical discipler/counselor may make a referral to other biblical disciplers/counselors, pastors, or teachers who are grounded and trained in biblical thought, perspective, methodology, and conduct. Referrals should be acknowledged and significant information obtained, and/or made available, that may assist in the process of biblical change.

E. The biblical discipler/counselor will maintain, as a trustworthy steward, all notes, records and information pertaining to the disciple/counselee. Records will be confidential and securely maintained, but it is recognized that confidentiality does not irrevocably prohibit the discipler/counselor from providing information in the utilization of church and/or state resources where necessary.

ARTICLE II — RELATIONSHIP OF THE BIBLICAL DISCIPLER/COUNSELOR TO THE DISCIPLE/COUNSELEE

The biblical discipler/counselor has no preconceptions concerning the needs of a disciple/counselee other than those already stated. The integrity of the disciple/counselee, and statements by the disciple/counselee, are accepted at face value as a truthful description of the problem. Confidentiality is respected where possible, information is safeguarded, and the best interest and well-being of the disciple/counselee is preserved.

A. It is a commitment on the part of the biblical discipler/counselor to maintain his conduct and relationship with the disciple/counselee above reproach and in accord with the highest standards of biblical ministry.

B. It is Scriptural to offer hope. However, the biblical discipler/counselor does not offer a quick panacea, but maintains a reasonable reservation as to biblical application until the full needs of the disciple/counselee have been identified and studied.

C. The biblical discipler/counselor stresses those requirements clearly stated in the Scriptures. His responsibility as a biblical discipler/counselor consists of:

1. Showing the disciple/counselee that in order to face and deal with his problem victoriously, his life must first be transformed by regeneration through Jesus Christ, and by the empowering of the Holy Spirit, his habits must conform to the standards of the Scriptures.

2. Pointing out clearly the requirements of the Scriptures as applied to everyday life and practice.

3. Helping the disciple/counselee change his conduct as God has instructed in the Scriptures in order that he may have peace and joy in his life and relationship with God.

D. The biblical discipler/counselor will protect the identity of a disciple/counselee in any spoken or written communication or publication.

ARTICLE III — CHURCH OR FAITH GROUP RELATIONSHIP

The biblical discipler/counselor shall have continuing fellowship with a church or faith group, and shall place himself under the authority and oversight of its ruling body.

ARTICLE IV — CONTINUING STUDY

The biblical discipler/counselor is committed to continuing study of the Scriptures with a view to applying them to all phases of spiritual growth, personal living, conduct, behavior, and interpersonal relationships.

ARTICLE V — COMMUNICATIONS AND REPRESENTATION

The biblical discipler/counselor exercises care in public utterances and writing to distinguish his ministry as a biblical discipler/counselor from his private views and denominational theological positions.

A. The biblical discipler/counselor will prepare himself to train believers to practice biblical discipleship/counseling in support of the local church ministry.

B. Biblical disciplers/counselors shall seek in every area of life to exemplify and otherwise promote the principles and practices of biblical faith and behavior with loving concern, and assist others to do the same.

C. The biblical discipler/counselor will demonstrate trustworthiness in spoken or written communications to avoid gossip. His evaluations or conclusions relating to individual cases or the general biblical discipleship/counseling ministry will build up others in a manner that is above reproach.

D. Biblical disciplers/counselors shall encourage churches and faith groups to institute training in the use of the Scriptures to help one another in overcoming the problems of personal, interpersonal, and family life.

STATEMENT OF FAITH
FOR THE MINISTRY OF BIBLICAL DISCIPLESHIP/COUNSELING

> The church of Jesus Christ is to be committed solely to the Old and New Testaments as the only written authority for faith and conduct. The biblical discipler/counselor's faith and conduct, which includes his discipling/counseling theory and practice, are established and defined only by the standards of Scripture. The following statement of faith and conduct sets forth the central doctrines, precepts, and principles of God's Word which, since the first century, have formed the basis for authentic and effective biblical discipleship/counseling in the Body of Christ.

BIBLICAL BASIS FOR STATEMENTS

I. We affirm the Bible to be the only infallible and authoritative Word of God, given by inspiration of God and devoid of error as originally written.[1] The Bible can be understood only through the regenerative power of the Holy Spirit[2] and is to be interpreted first and foremost by itself, using all relevant passages that relate to a particular subject. Since the Bible supplies all the resources necessary for godly living, it is totally sufficient to guide every individual in what to believe, how to think, speak, and act in every relationship and circumstance.[3] Nothing is to be added to or deleted from its teachings.[4]

A. This statement affirms the complete sufficiency of the Bible to provide for each individual all the guidance necessary to face, deal with, and endure every test and trial of life[5] and for each believer, provides all the help necessary to live in a way that pleases God and develops maturity as a faithful disciple of Jesus Christ.[6]

1. On any issue where God's Word speaks clearly by command, precept, or judgment, the biblical discipler/counselor uses Scripture alone, as a continuing basis of faith, hope, change, and perseverance in doing the Word.[7]

2. The biblical discipler/counselor assembles the full range of biblical commands, precepts, descriptions, and judgments[8] that contrast man's erroneous thinking, judgment, and ways[9] — which demonstrate a preoccupation with self[10] — with a commitment to please God and obey His Word regardless of feelings, circumstances, or other people.[11]

[1] Psalm 19:7; 119:160; John 17:17; II Timothy 3:16; II Peter 1:21
[2] I Corinthians 2:14
[3] I Timothy 3:15-17; II Peter 1:3-4
[4] Deuteronomy 4:2; Proverbs 30:5-6; II Peter 3:16; Revelation 22:18-19
[5] I Thessalonians 2:13; II Timothy 3:15-17; I Peter 1:23
[6] I Peter 2:1-5; II Peter 1:3-4
[7] Romans 15:4; Hebrews 4:12; 5:13-14; James 1:22-25
[8] Psalm 19:7-11; II Timothy 3:15b-17
[9] Isaiah 55:8-11
[10] Matthew 7:1-5; 10:38-39; Luke 18:9-14
[11] Proverbs 3:5-7; Jeremiah 17:5-8; Colossians 1:10; I Thessalonians 2:4; 4:1

BIBLICAL BASIS FOR STATEMENTS

3. Even on issues where the wisdom of man seems to correspond to the truth of God's Word, the biblical discipler/counselor continues to refer only to Scripture as the ultimate authority for living and disregards any so-called validation of scriptural truths outside the Bible.[12]

[12] *Isaiah 55:11;*
John 17:17;
Titus 1:9; 2:1, 7

B. This affirmation also is meant to reject all philosophies that contain any ideas that are in opposition to Scripture as to how God deals with mankind.[13] Specifically, God's Word defines the sinful basis for man's problems as originating in the heart[14] and leading to an orientation to live for self instead of the Lord.[15] Therefore the biblical discipler/counselor rejects as superficial, futile, and unbiblical, methodologies that do not deal with issues of the heart but instead focus on other persons or circumstances as the reason for not overcoming difficulties in life.[16]

[13] *Psalm 1:1-3;*
I Samuel 16:7;
I Corinthians 1:30;
Colossians 2:8

[14] *Jeremiah 17:9;*
Matthew 15:18-20;
Mark 7:20-23;
Luke 6:45

[15] *Luke 9:23-24*

[16] *Colossians 2:8;*
I Timothy 1:3b-7; 4:7a

II. We affirm the one God,[17] eternally existent[18] in the triune Godhead: Father, Son and Holy Spirit.[19]

[17] *Deuteronomy 6:4*

[18] *Deuteronomy 33:27a;*
Psalm 90:1-2;
Hebrews 1:8-12;
7:24-25; 9:14

[19] *Matthew 3:16-17;*
28:19;
John 14:16-18;
II Corinthians 13:14;
Ephesians 4:4-6

III. We affirm the deity of our Lord Jesus Christ,[20] His virgin birth,[21] His sinless life,[22] His miracles,[23] His vicarious and atoning death through His shed blood,[24] His bodily resurrection,[25] His ascension to the right hand of the Father,[26] and His personal return in power and glory.[27]

[20] *Isaiah 9:6-7;*
John 10:30;
Colossians 1:15-17

[21] *Isaiah 7:14;*
Matthew 1:23

[22] *Hebrews 4:15*

[23] *John 20:30-31*

[24] *II Corinthians 5:21;*
Ephesians 1:7

[25] *Romans 1:4; 4:25; 8:11;*
I Corinthians 15:4

[26] *Romans 8:34;*
Hebrews 8:1

[27] *Acts 1:11;*
I Thessalonians 4:13-18;
Hebrews 9:28

IV. We affirm that mankind was created in the image of God[28] but fell into sin by being disobedient to God's will.[29]

[28] *Genesis 1:27*

[29] *Genesis 2:15-17;*
3:1-7

	BIBLICAL BASIS FOR STATEMENTS
As a result, all individuals are sinful by nature[30] and are unable to save themselves,[31] live righteously,[32] or understand the things of God.[33] Therefore, no one has any inherent justification as he appears before a holy and righteous God, since every person is subject to death[34] and God's judgment.[35]	[30] *Romans 5:12; Ephesians 2:1-3*
	[31] *Psalm 49:7; Proverbs 20:9; Ephesians 2:8-9; Titus 3:5*
	[32] *Psalm 143:2; Ecclesiastes 7:20; Isaiah 64:6; Romans 3:9-12*
	[33] *Proverbs 14:12; Isaiah 55:8-9; I Corinthians 2:14*
	[34] *Ezekiel 18:4; Romans 3:23; 6:23a*
	[35] *Romans 1:18; 5:16, 18; Hebrews 9:27; II Peter 3:7*
A. This affirmation emphasizes that the foremost problem faced by natural man is separation from God and not merely an inability to face, deal with, and endure problems of life.[36]	[36] *Ephesians 2:1-4*
B. This affirmation indicates the futility of trying to disciple/counsel individuals with a view to Christlike change apart from dealing with their basic sinfulness.[37]	[37] *John 3:18; 8:34; Romans 6:17-18; 8:5-8*
C. This affirmation also concludes that it is impossible to please God in one's thoughts, words, or actions apart from conversion through Jesus Christ.[38]	[38] *Romans 8:5-9*
V. We affirm that God, by His gracious and merciful love, gave His one and only begotten Son, Jesus Christ, as the only answer for mankind's helpless spiritual condition.[39] Jesus voluntarily accepted the punishment for sin and died on the cross to pay the full price of redemption.[40]	[39] *Isaiah 53:2-12; John 3:16; 14:6; Acts 4:12; Romans 5:6; I Timothy 2:5-6; I John 4:10*
	[40] *John 10:17-18; II Corinthians 5:21; Ephesians 1:7; Hebrews 10:10-14; I Peter 1:18-19; 3:18*
VI. We affirm that each member of the Triune Godhead is jointly involved in the plan of redemption for lost and sinful mankind[41] and that this redemption is provided to those who receive a spiritual new birth[42] by God's grace	[41] *Hebrews 9:14; I Peter 1:1-2*
	[42] *John 3:5-8; Romans 5:17*

BIBLICAL BASIS FOR STATEMENTS

and mercy.[43] This spiritual transformation[44] is initiated and maintained by God[45] and enables a believer to be an overwhelming conqueror through Christ Jesus.[46]

[43] *Ephesians 2:8-9; Titus 3:5-7*

[44] *Romans 6:6-11; II Corinthians 5:17*

[45] *Philippians 1:6*

[46] *Romans 8:31-39; I John 4:4*

A. This affirmation highlights the necessity of salvation in Jesus Christ as a prerequisite for enablement to face, deal with, and endure problems in a biblical manner.[47] Thus a biblical discipler/counselor is to present the Good News of Jesus Christ to an unbeliever,[48] which must be appropriated before any further biblical discipling/counseling can be effective.[49]

[47] *John 15:5; Romans 6:16-19*

[48] *II Corinthians 5:18-20*

[49] *I Corinthians 2:14*

B. This affirmation emphasizes that the divine resources of God are available and completely sufficient for a believer in Christ to endure in a Christlike manner any trial or test, including those involving painful emotional distress, agonizing physical discomfort, or physical care by medical personnel.[50]

[50] *I Corinthians 10:13; II Corinthians 1:3-5; Philippians 4:13; Hebrews 4:15-16; James 1:2-4; II Peter 1:2-4*

C. This affirmation is meant to convey that a biblical relationship with God through Jesus Christ provides the only way for one to experience lasting peace and joy in the midst of the adversities of life.[51]

[51] *John 14:27; 15:11; 16:33; 17:13*

VII. We affirm the present work of the Holy Spirit as convicting the world of sin, righteousness and judgment.[52] The Holy Spirit indwells a believer[53] to help him understand the things of God[54] and to empower him for godly living[55] that results in further Christlikeness.[56]

[52] *John 16:8*

[53] *John 14:16-17; Romans 8:9-11; I Corinthians 3:16*

[54] *John 14:26; I Corinthians 2:9-16; I John 2:18-27*

[55] *Acts 1:8; Romans 8:13; Galatians 5:16; Ephesians 5:18*

[56] *II Corinthians 3:18; Galatians 5:22-23*

A. This affirmation is meant to convey that focusing on interpreting or living in one's past is not necessary for biblical change.[57]

[57] *I Corinthians 3:19-20; Philippians 3:13-14*

B. This affirmation also emphasizes the need for a biblical discipler/counselor to reject any reliance on self-adequacy when dealing in the life of another. Instead, he is to rely on God's Spirit totally apart from man-made techniques or practices that supposedly help one disciple/counsel others.[58]

[58] *Zechariah 4:6; II Corinthians 3:5-6*

BIBLICAL BASIS FOR STATEMENTS

VIII. We affirm the resurrection of both the saved and the lost, they that are saved to the resurrection of life and they that are lost to the resurrection of damnation.[59] Each shall be responsible to give an account of deeds done in the body.[60]

> This affirmation emphasizes the importance of being a doer of the Word to please the Lord, not only for the blessings of the Lord in this life[61] but also for God's rewards in the life to come.[62]

IX. We affirm the spiritual unity of believers in our Lord Jesus Christ.[63] We believe that all professing Christians should be baptized,[64] be in ministry in conjunction with other believers,[65] be in biblical submission to one another,[66] be subject to and participate in the care and restorative discipline of the church,[67] and be in submission to godly leadership that God has ordained in a church.[68]

X. We affirm the responsibility of church leaders to train believers to carry out the work of ministry including that of counseling based on God's Word as an integral part of discipleship/counseling training.[69] Each church family, in fulfilling the biblical responsibilities of teaching, reproof, correction, and training in righteousness[70] will equip its members towards Christlike maturity[71] and the ministry of discipleship/counseling.[72] Fulfilling this normal responsibility of discipleship in a church enables the Body of Christ to fulfill the Great Commission of Jesus — making disciples in all nations.[73]

   A. This affirmation points out that the ministry of counseling/discipleship is not relegated to a select group of counseling professionals but instead is to be a normal function of every believer who is growing in Christlikeness.[74]

---

[59] *Daniel 12:2; John 5:28-29; 6:40; I Corinthians 15:51-52; Revelation 20:11-15*

[60] *Ecclesiastes 12:13-14; Matthew 12:35-37; 16:27; Romans 2:6; 14:10-12; II Corinthians 5:10; I Peter 1:17; Revelation 20:12-13*

[61] *John 15:10-11; James 1:22-25; I John 3:22*

[62] *Matthew 16:27; Colossians 1:10-12; 3:23-24*

[63] *John 17:22-23; Ephesians 4:3-6, 12-16*

[64] *Matthew 28:19; Acts 2:38*

[65] *Romans 12:4-5; I Corinthians 12:4-6; Ephesians 4:4-16; I Peter 4:10*

[66] *Ephesians 5:21*

[67] *Matthew 18:15-17; Galatians 6:1-5*

[68] *I Thessalonians 5:12-13; Hebrews 13:17*

[69] *Ephesians 4:12; II Timothy 2:2*

[70] *Colossians 3:16; II Timothy 3:16*

[71] *II Timothy 3:17; II Peter 1:2-4*

[72] *Romans 15:14; Galatians 6:1-2*

[73] *Matthew 28:19-20*

[74] *Romans 15:14; Galatians 6:1-2; II Timothy 3:16-17*

		BIBLICAL BASIS FOR STATEMENTS
B.	This affirmation further proclaims that God has provided all that is necessary for His people to face and deal with any problem of life by using the divinely ordained resources already given to His Church.[75]	[75] *Psalm 19:7-11; Romans 8:9, 11, 26-27, 34; II Thessalonians 3:3; II Timothy 3:16-17; II Peter 1:2-4; I John 2:1*

Made in the USA
Columbia, SC
28 July 2024

39568554R00154